FLAPPER

FLAPPER

A Madcap Story of Sex, Style,
Celebrity, and the Women
Who Made America Modern

JOSHUA ZEITZ

B\D\W\Y
Broadway Books
New York

Published in the United States by Broadway Books, an imprint of the
Crown Publishing Group, a division of Penguin Random House LLC, New York.
www.crownpublishing.com

BROADWAY BOOKS and its logo, B \ D \ W \ Y, are trademarks of
Penguin Random House LLC.

Originally published in hardcover in the United States by Crown Publishers, an imprint of the
Crown Publishing Group, a division of Penguin Random House LLC, New York, in 2006.

Grateful acknowledgment is made to the following for permission to reprint
previously published material:

Alfred A. Knopf: Excerpts from *Lulu in Hollywood,* by Louise Brooks,
copyright © 1974, 1982 by Louise Brooks. Reprinted by permission of
Alfred A. Knopf, a division of Random House, Inc.

Dell Publishing: Excerpt from *Exiles from Paradise* by Sara Mayfield, copyright © 1971
by Sara Mayfield. Reprinted by permission of Dell Publishing, a division
of Random House, Inc.

Doubleday: Excerpt from *Silent Star* by Colleen Moore, copyright © 1968 by
Colleen Moore. Reprinted by permission of Doubleday, a division of Random House, Inc.

The New Yorker/The Condé Nast Publications Inc.: Excerpts from *The New Yorker—
Talk of the Town: Tables for Two* and *On and Off the Avenue,* courtesy of The New Yorker/
The Condé Nast Publications Inc. www.newyorker.com

Library of Congress Cataloging-in-Publication Data
Zeitz, Joshua.
Flapper : a madcap story of sex, style, celebrity, and the women who
made America modern / Joshua Zeitz.
Includes bibliographical references and index.
1. United States—History—1919–1933—Biography. 2. Women—United States—
Biography. 3. Celebrities—United States—Biography. 4. Artists—United States—
Biography. 5. United States—Social life and customs—1918–1945. 6. Women—United
States—Social life and customs—20th century. 7. Sex customs—United States—
History—20th century. 8. Sex role—United States—History—20th century.
9. Popular culture—United States—History—20th century. 10. Consumption
(Economics)—Social aspects—United States—History—20th century. 1. Title.
E784.Z45 2006
813'.52—dc22
[B]
2005024297

ISBN 978-1-4000-8054-0
eBook ISBN 978-0-307-52382-2

Design by Lauren Dong

149137329

For Juli-anne

The world broke in two in 1922 or thereabouts . . .

——WILLA CATHER

Contents

Introduction: Tango Pirates and Absinthe   *1*

Part One

1   The Most Popular Girl   *13*
2   Sex o' Clock in America   *21*
3   Will She Throw Her Arms Around Your Neck and Yell?   *29*
4   Flapper King   *39*
5   Doing It for Effect   *51*
6   I Prefer This Sort of Girl   *61*
7   Straighten Out People   *71*
8   New York Sophistication   *79*
9   Miss Jazz Age   *87*
10   Girlish Delight in Barrooms   *95*
11   These Modern Women   *105*
12   The Lingerie Shortage in This Country   *115*

Part Two

13   A Mind Full of Fabulations   *127*
14   An Athletic Kind of Girl   *135*
15   Let Go of the Waistline   *147*
16   Into the Streets   *161*

17   WITHOUT IMAGINATION, NO WANTS   *173*

18   10,000,000 FEMMES FATALES   *185*

19   APPEARANCES COUNT   *197*

PART THREE

20   PAPA, WHAT IS BEER?   *211*

21   OH, LITTLE GIRL, NEVER GROW UP   *223*

22   THE KIND OF GIRL THE FELLOWS WANT   *231*

23   ANOTHER PETULANT WAY TO PASS THE TIME   *245*

24   THE DREAMER'S DREAM COME TRUE   *257*

25   SUICIDE ON THE INSTALLMENT PLAN   *267*

CONCLUSION: UNAFFORDABLE EXCESS   *277*

Notes   *293*

Photography Credits   *321*

Acknowledgments   *323*

Index   *327*

FLAPPER

Living life on the edge, two young flappers demonstrate the Charleston on the roof of Chicago's Sherman Hotel, December 11, 1926.

INTRODUCTION

TANGO PIRATES AND ABSINTHE

O N MAY 22, 1915, amid a flurry of cameras and a battery of outstretched hands, most bearing autograph books and pens, Eugenia Kelly, the young heiress to a sizable New York banking fortune, pushed past waves of idle celebrity watchers and slowly wound her way up the marble staircase at the Yorkville Magistrate's Court, on Manhattan's fashionable Upper East Side.

Walking beside her lawyer, nineteen-year-old Eugenia impressed bystanders as unexpectedly well poised and confident. She sported "a green shade Norfolk suit," one courtroom observer reported, "a white silk shirt waist with a loose, rolling collar, and a bright red necktie. Her wavy hair was covered by a tri-cornered brimless hat of black straw, decorated with yellow and a rosette."

Eugenia couldn't have struck a sharper contrast with her mother, Helen Kelly, a matronly widow of ambiguous middle age who arrived at the magistrate's building just moments after her daughter. Mrs. Kelly was clad in an old-fashioned, long-necked black dress whose severity found only the slightest relief from the touch of white lace that wrapped around her collar. As she took her seat in the courtroom, Mrs. Kelly fixed her gaze nervously on Eugenia, who refused to acknowledge her mother.

And no wonder. Just two nights earlier, Mrs. Kelly had sworn out an arrest warrant against Eugenia and asked that a judge commit her to a correctional institution. After hearing Mrs. Kelly's woeful tale, a local magistrate immediately consented to the request. That evening, without warning, two plainclothes detectives confronted and arrested Eugenia inside a restaurant at Pennsylvania Station. She spent several late hours in lockup until her older sister arrived with bail money.

Eugenia, it seemed, had turned overnight from a sweet young society belle into an irredeemable wild child. By her mother's estimation, she was even "likely to become depraved."

For months, Eugenia had been frequenting the dance halls on Broadway, where she acquired an insatiable appetite for jazz, cigarettes, absinthe, and brandy. She was also keeping company with an older married man, Al Davis, whom authorities described as a "tango pirate"—a confidence man who preyed on unsuspecting rich girls.

Though money was the primary motive driving Mrs. Kelly's concern—Eugenia would inherit $10 million on her twenty-first birthday, and the family was hell-bent on stopping her from squandering her bequest on a miscreant like Al Davis—she shrewdly justified her case by highlighting Eugenia's antisocial behavior.

What to do with a young woman who stayed out until three or four in the morning? Every night. With the exception of her lawyer, all parties concerned, including the state magistrate, seemed to agree that Eugenia was out of control. Maybe even criminally wayward.

"Why, if I didn't go to at least six cabarets a night," she allegedly told her mother, "I would lose my social standing."

The weepy-eyed Mrs. Kelly had tried everything: increasing Eugenia's allowance, docking her allowance, begging her to stay home, ordering her to stay home. She had even tried locking the front door of her East Side town house after midnight, in the hope that Eugenia wouldn't risk spending a long, cold night on the front porch stoop. No use. Eugenia had smashed out the glass window above the brass handle and unlocked the door from the inside.

In vain, Eugenia's lawyer, Frank Crocker, asked that the charges against his client be dismissed. She was nineteen years old, after all— an adult, legally entitled to make her own mistakes. This motion only infuriated the magistrate, who dressed down Crocker in no uncertain terms. "The issue is plain," he bellowed, "as to whether the defendant is disobedient to the reasonable commandment of her mother, who is her natural and legal guardian; whether she associates with vicious and depraved people; and whether she is liable to become morally depraved." The trial would proceed.

To the public's delight, Eugenia was in fine form the next day when she took the witness stand.

"You are too nice a girl, Eugenia," said John McIntyre, counsel to Mrs. Kelly, "to be hauled into court this way, and to have your name daily blemished by this notoriety. You are breaking your mother's heart. If you will promise now to go home to her, to cut out this Broadway crowd, to eliminate this man Al Davis from your mind, I will drop this thing right now."

"I will not go home to my mother," Eugenia snapped back. "I am not going to apologize to any one for anything that I have done. I am not going to give up my acquaintance with Al Davis. My mother started the ball rolling, and I will see this thing through to the end." With steely-eyed conviction, Eugenia declared, "I do not think they can send me away."

Clearly uncomfortable with his role in the case, Maurice Spies, the deputy assistant district attorney, tried to reason with Eugenia. "Do you realize what this means to you?" he pleaded. "Do you know that you are in danger of being sent to some institution?"

"Well, I am the one that will be sent away," she rejoined, "not you, so this is my business and not yours."

Captivated newspaper readers were just getting acquainted with the strange case of Eugenia Kelly when, on the third day of the trial, in a sudden and disappointing about-face, the defendant yielded to the state's demands and formally repudiated her lifestyle.

"I was wrong and mother was right," she told the judge, somewhat unconvincingly, in court.

It seemed that, following a marathon negotiation session, mother and daughter had come to a mutual understanding, brokered by lawyers for Mrs. Kelly, as well as several Catholic priests who were longtime associates of the family. Realizing that her inheritance was in jeopardy, Eugenia agreed to cut off all contact with Al Davis and the Broadway crowd. In turn, her mother would drop all charges.

"Eugenia is not innately bad," Mrs. Kelly assured members of the press. "She is a good girl, but she was *blinded* to a true perception of life by the white lights of Broadway."

Her daughter agreed, summoning almost identical language in her apology to the court. "I realize now," she admitted, "that I was dazzled by the glamour of the white lights and the music and the dancing of Broadway."

It wasn't enough for the magistrate, who was determined to use the case to issue a sweeping moral judgment from the bench. He ordered Eugenia to stand before him and, with court reporters working furiously to record his every word, tore into the young defendant for what must have seemed an interminable length of time.

"You come from one of the best families in the city," he chided. "I can remember, as a young man, that your grandfather stood so high in this community that when men passed him in the street they lifted their hats out of respect to him. Your father was a high type of man, and one of the city's best citizens. I am afraid you have acted a little foolishly. The best friend you have is your mother. Sometimes we may disagree as to what a mother says, but when we think it over calmly we realize all she does is for our interest and benefit. After you think this over you will realize that your mother was guided by the right motives in trying to do what she could to save you.

"I think you will agree with me in the end," he concluded, "that she is entitled to a great deal of consideration on your part for bringing you to a realization that you were doing something that is not going to benefit you. Bear that in mind, please, and realize that, after all, your mother is the best friend you have. Will you promise to do that?"

"Yes, yes, your Honor," Eugenia replied, though probably not without digging her nails into the palm of her hand.

Eugenia didn't keep her promise for very long. Within the space of three months, she eloped to Elkton, Maryland—the North American capital of eleventh-hour marriages—with the recently divorced Al Davis. Sporting a plain suit coat and carrying a large bouquet of roses, the incorrigible Miss Kelly found that her reputation preceded her, even below the Mason-Dixon Line. In vain, she and Davis spent several frantic hours trying to find a clergyman who would perform the ceremony until, finally, the Reverend Henry Carr, a minister who specialized in last-minute wedding ceremonies, agreed to consecrate their union.

The story didn't end happily ever after. Two years later, as America made a fateful break with its isolationist heritage and sent the first round of doughboys off to the Great War, Eugenia Kelly quietly inherited her fortune. Before the 1920s were out, she and Al Davis had divorced.

By then, nobody cared. The guardians of feminine virtue and Victorian morality had much bigger problems with which to contend. Every girl, it seemed, wanted to be Eugenia Kelly.

It was the age of the flapper.

IT's NOT CLEAR how or when the term *flapper* first wound its way into the American vernacular. The expression probably originated in prewar England. According to a 1920s fashion writer, "flapper" initially described the sort of teenage girl whose gawky frame and posture were "supposed to need a certain type of clothing—long, straight lines to cover her awkwardness—and the stores advertised these gowns as 'flapper-dresses.'"

Shortly after the closing shots of World War I, the word came to designate young women in their teens and twenties who subscribed to the libertine principles that writers like F. Scott Fitzgerald and actresses like Clara Bow popularized in print and on the silver screen.

An early reference in *Webster's Collegiate Dictionary* defined the flapper as "A young girl, esp. one somewhat daring in conduct, speech and dress," a designation that at least one eighteen-year-old woman in 1922 seemed ready to embrace. "Of all the things that flappers don't like," she boldly explained to readers of *The New York Times Book Review and Magazine,* "it is the commonplace."

If historians still disagree about how and when the term came into vogue, by the early 1920s it seemed that every social ill in America could be attributed to the "flapper"—the notorious character type who bobbed her hair, smoked cigarettes, drank gin, sported short skirts, and passed her evenings in steamy jazz clubs, where she danced in a shockingly immodest fashion with a revolving cast of male suitors. She was the envy of teenage girls everywhere and the scourge of good character and morals. Nobody could escape the intense dialogue over the flapper. "Concern—and consternation—about the flapper are general," observed a popular newspaper columnist of the day. "She disports herself flagrantly in the public eye, and there is no keeping her out of grownup company or conversation. Roughly, the world is divided into those who delight in her, those who fear her and those who try pathetically to take her as a matter of course."

The U.S. secretary of labor decried the "flippancy of the cigarette-smoking, cocktail-drinking flapper." A Harvard psychologist reported that flappers possessed the "lowest degree of intelligence" and posed "a hopeless problem for educators." In 1929, the Florida State Legislature even considered banning use of the term *flapper,* so infamous was her character.

It's easy, in retrospect, to lose sight of just how radical the flapper appeared to her elders. Until World War I, few women other than prostitutes ventured into saloons and barrooms. As late as 1904, a woman had been arrested on Fifth Avenue in New York City for lighting up a cigarette. It wasn't until 1929 that some railroad companies formally abolished their prohibition against women smokers in dining cars.

Given how new the "New Woman" really was in America, it's little wonder that she dominated the public debate in the 1920s. Throughout the decade, headlines reported terrible stories of young girls driven to ruin, like a fourteen-year-old from Chicago who committed suicide after her mother forbade her to don flapper wear. "Other girls in her class rolled their stockings, had their hair bobbed and called themselves flappers," readers learned. "She wanted to be a flapper, too. But her mother was an old fashioned mother, who kindly but firmly said 'No.' So the girl put a rubber hose in her mouth and turned on the gas."

NOT EVERYONE THOUGHT the flapper's triumph represented civilization's decline. Writing in September 1925, at the height of the Jazz Age, Bruce Bliven, editor of *The New Republic,* penned a lighthearted profile of "Flapper Jane," a nineteen-year-old representative of the youth generation and exemplar of the New American Woman who seemed everywhere on display in the years just following World War I. Maybe "Jane" was real. Maybe she was the work of Bliven's imagination. In all probability, she was a composite figure.

Her minister, wrote Bliven, "poor man," condemned Jane as "a perfectly horrible example of wild youth—paint, cigarettes, cocktails, petting parties—oooh!" Her critics linked her with "prohibition, the automobile, the decline of Fundamentalism," and any number of other sweeping social changes. She was one of those reckless youths who "strolls across the lawn of her parents' suburban home, having just put the car away after driving sixty miles in two hours." A "very pretty girl" made up "for an altogether artificial effect—pallor mortis, poisonously scarlet lips, richly ringed eyes," Jane imitated the "swagger supposed by innocent America to go with the female half of a Paris Apache dance."

To Bliven's rhetorical question—"Jane . . . why do all of you dress the way you do?"—the young flapper replied, "In a way, it's just honesty. Women have come down off the pedestal lately. They are tired of this mysterious feminine charm stuff. Maybe it goes with independence, earning your own living and voting and all that. There was always a bit of the harem in that cover-up-your-arms-and-legs business, don't you think? Women still want to be loved, but they want it on a 50-50 basis, which includes being admired for the qualities they really possess."

Ultimately, Bliven ventured that there was "a good deal more smoke than fire" in the flapper's general conduct. Rather than evidence of a great unloosening of morals, she was proof positive that "women today are shaking off the shreds and patches of their age-old servitude. 'Feminism' has won a victory so nearly complete that we have even forgotten the fierce challenge that once inhered in the very word.

"Women have highly resolved that they are just as good as men," Bliven continued, "and intend to be treated so. They don't mean to have any more unwanted children. They do not intend to be barred from any profession or occupation which they choose to enter. . . . If they should elect to go naked nothing is more certain than that naked they will go, while from the sidelines to which he has been relegated mere man is vouchsafed permission only to pipe a feeble Hurrah!"

To which, the editor concluded, "Hurrah!"

STRIP AWAY THE sensational headlines and popular warnings of moral calamity and decay, even look past the coolheaded assessments of progressive writers like Bruce Bliven, and the flapper was a complex figure.

She was distinctly real, the product of compelling social and political forces that converged in the years between the two world wars. Gainfully employed and earning her own keep, free from family and community surveillance, a participant in a burgeoning consumer culture that counseled indulgence and pleasure over restraint and asceticism, the New Woman of the 1920s boldly asserted her right to dance, drink, smoke, and date—to work, to own her own property, to live free of the strictures that governed her mother's generation.

Growing up in an urban environment that afforded Americans opportunities for anonymity and leisure, born in the era of mass production and mass reproduction, the flapper experimented openly with sex and with style. She redefined romance and courtship in ways that expanded and—sometimes unknowingly—contracted her autonomy. She flouted Victorian-era conventions and scandalized her parents. In many ways, she controlled her own destiny.

But if the flapper faithfully represented millions of young women in the Jazz Age, she was also a character type, fully contrived by the nation's first "merchants of cool." These artists, advertisers, writers, designers, film starlets, and media gurus fashioned her sense of style, her taste in clothing and music, the brand of cigarettes she smoked, and the kind of liquor she drank—even the shape of her body and the placement of her curves. Their power over the nation's increasingly centralized print and motion picture media, and their mastery of new developments in group psychology and the behavioral sciences, lent them unusual sway over millions of young women who were eager to assert their autonomy but still looked to cultural authorities for cues about consumption and body image. Like so many successor movements in the twentieth century, the flapper phenomenon emphasized individuality, even as it expressed itself in conformity.

The pioneer merchants of cool invented the flapper for fun, for profit, and for fame. In branding and selling her, they inaugurated that curious, modern cycle by which popular culture imitates life and life imitates popular culture.

By the mid-1920s, few flappers knew whether they were a grass-roots or elite invention. Neither could they appreciate the steep price they paid for their new freedoms. In return for measuring the good life in material terms, they forfeited a degree of political and social power; in return for new romantic, heterosexual liberties, they lost some of the intimacy that women once shared with one another.

Above all, the history of the flapper isn't just about America's first sexual revolution, though certainly the New Women of the 1920s represented a dramatic break with traditional American values and ethics. Indeed, the flapper's importance ranged far beyond the bedroom or the dance hall. Her story is the story of America in the 1920s—the first "modern" decade, when everyday life came under the full sway of mass media, celebrity, and consumerism, when public rights gave way to private entitlements, and when people as far and wide as Muncie, Indiana, and Somerset, Pennsylvania, came to share a national standard of tastes and habits.

The people who made and embodied the flapper were a diverse lot.

There was Coco Chanel, the French orphan who built a fashion empire and singularly redefined the feminine form and silhouette.

Three thousand miles away, Lois Long, the daughter of a Connecticut clergyman, emerged as one of the most insightful observers of sex and style in Jazz Age America.

In California, where orange groves gave way to studio lots and fairy-tale mansions, Clara Bow, Colleen Moore, and Louise Brooks, Hollywood's great flapper triumvirate, fired the imagination of millions of filmgoers with their distinct variations on the New Woman.

Gordon Conway, a Texas-born fashion artist, and John Held, a Utah-born cartoonist, designed magazine covers that gave visual expression to the social revolution sweeping the United States.

In New York, Bruce Barton and Edward Bernays, pioneers in the new art of advertising and public relations, taught big business how to harness the dreams and anxieties of a growing industrial nation.

Their story—a tale of the fascinating characters who were present for America's rendezvous with modernity—begins in the most unlikely of places: at a small country club in the summer of 1918, where a young army officer is mustering up the courage to ask someone to dance.

PART ONE

Zelda Sayre, shortly before she caught the eye of F. Scott Fitzgerald.

1

THE MOST POPULAR GIRL

OR ALL INTENTS and purposes, and purely by virtue of chance, America's Jazz Age began in July 1918 on a warm and sultry evening in Montgomery, Alabama. There, at the Montgomery Country Club—"a rambling brown-shingled building," as one contemporary later remembered it, "discreetly screened from the public eye by an impenetrable hedge of mock oranges"—a strikingly beautiful woman named Zelda Sayre sauntered onto the clubhouse veranda and caught the eye of First Lieutenant Francis Scott Fitzgerald.

At seventeen, Zelda was "sophisticated for her age," recalled one of her friends, but "she still had the charm of an uninhibited, imaginative child."

As she stood outside the clubhouse amid the dull murmur of the brass dance music emanating from within, bathed by the Alabama moonlight, her "summer tan gave her skin the color of a rose petal dripped in cream. Her hair had the sheen of spun gold. Wide and dark-lashed, her eyes seemed to change color with her prismatic moods; though in reality they were deep blue, at times they appeared to be green or even a dark Confederate gray." Just one month out of high school, Zelda was "slender and well-proportioned," "lithe," and "extraordinarily graceful."

Among the younger set, Zelda Sayre was commonly acknowledged as something of a wild child. She particularly delighted in scandalizing her father, Judge Anthony Sayre, a staid Victorian who, in his capacity as an associate justice of the Alabama Supreme Court, was one of Montgomery's leading citizens.

Given her family's standing in the community, Zelda's frequent exploits were sure fodder for gossip. There was the day she climbed to the roof of her house, kicked away the ladder, and compelled the fire company to rescue her from certain injury and disgrace. Or the time she borrowed her friend's snappy little Stutz Bearcat to drive down to Boodler's Bend, a local lover's lane concealed by a thick orchard of pecan trees, and shone a spotlight on those of her schoolmates who were necking in the backseats of parked cars. Or those other occasions when she repeated the same trick, but at the front entrance to Madam Helen St. Clair's notorious city brothel.

Most disturbing to Judge Sayre was Zelda's well-earned reputation for violating the time-honored codes of sexual propriety that seemed everywhere under attack by the time the opening shots were fired in World War I. Already a veritable legend among hundreds of well-heeled fraternity brothers as far and wide as the University of Alabama, Auburn University, and Georgia Tech, Zelda was "the most popular girl at every dance," as a would-be suitor remembered years later.

Part of Zelda's renown surely was owed to her habit of sneaking out of country club dances—and sometimes her bedroom window— to join Montgomery's most eligible bachelors for a few hours of necking, petting, and drinking in secluded backseat venues. On more than a few occasions, the inviting aroma of pear trees, the dim glow of a half-moon, and the tentative sound of a boyfriend's car horn were all the inspiration Zelda needed to walk quietly across her plain whitewashed room, draw open the curtains, and creep down to the tin roof that protected the Sayre family's front porch.

After that, she was gone into the night.

During her four years at Sidney Lanier High School, Zelda was an average student, but she was well ahead of the learning curve in most other matters. She habitually rouged her cheeks and stenciled her eyes with mascara, giving her friends' parents great cause for concern.

A regular at the local soda fountain, she alternated between double banana splits (innocuous) and a "dopes" (not so innocuous), a combination of Coca-Cola and aromatic spirits.

When the entire senior class cut school on April 1, it was Zelda who pooled everyone's money and flirted with the nice agent at the Empire Theatre, who happily granted the students admission at a cut rate. And it was Zelda who triumphantly organized a group photo in front of the ticket box.

When her English teacher assigned a poetry-writing exercise for homework, Zelda immediately volunteered to read her original composition—scratched out the next morning in homeroom—aloud.

> *I do love my Charlie so.*
> *It nearly drives me wild.*
> *I'm so glad that he's my beau*
> *And I'm his baby child!*

It was a big hit with her classmates, but not exactly what the teacher was looking for.

For all of Zelda's purported daring, Sara Mayfield, her loyal childhood friend, averred that she was no better or worse than most young women of her time. "Zelda would have been the last to deny that she danced cheek to cheek and did the Shimmy, the Charleston, and the Black Bottom," Mayfield admitted. But "if she gave a demonstration of the Hula at a midterm dance at the University of Alabama, had not Alice Roosevelt, the President's daughter, been similarly criticized for doing the same thing . . . ?"

To be sure, Zelda "rode behind her admirers . . . on their motorcycles with her arms around them, raised her hemlines to the knee, bobbed her hair, smoked, tippled, and kissed the boys goodbye." But this sort of "flirtation was an old Southern custom; 'going the limit' was not. Zelda was a reigning beauty and 'a knockout' in the paleolithic slang of the day, far too popular to have 'put out' for her beaux, far too shrewd in the tactics and strategy of popularity to grant her favors to one suitor and thereby alienate a regiment of them."

Maybe so, maybe not. But Zelda did her best to cultivate a scandalous reputation. She encouraged reports of skinny-dipping excursions and multiple romantic entanglements. During the summer, when it got too hot, she slipped out of her underwear and asked her date to hold it for the evening in his coat pocket. And at a legendary Christmas bop, when a chaperone reproached her for dancing too closely and too wantonly with her date, Zelda retaliated by swiping a band of mistletoe and pinning it to her backside.

Long after the last chords of the Jazz Age had been struck, Zelda admitted in her own autobiographical novel that "I never let them down on the dramatic possibilities of a scene—I give a damned good show."

Scott Fitzgerald certainly thought so.

Just shy of his twenty-first birthday, the young army lieutenant was stationed at nearby Camp Sheridan, where he spent most of his time devouring novels and cavorting with the sons and daughters of Montgomery's first citizens. Smartly clad in a new dress uniform, Fitzgerald cut an impressive figure. Shortly after the war, when Scott's first book became a best-seller, an interviewer described him as bearing "the agreeable countenance of a young person who cheerfully regards himself as the center of everything." His eyes were "blue and domineering," his nose "Grecian and pleasantly snippy; mouth, 'spoiled and alluring,' like one of his own yellow-haired heroines; and he parts his wavy fair hair in the middle, as Amory Blaine"—the fictional hero of Fitzgerald's first novel—"decided that all 'slickers' should do."

Fitzgerald was a native of St. Paul, Minnesota, who had spent four years at Princeton without earning his undergraduate degree. An indifferent student, he received poor marks from his professors and made little contribution to classroom discussion. To his credit, Fitzgerald was an accomplished amateur playwright and a frequent contributor to the university literary magazine. But on balance, his academic career fell far short of even his expectations.

Lazy in all things but reading and writing, vaguely ambitious but hopelessly lacking direction, Fitzgerald escaped the indignity of a fifth year at Princeton by enlisting in the army in late 1917. First stationed at Fort Leavenworth for officer's training, he made a poor impression on his platoon captain, a serious young West Point man named Dwight D. Eisenhower. Scott's attention simply wasn't on soldiering, and it showed. He fully expected that he would be sent to the European front, and fearing that he might return in a pine box, he accelerated work on his first novel, *The Romantic Egotist*. It consumed much of his time and all of his energy.

On short leave from the army in early 1918, Scott enjoyed a brief hiatus in Princeton, where he managed to finish the novel and send it off to an editor at Charles Scribner's Sons. After reporting back for duty in March, he was transferred to the Forty-fifth Infantry Regiment at Camp Alexander in Kentucky. Though he was trained to lead a platoon, his commanding officers found Scott so deficient as a soldier that they consigned him to stateside duty—first at Camp Gordon in Georgia and then, in June 1918, at Camp Sheridan.

With his novel under review and combat service safely at bay, Fitzgerald was free to immerse himself in local revelries. Almost from the start, he began working his way through a list of Montgomery's most eligible debutantes, generously supplied by Lawton Campbell, a local boy he had known at Princeton. In a more candid moment years later, Fitzgerald admitted that he had been naturally endowed with neither "great animal magnetism nor money," two certain keys to success among the well-bred collegiate circles in which he moved back in the early days. Still, he knew that he had "good looks and intelligence," qualities that generally helped him get the "top girl" wherever he went.

Lawton Campbell was several years older than Zelda Sayre and had left Montgomery before she entered high school; consequently, he didn't include her on Scott's roster of southern belles. It was purely by chance that she and Scott Fitzgerald happened upon each other that evening in July.

The moment his eyes locked on her, Scott was taken by Zelda's beauty. Had he asked around, he would have learned of her dangerous reputation. As one contemporary remembered, "There were two kinds of girls, those who would ride with you in your automobile at night and the nice girls who wouldn't. But Zelda didn't seem to give a damn."

At the first opportunity, Scott elbowed his way to her side and, finding that her dance card was full for the evening, asked if he might take her out after the country club festivities wound down. The faux East Coast drawl that he studiously cultivated at Princeton just barely concealed his flat Minnesota burr.

"I never make late dates with fast workers," she replied sharply in the most properly southern of southern accents.

Nevertheless, she gave Scott her telephone number and subtly encouraged him to ply his charms another time.

Scott called Zelda at home the next day—and the next day after that, and again every day for the better part of two weeks until she relented. Not that it took a great deal of convincing. Scott was "a blond Adonis in a Brooks Brothers uniform," one of their contemporaries remarked. He was, by Lawton Campbell's estimation, "the handsomest boy I'd ever seen. He had yellow hair and lavender eyes" and a confident swagger that won over even his deepest skeptics.

In her autobiographical novel, Zelda evoked the sensation of dancing with Scott on one of their first dates. "[H]e smelled like new goods," she wrote all those years later. "Being close to him, [my] face in the space between his ear and his stiff army collar was like being initiated into the subterranean reserves of a fine fabric store exuding the delicacy of cambrics and linen and luxury bound in bales." Zelda was jealous of Scott's "pale aloofness," and when she watched him stroll arm in arm off the dance floor with other women, she felt a dull pang of resentment that he was "leading others than [me] into those cooler regions which he inhabited alone."

To be fair, Zelda saw to it that Scott did most of the chasing. As one of Montgomery's most popular debutantes, she already enjoyed scores of romantic opportunities from the usual college and business crowds. In normal times, Scott would have faced stiff competition from the likes of Dan Cody, the dashing young scion of a prominent Montgomery banking family, or Lloyd Hooper, an even wealthier son of an even wealthier Alabama line. Now, with America fully mobi-

2

ʃEX O'CLOCK IN AMERICA

ONE OF ZELDA'S close friends from Montgomery noted that Minnie Sayre, Zelda's mother, "had been carefully schooled in the axioms of Victorian etiquette that we called the 'no ladies': no lady ever sits with her limbs crossed (and *limbs* it was; *legs* was still a four-letter word); no lady ever lets her back touch the back of a chair; no lady ever goes out without a clean linen handkerchief in her purse; no lady ever leaves the house until the last button on her gloves is fastened; no lady ever lets her bare foot touch the bare floor, and so forth."

By the eve of World War I, Victorians like Minnie and Anthony Sayre were beside themselves with grief over the younger generation's apparent lack of restraint. Zelda Sayre certainly wasn't the only girl in Montgomery—or America—who was sliding out her bedroom window and driving off into the night with her boyfriend.

Since the early twentieth century, the sexual habits of American women had changed in profound ways. Surveys later revealed that whereas only 14 percent of women born before 1900 engaged in premarital sex by the age of twenty-five, somewhere between 36 percent and 39 percent of women who came of age in the 1910s and 1920s lost their virginity before marriage. What's more, the New Woman of the 1920s was more than twice as likely to experience an orgasm while having premarital sex than her mother before her. In short, a

A typical Jazz Age couple displaying the new comfort level with romance and sexuality, 1928.

lot more women of the younger generation were having premarital sex, and many of them were enjoying it.

As early as 1913, social commentators observed that the bell had tolled "Sex o'clock in America," signaling a "Repeal of Reticence" about matters both carnal and romantic. Writers noted with disapproval that "making love lightly, boldly and promiscuously seems to be part of our social structure" and that a new set of concerns like " 'To Spoon' or 'Not to Spoon' Seems to Be the Burning Question with Modern Young America." They lamented that it was now "literally true that the average father does not know, by name or sight, the young man who visits his daughter and who takes her out to places of amusement," a practice that grew ever more common as more men acquired automobiles, which a disapproving Victorian scorned as the "devil's wagon."

"Where Is Your Daughter This Afternoon?" asked another spokesman for the elder generation. "Are you sure that she is not being drawn into the whirling vortex of afternoon 'trots' . . . ?"

In a disturbing magazine exposé, "From the Ballroom to Hell," Mrs. E. M. Whittemore estimated that 70 percent of all prostitutes in New York had been spoiled by jazz music. In Cleveland, Ohio, a municipal ordinance prohibited revelers at any city dance hall "to take either exceptionally long or short steps. . . . Don't dance from the waist up; dance from the waist down. Flirting, spooning, and rowdy conduct of any kind is absolutely prohibited." And Cleveland was *liberal*. In Oshkosh, Wisconsin, couples were barred from "looking into each other's eyes while dancing."

But the Victorians were fighting a losing battle, and the most perceptive among them knew it. By the time Scott Fitzgerald left Zelda Sayre for New York in early 1919—well before the heyday of the Jazz Age—millions of American daughters were already hiking up their skirts, wearing makeup, bobbing their hair, and partaking of heretofore forbidden delights like alcohol, cigarettes, and mixed-sex dancing.

Not everyone found fault with the emerging New Woman. In the immediate prewar years, she was feted in such popular songs as "A Dangerous Girl" and serenaded with lines like "You dare me, you scare me, and still I like you more each day. But you're the kind that will charm; and then do you harm; you've got a dangerous way." A particularly scandalous magazine advertisement featured a young woman with rouged, puckered lips. The caption below her picture read simply: "Take It from Me!" Even with the benefit of hindsight, it's hard to imagine just how shocking these developments were in the late 1910s and 1920s.

Even before she became the archetype of the 1920s flapper— the term that she and Scott would do so much to popularize and define—Zelda adopted the same increasingly casual approach to romance and sexuality that many young women exhibited in the pre-war decade.

In later years, all of this made good fodder for Scott's literary imagination. But in the meantime, it caused him a world of pain. Scott's trouble started even before he boarded the train for New York. Though Scott secured her vague commitment of engagement by early 1919, within the space of a few weeks Zelda returned to the habit of dating several men at once. Just as Scott embarked for his new job that February, they quarreled bitterly over her plan to attend a dance at Auburn University in the company of Francis Stubbs, the school's well-chiseled star quarterback.

During a stopover in North Carolina, en route to New York, Scott sent Zelda a conciliatory telegram—in care of Stubbs—assuring her: YOU KNOW I DO NOT DOUBT YOU DARLING. The next day, writing from New York, he wired her an even more elaborate note of contrition: DARLING HEART . . . THIS WORLD IS A GAME AND [WHILE] I FEEL SURE OF YOU[R] LOVE EVERYTHING IS POSSIBLE[.] I AM IN THE LAND OF AMBITION AND SUCCESS AND MY ONLY HOPE AND FAITH IS THAT MY DARLING HEART WILL BE WITH ME SOON.

The dust from the Auburn incident had barely settled when Scott discovered that Stubbs had given Zelda his prized golden football insignia. Still more grief ensued when he learned that Zelda had also attended a dance in Sewanee with John Dearborn and sat up half the night with him in front of a rustic log fire at his fraternity house.

Zelda was a master of the mixed signal. At times, her letters could be encouraging and even winsome. "All these soft, warm nights going to waste when I ought to be lying in your arms, under the moon," she wrote, "—the dearest arms in all the world—darling arms that I love so to feel around me— How much longer—before they'll be there to stay?"

But as Scott grew alarmed that her letters were too few and far between, Zelda, either by design or accident, only fed his darkest suspicions of betrayal. *"Please, please* don't be so depressed," she told him. "We'll be married soon, and then these lonesome nights will be over forever—and until we are, I am loving, loving every minute of the day and night."

It's easy to imagine Scott cooping himself up for hours in his cold and dingy apartment at 200 Claremont Avenue, just on the border between Morningside Heights and Harlem. There, amid the steady rumble of the Seventh Avenue elevated train, he scratched out nineteen short stories in less than four months and received 122 rejection letters from mass circulation magazines that simply weren't ready for F. Scott Fitzgerald.

"I had about as much control over my own destiny," he later mused, "as a convict over the cut of his clothes." New York in early 1919 "had all the iridescence of the beginning of the world." But as he "hovered ghost-like in the Plaza Red Room of a Saturday afternoon, or went to lush and liquid garden parties in the East Sixties or tippled with Princetonians in the Biltmore Bar I was haunted always by my other life—my drab room . . . my square foot of the subway, my fixation upon the day's letter from Alabama—would it come and what would it say?"

It couldn't have made matters any better when Zelda alluded dimly to her romantic exploits. "I must leave now," she closed a short dispatch, "or my date (awful boob) will come before I can escape—" On another occasion, she wrote that "yesterday Bill LeGrand and I drove his car to Auburn and came back with *ten* boys to liven things up— Of course [*sic*], the day was vastly exciting—and the night more so— Thanks to a jazz band that's been performing at Mays between Keith shows. The boys thought I'd be a charming addition to their act, and I nearly entered upon a theatrical career." Still another letter explained that " 'Red' said last night that I was the pinkest-whitest person he ever saw, so I went to sleep in his lap. Of course, you don't mind because it was really very fraternal, and we were chaperoned by three girls—"

However much she gestured at fidelity—"Scott," she wrote, "you're really awfully silly— In the first case, I haven't kissed anybody goodbye, and in the second place, nobody's left in the first place"—Zelda couldn't resist leaving her fiancé in limbo. She made passing references to her own trysts and encouraged Scott to have a few of his own. *"Please—please,"* she demanded shortly after his second visit to Montgomery that spring, "aren't you ever going to learn that boys never appreciate things other men tell them on their girls? At least five men have suffered a bout behind the Baptist Church for no other offense than you are about to commit, only I was the lady concerned—in the dim past. Anyway, if she is good-looking, and you want to one bit—I know you could and love me just the same—"

Certainly, Scott could claim his share of past sexual conquests. Before he met Zelda, he had been involved with another young Montgomery belle, a fellow Catholic with whom he once visited St. Peter's Church to pay penance. After Scott had cleansed away his sins, his girlfriend stepped into the confession box and ticked off a number of minor transgressions against God and man. When she finished, the priest asked, "Is that all, my daughter?"

"I . . . I . . . think so," she replied tentatively.

"Are you sure, my daughter?"

"That's all I can remember."

"No, that's not all, my daughter," he answered severely. "I fear I shall have to prompt you. . . . Because I heard your young man's confession first."

In Zelda, Scott met his match. He wasn't the only person ripping his hair out over her wild ways. Mrs. Sayre frequently deposited reproachful notes on Zelda's pillow, like one that warned, "If you have added whiskey to your tobacco you can subtract your Mother. . . . If you prefer the habits of a prostitute don't try to mix them with gentility. Oil and water do not mix."

Matters finally came to a head in May when Zelda accidentally mailed Scott a "sentimental" note intended for Georgia Tech's star golfer, Perry Adair, who had "pinned" her at a recent university dance. Even Zelda seemed to agree that the slipup went beyond the pale. "You asked me not to write," she began sheepishly, "but I had to explain— That note belonged with Perry Adair's fraternity pin which I was returning. Hence, the sentimental tone. He has very thought-fully contributed a letter to you to the general mix-up. It went to him, with his pin. I'm so sorry, Scott. . . ."

Scott's reaction to Perry's letter is lost to the ages, but it probably wasn't a happy one. And he wouldn't have enjoyed knowing that another member of the weekend party had walked in on Perry and Zelda at the fraternity house, both drunk beyond recognition and smashing Victrola records over each other's heads.

In June, Scott paid a third visit to Montgomery to pressure Zelda into marrying him. They quarreled again, and she broke off the engagement definitively. Scott stormed off for one last legendary bender up north.

"While my friends were launching decently into life," he wrote of his return to New York, "I had muscled my inadequate bark into mid-stream. The gilded youth . . . the classmates in the Yale-Princeton Club whooping up our first after-the-war reunion, the atmosphere of the millionaire's houses that I sometimes frequented—these things were empty for me. . . ." Scott wandered around 127th Street and took full stock of his situation.

"I was a failure—mediocre at advertising work and unable to get started as a writer. Hating the city, I got roaring, weeping drunk on my last penny and went home. . . ."

That June, he quit his job and moved back to his parents' house in St. Paul, Minnesota. There, sequestered in a third-floor attic and sur-viving on a steady diet of Coca-Cola and cigarettes—all purchased with money he bummed off of old friends from the neighborhood—he revised his manuscript, now entitled *This Side of Paradise*. On Sep-tember 16, success finally beckoned. Maxwell Perkins, an editor at Charles Scribner's Sons, delivered the news he had been waiting for so desperately. Scott Fitzgerald was going to be a published author.

It was time to go win back Zelda.

Two young couples enjoy a romantic picnic.

3

WILL ʃHE THROW HER ARMʃ AROUND YOUR NECK AND YELL?

O F ALL PEOPLE, Scott Fitzgerald—soon to be heralded as
the premier analyst of the American flapper—should have
taken things in better stride. After all, Zelda Sayre was only
marching in lockstep with millions of other American women who
claimed new sexual and romantic freedoms in the years just before
World War I.

Much of this revolution in morals and manners had to do with the
subtle but steady pull of economic and demographic forces. By 1929,
more than a quarter of all women—and more than half of all *single*
women—were gainfully employed. In large cities like Chicago,
Philadelphia, and St. Paul, anywhere between one-quarter and one-
third of adult women workers lived alone in private apartments or
boardinghouses, free from the close surveillance of their parents.

Despite deep and abiding discrimination in wages and employment, working women often found that real money could buy real
freedom. As an observer noted, "In those cities where women
twenty-five to thirty-five can control their own purse strings many of
them are apt to drift into casual or steady relationships with certain
men friends which may or may not end in matrimony."

The mass entry of women into the workforce was part of a longer
trend toward industrialization and urbanization, a process that reached

its crescendo in 1920, when the Census Bureau announced that the United States was no longer a nation of small farmers. For the first time ever, more Americans (51 percent) lived in cities than in the countryside. Though the Census Bureau counted any municipality with more than 2,500 residents as "urban," most of the country's new urban majority lived in cities with more than 100,000 residents. In real numbers, the change was staggering. Between 1860 and 1920, the number of people living in cities with a population of at least 8,000 jumped from 6.2 million to 54.3 million.

Critically, a great many of those new urban migrants were women. Popular literature notwithstanding, a 1920 government survey found that "the farmer's daughter is more likely to leave the farm and go to the city than is the farmer's son." Many of these young women surely fled rural America in pursuit of better economic opportunities. Others abandoned their small towns in search of excitement and glamour or because their parents chastised them for going out publicly with men. One urban pioneer told an interviewer that she "wanted more money for clothes than my mother would give me. . . . We were always fighting over my pay check. Then I wanted to be out late and they wouldn't stand for that. So I finally left home."

Another woman explained that she and her stepfather "kept having fights back and forth about the boys I went out with and the hours that I kept. He even accused me of wanting to do things which I'd not even thought of doing *up to that time*." After a particularly angry row, she packed her bags and moved to Chicago. "I was always willing to stand up for my rights," she explained.

If excitement and freedom were what she craved, her timing was perfect.

As late as the 1890s, there had scarcely been such a thing as an urban nightlife. Young romance had been captive to the sun, and once it set, towns and cities could rely only on gas lamps, which cast a short and dim glow. Against this shadowy backdrop, no respectable citizen was safe. George Foster, a popular writer for the *New-York Tribune,* warned Victorian Americans of "the fearful mysteries of darkness in the metropolis—the festivities of prostitution, the orgies of pauperism, the haunts of theft and murder, the scenes of drunkenness and beastly debauch . . ."

By 1900, all of that had changed.

Across America, one journalist cheered, "the field where but yesterday the flickering gas flame held full sway now blazes nightly in the glow of myriads of electric lamps, aggregating in intensity the power of 15,000,000 candles." Out of the darkness had come light. What's more, by 1902 nearly all urban streetcars were electrified. It was a new dawn of freedom for both town and city.

When young women moved to the city alone, they were able to elude the familiar scrutiny of their parents and neighbors. Even when young women still lived at home, towns and cities afforded them a greater measure of anonymity and social freedom than they enjoyed in the sleepy villages that dotted America's landscape throughout the nineteenth century. Thanks to mechanization, in the opening decades of the new century, the number of hours the typical American worked each week dropped, even as real wages, adjusted for inflation, rose. Free from the round-the-clock demands of farm life, ordinary people found themselves with more money and more time to spend on themselves.

And spend it they did, on a host of public amusements that were scarcely imaginable twenty years before: dance halls both grand and modest; plush movie palaces like Chicago's Oriental Theatre and New York's Rialto; fun parks like Luna and Steeplechase, each magnificently lit by as many as 250,000 electric bulbs; inner-city baseball stadiums like Ebbets Field and Shibe Park, easily accessible by public transportation.

This innovative leisure culture was meant for men and women to enjoy together, and it ushered in a new frankness about sex and romance. Popular concessions at amusement parks included machines that gauged the intensity of a couple's kiss and rides like the Cannon Coaster. "Will she throw her arms around your neck and yell?" the ads wondered. "Well, I guess yes." Each year, millions of visitors to these urban fantasylands coupled up and rode into the dark welcome of the Canals of Venice and the Tunnel of Love. The owner of Steeplechase Park at Coney Island only stated the obvious when he observed, "The men like it because it gives them a chance to hug the girls, the girls like it because it gives them a chance to get hugged."

Amusement parks were just the tip of the iceberg. In 1910, Ruth True, an urban sociologist, chronicled the story of Louisa, a typical Irish working girl from the West Side of Manhattan. Earning $5 per week from her job at a candy factory, Louisa felt entitled to stay out late at dance halls, often in the company of strange men. "The costume in which she steps out so triumphantly has cost many bitter moments at home," True observed. Indeed, Louisa's poor mother was beside herself with grief. "She stands up and answers me back," she lamented. "An' she's comin' in at 2 o'clock, me not knowin' where she has been. Folks will talk, you know, an it ain't right fer a girl."

Louisa's mother probably didn't *want* to know everything that went on at the dance halls her daughter frequented. A high-minded reformer described with horror a scene at a typical venue, where "one of the women [was] smoking cigarettes, most of the younger couples were hugging and kissing, there was a general mingling of men and women at the different tables," and the customers "kept running around the room and acted like a mob of lunatics."

An observer at another dance hall noted with similar disapproval that "one of the girls while in the middle of a dance stopped on [the] floor and went to different tables and kept saying, 'You didn't kiss me for New Year's.'"

None of this made any sense to the aging Victorians. Twenty years earlier, when Minnie Sayre was a young woman, American courtship had been a carefully orchestrated affair that allowed mothers and fathers to exercise considerable control over their children. A teenage girl received gentleman callers on the front porch or in the family parlor, all under the vigilant eye of an adult chaperone.

Such was the case for Ina Smith, age eighteen, and John Marean, age twenty-four, who grew up on adjacent farms in New York State's rural Nanticoke Valley. Beginning in 1899, when the young couple started courting, John would visit the Smith homestead a few times a week. With Ina's parents keeping close watch, they would pass the hours in conversation, playing tiddlywinks, reading to each other, or making fudge in the kitchen. Sometimes, when the opportunity presented itself, they went out unaccompanied to church socials and musical performances. On rare occasions they even ventured fifteen miles away, to Binghamton, for events like Casino Night or Buffalo Bill's Wild West Show. "Got home at half past three," Ina recorded in her diary after one such excursion. "I've been awfully sleepy today."

But this was an exception. Most of the time, Ina and John were under lock and key.

The Victorians were hardly all prudes. In fact, theirs was an intensely romantic culture. Looking back on his boyhood in rural Indiana, the novelist Theodore Dreiser remembered that young men and women were always seen "walking under the trees or rowing on the lakes, holding hands or kissing or whispering sweet nothings." "Fiery tales" abounded of "sweet trysts and doings in unlighted parlors and groves." Still, those moments were tame by later comparison. For most young lovers in the Victorian era, romance was a closely guarded and circumscribed affair.

All of this came under assault at the turn of the century, even before most American towns went electric. The first sign of trouble came in the 1890s, when Americans fell in love with the bicycle.

For young people like Otto Follin and Laura Grant, who grew up in Illinois, these new contraptions made all the difference. "We rode till half past nine," Otto recorded, "and then we sat down to rest by the lake and were alone and I knew that I could touch her if I wanted to and I did, just a little. . . ."

It got worse.

Parents who were just coming to terms with the bicycle woke up one day to discover the deleterious effects of the telephone, which came into wider use in the first decades of the new century. Now, lovelorn teenagers like Marian Curtis and Lawrence Gerritson, who lived in the suburbs of Boston, could speak daily by phone, even as they continued to see *and* write each other several times a week. Doubtless, their parents came to rue the day when the uniformed agent came over to install the magic black box and handset.

Then came the automobile.

At the dawn of the twentieth century, cars were still viewed as impractical and unsafe. Their tires fell off; they buckled and spun out at the slightest provocation; when it rained, their wheels got mired in the mud and the muck. At best, they were playthings of oil tycoons and bankers' sons. San Francisco, Cincinnati, and Savannah slapped drivers with a maximum speed limit of eight miles per hour. Vermont required all motorists to hire "persons of mature age" to walk one-eighth of a mile ahead of their cars, waving red warning flags for the benefit of innocent pedestrians.

The technology revolution hit America almost overnight. In the years before World War I, Ransom Olds inaugurated the mass production of automobiles, Henry Leland experimented with interchangeable car parts, and Henry Ford took advantage of both advances to usher in a radical phase in the ongoing transportation revolution. By the late 1920s, the automobile industry was turning out nearly five million cars each year and Americans collectively owned twenty-six million automobiles, which translated to one car for every five persons. To support this new car culture, state and local governments saddled themselves with over $10 billion of debt to construct modern highways, roads, tunnels, and bridges. Florida cut through the everglade swampland to raise the Tamiami Trail; Arizona bisected its vast desert; Utah paved a road over Lake Bonneville; and New York erected the Bronx River Parkway.

The triumph of the mass-produced automobile signaled the end of the Victorian era's courtship system. Just ask the father of a teenage girl in Muncie, Indiana, who vainly warned his daughter against "going out motoring for the evening with a young blade in a rakish car waiting at the curb." "What on earth *do* you want me to do?" the young woman replied with exasperation. "Just sit around home all evening!"

Parents worried that their kids never spent time with their families anymore. "They always have something else going on," one mother complained. "In the nineties we were all much more together," another woman sighed.

A survey of Muncie's high school students in the 1920s revealed that the five most frequent sources of disagreement between teenagers and their parents were, in order: (1) "the number of times you go out on school nights during the week"; (2) "the hour you get in at night"; (3) "grades at school"; (4) "your spending money"; and (5) "use of the automobile." It didn't take a genius to realize that items one, two, and four were all intimately related to item five.

It wasn't just the erosion of family spirit that bothered parents. The car was "an incredible engine of escape," as Dorothy Bromley and Florence Britten observed in their 1938 tract, *Youth and Sex*. It meant that young couples could be "off and away, out of reach of parental control. A youth now . . . has a refuge . . . complete privacy. He has taken full advantage of it, not only as a means of going places, but as a place to go where he can take a girl and hold hands, neck, pet, or if it's that kind of affair, go the limit." Not that teenage boys were the only ones titillated by automotive possibilities. A Rhode Island woman remarked, "You can be so nice and all alone in a machine, just a little one that you can go on crazy roads in and be miles away from anyone but each other."

By 1925, when the husband-and-wife sociologist team of Robert and Helen Lynd arrived in Muncie to conduct their famous study of an ordinary American town, the destructive effects of the automobile were pretty well established. Between September 1923 and September 1924, thirty young women were hauled into the Muncie courthouse and charged with "sex crimes." Of that total, nineteen had been apprehended in parked cars.

The Lynds observed a Sunday school teacher ask his students to list temptations that "we have today that Jesus didn't have." To this challenge, a quick-witted boy replied, "Speed!"

All of this boded poorly for the old order. As late as 1907, *Harper's Bazaar* could still find a captive audience for articles like "Etiquette for Men," which considered in minute detail the protocols of Victorian courtship. But the swift breakdown of the "calling system" gave rise to a new romantic lexicon by the early 1910s. Now, boys and girls were going out on "dates," a term that appeared as early as 1896 in George Ade's columns for the *Chicago Record* but that most prewar writers continued to place safely between quotation marks so as to impart the experimental and faddish quality of the emerging system.

The new dating culture lent itself to greater sexual experimentation and frankness on the part of young people like Katherine Dummer, a typical middle-class teenager from Chicago. In the summer of 1915, Katherine's family took her on a camping trip out west. Writing to her fiancé, a law student named Walter Fisher, Katherine spoke of her "starvation" for physical intimacy. "I'll be patient, dear," she assured him, "but I'm awfully hungry. . . . If this hideous restless feeling keeps up I don't know what I'll do."

As the summer wore on, Katherine's notes grew edgier. "If I get much hungrier," she told Walter, "I'm awfully afraid I'll start something." She must have been unusually relentless, because by mid-July Mr. and Mrs. Dummer agreed to have Walter join the family in California for the last leg of the trip. "If I only see you for two weeks in September, with nothing particular to do & the thought of separation again the uppermost thing," Katherine confided, "we may have more or less a debauch, we'll be a lot more likely to do crazy things."

Clearly, Zelda Sayre wasn't the only girl in America who liked to do "crazy things." Young women growing up right before the Jazz Age were equal partners in pioneering a new set of customs governing romance and sexuality.

This new system wasn't necessarily stacked in a girl's favor, though. Working women faced rampant wage and employment discrimination that sharply curtailed their spending power. A study conducted in Chicago found that the average female factory worker or clerk in the 1920s earned not much more than $22 per week, yet *bare minimum* living costs ranged between $20 and $25 a week. At best, if she had a boyfriend who treated her to the occasional dinner or lunch, the working girl could keep her head above water; at worst, she fell below the poverty line. This was the case for Cora, a typical twenty-five-year-old laundress whose sixty-hour work week afforded her little more than a dark, grimy room in a boardinghouse and solitary meals of stew, potatoes, and apple pie at a cheap neighborhood cafeteria.

Even when working women lived with their families, they faced a crude double standard: They were expected to hand over all of their weekly pay to their parents—a practice with which most women wage earners in New York complied. By comparison, their brothers normally retained at least half their earnings for personal expenses.

On their own, working-class women could scarcely afford to indulge themselves with fancy clothes, movie tickets, or a thrilling afternoon at Coney Island. For them, city life held out the promise of social freedom, but not always the reality. The same could also be true for many middle-class teenagers like Zelda Sayre and Katherine Dummer, who grew up in considerably greater comfort but were still dependent on their parents for money.

This was where men came into the picture.

A central component of the new dating system came to be known as "treating," whereby men paid cash for dinners, theater tickets, and amusement park admissions and women carefully estimated how much physical and romantic attention they needed to provide in turn. "If they didn't take me," a young department store clerk explained, "how could I ever go out?" More to the point, a young waitress offered, "If I did not have a man, I could not get along on my wages."

This was an entirely new dynamic. In the old days, courting took place at home. There simply wasn't anywhere else to go. In effect, the Victorian system of romance, centered as it was around the front parlor or porch, put women in the driver's seat: They did the inviting, they set the hour and day of the visit, and they called the limits. Dating was something completely different. It revolved around a new public leisure culture that cost money; it therefore placed men, who *had* more money, in greater control. The result was a complex interplay among commerce, sexuality, and love.

Sometimes the dating system could be purely mercenary. "Most of the girls quite frankly admit making 'dates' with strange men," a Consumer's League report found in the early 1910s. "These 'dates' are made with no thought on the part of the girl beyond getting a good time which she cannot afford herself."

Many men resented this commercialization of romance, as was fully evident in a 1919 article that appeared in the *Chicago Tribune* under the headline MAN GETTING $18 A WEEK DARES NOT FALL IN

LOVE. The young man in question was a returning World War I veteran whose meager wages "could not even buy a young lady an ice cream cone," let alone an expensive night out on the town.

The trade-off was even worse for women. Implicit in the exchange was a sexual return, and this took some getting used to. A social investigator named Clara Laughlin reported the story of a young working girl in New York who was puzzled by her inability to keep a boyfriend after the first few dates. "Don't yeh know there ain't no feller goin' t'spend coin on yeh for nothin'?" explained one of her more savvy coworkers. "Yeh gotta be a good Indian, Kid—we all gotta!"

Still, for many women, as for many men, the new system was often exciting. It was complex, it was inherently adversarial, it placed women in a tough spot . . . but it could be fun. "Smoking, dancing like Voodoo devotees, dressing décolleté, 'petting' and drinking," a coed at Ohio State began. "We do these things because *we honestly enjoy the attendant physical sensations. . . .* The girl with sport in her blood . . . 'gets by.' She kisses the boys, she smokes with them, drinks with them, and why? Because *the feeling of comradeship is running rampant.*"

It was a new age, and for millions of young women it offered not only new challenges, but also an unprecedented scale of freedom for personal exploration and self-fulfillment.

Scott Fitzgerald would make his career by describing it all.

4

FLAPPER KING

ROM ALMOST THE day his first novel hit bookstores in early 1920, F. Scott Fitzgerald was anointed "the recognized spokesman of the younger generation—the dancing, flirting, frivoling, lightly philosophizing young America," as one Hollywood journalist put it. After all, the semiautobiographical book was a classic coming-of-age tale following the trials and tribulations of one Amory Blaine—a young midwesterner who, like Fitzgerald, attends Princeton, falls in love with a wild and bewitching young woman, and aimlessly seeks fame and fortune in the big city.

This Side of Paradise was properly credited with opening a portal to the hidden lives of America's collegiate crowd, a growing portion of the population that many ordinary readers were eager to learn more about.

The irony was that the young author also found himself billed as "F. Scott Fitzgerald, who originated the flapper," "Flapperdom's Fiction Ace," and, only somewhat more modestly, the nation's "Expert on Flappers." "He draws with knowledge, with divination," crowed the *Minneapolis Tribune* shortly after the novel was released. "Mr. Fitzgerald presents more and better than the manners of the girl of the period of jazz and free speech. He really has 'the eternal feminine' caught."

In fact, *This Side of Paradise* didn't have a great deal to say about

By 1920, it was no longer clear whether Scott Fitzgerald created
the flapper or she created him.

women. It was really a book about a young man. More to the point, Fitzgerald never even used the term *flapper* in the whole of the text.

Still, by the year's end, Scott's name grew so synonymous with the New Woman that one newspaper paid a toast:

> *To Scott Fitzgerald,*
> *flapper King,*
> *A Flappy New Year*
> *do I sing.*

At Wellesley College, the venerable all-women's school outside Boston, the student newspaper ran a satirical poem entitled "The Transformation of a Rose," in which a "winsome lass, a maiden pure and sweet," falls under the sway of Fitzgerald's novel. By the last few stanzas, she has been thoroughly corrupted:

> *. . . Her fortune went in purchases—*
> *Cosmetics, clothes and such,*
> *Her time all went into a line*
> *She needed one so much.*
>
> *Rosemary's name is not the same*
> *Nor is her face or form.*
> *She's reckless Rose of many beaux*
> *The envy of her dorm.*
>
> *They ask her where she got her pep,*
> *Her snappy, Frenchy air*
> *And where she learnt to wear her clothes*
> *And henna rinse her hair.*
>
> *Her answer is—"I bought it all*
> *And at the cheapest price.*
> *I bought the book that tells the tricks,*
> *'This Side of Paradise.'"*

By later standards, Fitzgerald's exposé of the flapper was tame. But it was provocative enough for its time. "None of the Victorian mothers . . . had any idea how casually their daughters were accustomed to be kissed," opened an oft quoted chapter.

Perhaps thinking of Zelda, Fitzgerald claimed that the "popular daughter" "becomes engaged every six months between sixteen and twenty-two, when she arranges a match with young Hambell, of Cambell & Hambell, who fatuously considers himself her first love, and between engagements [she] has other sentimental last kisses in the moonlight, or the firelight, or the outer darkness."

Throughout the novel, Fitzgerald's protagonist—young Amory Blaine—"saw girls doing things that even in his memory would have been impossible." In this new and startling environment, virtually any girl could be found "deep in an atmosphere of jungle music and the questioning of moral codes. Amory found it rather fascinating that any popular girl he met before eight he might quite possibly kiss before twelve."

The young women in Scott's book whisper lines like "I'm just full of the devil." They wear "hand-knit, sleeveless" jerseys—which Amory aptly dubs "petting-shirts"—that offer easy access to the forbidden regions of their bodies. They scoff at their parents' prudery and remind them that "Mother, it's done—you can't run everything now the way you did in the early nineties."

As Fitzgerald's fame grew—and it grew quickly: Within a year, *This Side of Paradise* had sold forty thousand copies and topped waiting lists at libraries across the nation—journalists took to calling him the premier analyst of the American flapper. "Before he started to analyze this young person," wrote one critic, "to interpret her . . . to make familiar [her] weird vocabulary and to reveal what even fifteen or twenty years ago would have been considered 'scandalous goings-on,' the older generation had had only glimpses of what was doing in 'flapper' circles."

Even if he didn't invent the flapper, it didn't take Scott long to figure out that writing about her would pay handsome dividends. Eager to cash in on the hullabaloo surrounding *This Side of Paradise,* in 1920 *The Saturday Evening Post* began publishing Fitzgerald's short stories.

With a weekly circulation topping 2.75 million and a total readership probably amounting to several times that figure, the magazine was an important arbiter of middle-class culture during the Jazz Age. It was also a cash cow for its feature writers.

In 1920, Scott earned a whopping total of $18,850 for his writing, a sum equivalent in today's money to about $176,000. Only $6,200 of his income came from royalties on the novel. The rest derived from eleven short stories that he published that year, including $7,425 that Hollywood studios paid for the rights to three of his stories and options on future works.

In fact, Scott's short stories—and the movie rights associated with them—would always be the major source of his income. *This Side of Paradise* was regarded as a great success, but its total sales by the end of 1921—49,075 copies—didn't earn the book a spot among America's top ten best-sellers. By comparison, Sinclair Lewis's runaway success *Main Street,* also published in 1920, had sold 295,000 copies by the following year.

Unlike *This Side of Paradise,* many of Fitzgerald's early short stories, which were wildly popular among middle-class readers, featured young women as lead characters. The typical young woman in Scott's magazine stories—who came, in turn, to represent the typical American flapper—was an explicitly sexual being. "She was about nineteen, slender and supple, with a spoiled alluring mouth and quick gray eyes full of radiant curiosity," he described one of them. "Her feet, stockingless, and adorned rather than clad in blue-satin slippers which swung nonchalantly from her toes, were perched on the arm of a settee adjoining the one she occupied. And as she read she intermittently regaled herself by a faint application to her tongue of a half-lemon that she held in her hand."

Ardita, the flapper heroine of "The Offshore Pirate," which ran in *The Saturday Evening Post* in May 1920, was like many of Scott's lead women. She knew the value of her own sex appeal. The calves of her legs, she informs one suitor, are "worth five hundred dollars." "When a man's in love with me," she boasts, "he doesn't care for other amusements."

Another of Scott's flapper creations, Myra—the lead character in

"Myra Meets His Family," which Fox Studios adapted for the silver screen—was a midwestern debutante "with a becoming pallor and new shadows under her eyes [who] throughout the Armistice year . . . left the ends of cigarettes all over New York on little china trays marked 'Midnight Frolic' and 'Coconut Grove'; and 'Palais Royal.' She was twenty-one now and Cleveland people said that her mother ought to take her back home—that New York was spoiling her."

In a typical moment of candor, Myra admits that she's "played around so much that even while I'm kissing the man I just wonder how soon I'll get tired of him." Like all of Scott's flappers, Myra knows that she "may be a bit blasé, but I can still get any man I want."

In these and other stories, Fitzgerald taught his readers about the rituals of 1920s youth culture, from joyrides in shiny new automobiles to necking sessions and petting parties in the dark crooks of hotel lobbies and country club verandas. Scott's female characters smoked, rouged their cheeks and lips, cut their hair short, and took swigs from the hip flasks of their world-weary boyfriends.

Not just among the big-city literary crowds, but in Middle American towns like Muncie, Indiana, where one in every five households subscribed to The Saturday Evening Post, Fitzgerald quickly developed a reputation as the nation's expert on flappers and their boyfriends. In this regard, he was the beneficiary of considerable dumb luck.

American youth were more visible and excited more popular interest in the 1920s than at any earlier moment in history. Magazines like The Atlantic Monthly pondered whether the "Younger Generation [Is] in Peril," while popular tracts like George Coe's What Ails Our Youth? and Ben Lindsey's The Revolt of Modern Youth became essential reading for anyone who wanted to be in the know.

In part, this fascination with teenagers and twenty-somethings stemmed from long-term trends. Between 1800 and 1920, the number of children borne by the average American woman fell from roughly seven to three. This didn't mean Americans were having less sex. On the contrary, women increasingly turned to a variety of birth control techniques, including coitus interruptus, the rhythm method, prophylactics, and abortion.

First, though birthrates fell across the board, as a general rule urbanites and white-collar professionals were more likely to practice family planning than rural folk and blue-collar workers. This made perfect sense. Urban, middle-class parents—a growing portion of the population—no longer needed small armies of children to tend the family farm. In fact, extra children were often an added expense rather than an economic asset in the cities. They cost money to feed, clothe, and shelter.

Second, as America's industrial economy grew more advanced, a great demand arose for managers, scientists, engineers, clerks, lawyers, salespeople, and other service-sector employees. These jobs required years of education and training.

Parents who took these trends into account had fewer children, which allowed them to invest more time and resources in their small families.

In subtle ways, this trend also helped ignite a sexual revolution. After all, in an emerging industrial society where it paid to have fewer children, men and women were free to redefine sex not merely as something procreative, but as a legitimate and pleasurable activity within marriage. From this discovery, it might take only a small leap of faith to conceive of sex as a legitimate activity *outside* marriage.

At first glance, the declining birthrate should have made young people *less* visible by the 1920s, since the twenty-five-and-under age group accounted for an ever smaller portion of the American population. But the demographic trends had the reverse effect. As the average household size fell, adults were free to lavish more time and attention on their small families. Whereas teenagers were formerly thrown into the world of work at the earliest possible age, now they lived at home into their teens and twenties. Smaller families also created a narrower age gap between first- and last-born children; this trend, in turn, meant that children shared more in common with one another than with their parents.

Contributing to the growing consciousness of youth was the need for a literate and educated workforce, which created a boom in secondary and higher education. Between 1900 and 1930, America's college enrollments increased threefold and high school attendance jumped by a whopping 650 percent; this meant that by the 1920s, about 75 percent of teenagers attended at least some high school, while at any given moment 20 percent of eighteen-to-twenty-two-year-olds were enrolled in postsecondary education. The result was the emergence of a vibrant and highly visible youth culture where none had really existed before.

As the Lynds observed of their time in Muncie, "High school, with its athletic clubs, sororities and fraternities, dances and parties, and 'extracurricular activities,' is a fairly complete social cosmos in itself. . . . Today the school is becoming not a place to which children go from their homes for a few hours daily but a place from which they go home to eat and sleep."

As teenagers and twentysomethings spent more time with one another and less time with adults, there emerged a fascination with the new youth culture. One young woman complained that "this tremendous interest in the younger generation is nothing more nor less than a preoccupation with the nature of that generation's sex life," and in some respects, she was right.

Now that they were spending so much time together, young men and women were apt to experiment more freely with sex and romance. Back in the old days, one parent remembered, "we all went to parties together and came home together. If any couple did pair off, they were considered rather a joke." Those days were long gone. In Muncie, nearly half the boys in the sophomore, junior, and senior classes, and about a third of girls, *admitted* to attending "petting parties." Another study of 177 college women found that 92 percent acknowledged "petting" or "spooning."

However liberating they might have found the new sexual ethic, young women of the twenties found that the old double standard still applied, and it was they who provoked the greater portion of scorn and blame.

"Girls aren't so modest nowadays; they dress differently," complained one mother. "It's the girls clothing," another agreed. "We can't keep our boys decent when girls dress that way." "Last summer six girls organized a party and invited six boys and they never got home until three in the morning," a concerned parent told the Lynds. "Girls are always calling my boys up trying to make dates with them."

Mrs. George Rose, an itinerant evangelist, warned parents in Butte, Montana, that "modern fashions, exposed necks, bare arms, yes, even exposed legs . . . you say they are worn innocently, with no thought of appeal to the lust of men. I wish I could think that this were so."

Throughout the early twenties, Scott Fitzgerald proved an avid observer of social trends and a cagey student of marketing strategy. He and his editor, Maxwell Perkins, had cleverly billed *This Side of Paradise* as "A Novel About Flappers Written for Philosophers," a line that Scribner's incorporated into its advertisements for the book. Building on this theme, in September 1920 Scribner's published a collection of Scott's short stories under the title *Flappers and Philosophers.* Scott confided to Max Perkins that he thought the volume sold well in bookstores because of the "timelessness" of its title.

In fact, Scott had it wrong. The title wasn't timeless. It was timely.

In dozens of well-placed interviews and column items, with titles like "Fitzgerald, Flappers and Fame" and "This Is What Happens to Naughty Flappers," Scott positioned himself as an expert on young American women. Magazine writers could hardly help noting that "insomuch as he is strictly responsible for the introduction into this country of a new and devastating type of girl whose movements, thoughts and actions—to say nothing of deeds—have become matters of international importance . . . anything Mr. Fitzgerald might have to say on the subject . . . would be worth hearing."

"I sometimes wonder whether the flapper made me or I made her," Scott admitted in a moment of candor.

Later in life, Scott noted with bemusement that he was essentially "pushed into the position not only of spokesman for the time but of the typical product of that movement." He and Zelda spent the better part of the decade being "quoted on a variety of subjects we knew nothing about."

This was just a little bit disingenuous. Almost everything Scott did or said was calculated to achieve maximum effect—even when he denied any expertise on the flapper. "I wish to state publicly that I cannot understand why, whenever the word flapper is mentioned, my name should be dragged headlong into the conversation," he protested halfheartedly. "I know nothing about flappers. The idea that I am in any way interested in the number of knees on exhibition at the Biltmore lobby is extremely distasteful to me. You'd think I invented bobbed knees. I deny it."

On other occasions, when asked to comment on whether the "flapper craze [was] passing," Scott eagerly reassumed his familiar role of cultural savant and insisted, "I don't think it is. . . . The flapper is growing stronger than ever; she gets wilder all the time. . . . She is continuously seeking for something new to increase her store of experience. She still is looking for new conventions to break— for new thrills, for sensations to add zest to life, and she is growing more and more terrible."

When asked whether his books had created the flapper phenomenon, Scott "smiled a bit ruefully" and slipped into a long discourse on women's suffrage, women in English literature, Sigmund Freud, and regional differences among American girls.

"The younger generation has been changing all thru the last twenty years," he told an interviewer. "Girls, for instance, have found the accent shifted from chemical purity to breadth of viewpoint, intellectual charm, and piquant cleverness." With every bit of confidence he could muster as a twenty-four-year-old connoisseur, Scott explained that "all, or nearly all, the famous men and women of history—the kind who left a lasting mark—were, let us say, of broad moral views. Our generation has absorbed all this."

Within two years of his first major publication, Scott's role in popular culture was so well-defined that readers of *Life* magazine surely got a knowing chuckle out of Dorothy Parker's whimsical poem "The Flapper."

> She nightly knocks for many a goal
> The usual dancing men.
> Her speed is great, but her control
> Is something else again.
> All spotlights focus on her pranks.

All tongues her prowess herald.
For which she may well render thanks
to God and Scott Fitzgerald.

Appropriately, Scott Fitzgerald and America were both still in their early twenties when his star was on the rise. All that remained was to win the one prize that still eluded him. In his greatest deed of literary license, Scott would turn Zelda into the prototype of the American flapper, all in the service of wedding her future to his.

Beginning *an Adventure in Motoring*

Lillian Gish observed that the Fitzgeralds "didn't make the twenties;
they were the twenties."

5

DOING IT FOR EFFECT

LOOKING BACK ON that momentous afternoon in September 1919, Scott Fitzgerald would remember that he "ran along the streets, stopping automobiles to tell friends and acquaintances about it—my novel *This Side of Paradise* was accepted for publication. That week the postman rang, I paid off my terrible small debts, bought a suit, and woke up every morning with a world of ineffable toploftiness and promise."

The dispatch that changed Scott's life read, simply, "I am very glad, personally, to be able to write you that we are all for publishing your book. . . . [It] is so different that it is hard to prophesy how it will sell but we are all for taking a chance. . . ."

In his early letters to "Mr. Perkins"—F. Scott Fitzgerald and Maxwell Perkins, the most celebrated writer-editor team in American history, wouldn't graduate to "Scott" and "Max" for some time—Fitzgerald betrayed a sense of urgency about seeing the book to print. "Terms, etc., I leave to you," he told Perkins after receiving his acceptance letter, "but one thing I can't relinquish without at least a slight struggle. Would it be utterly impossible for you to publish the book by Xmas—or, say, by February? I have so many things dependent on its success—including of course a girl. . . ."

It had been months since Scott and Zelda had exchanged words. "During a long summer of despair," he later explained, "I wrote a novel instead of letters." Confined by his own will to the makeshift den in his parents' attic on Summit Avenue, gazing out the window at the tops of the trees, Scott surely let his vivid imagination run wild as the months slipped by. Zelda had a casual enough relationship with fidelity in good times; now, with their engagement broken and a thousand miles of Middle America separating them, God only knew what she was up to.

When at last he wrote with his good news and they resumed their correspondence, Zelda once again showed her deft hand at provocation. "I'm mighty glad you're coming," she assured him, "—I've been wanting to see you (which you probably knew) but I couldn't *ask* you." Scott's timing was impeccable, in fact, since she was "just recovering from a wholesome amour with Auburn's 'starting quarterback,' so my disposition is excellent as well as my health." Zelda asked Scott to pick up a quart of gin on his way to Montgomery, as she professed to have been on the wagon all summer. In any event, Scott was "already *ruined* along alcoholic lines with Mrs. Sayre."

Scott waited until November, when he had sold some short stories for publication, before visiting Zelda in Montgomery. The combination of old passion and new success proved a winning formula, as the couple reaffirmed their engagement and reconsummated their affair.

January found Scott renting a small room in a New Orleans boardinghouse, where he continued to churn out material for *The Saturday Evening Post* and make weekend visits to Alabama. When Metro Pictures optioned "Head and Shoulders" for $2,500—it was an O'Henry-like tale of a serious young scholar who marries a sexually adventurous chorus girl, only to find his own intellectual career in shambles and his wife transformed overnight into a literary sensation—Scott used part of the windfall to buy a $600 platinum-and-diamond watch for Zelda. "O, Scott, it's so be-au-ti-ful," she crowed, "—and the back's just as pretty as the front. . . . I've turned it over four hundred times to see 'from Scott to Zelda.'"

Scott admitted that his friends were more or less "unanimous in frankly advising me not to marry a wild, pleasure loving girl like Zelda." More than a few of his Princeton classmates were simply baffled by his decision. "Called on Scott Fitz and his bride," recorded Alexander McKaig. "Latter temperamental small town, Southern

Belle. Chews gum—shows knees. I do not think the marriage can succeed."

Scott conceded that he might very well be in over his head, but "no personality as strong as Zelda's could go without getting criticisms and as you say she is not above reproach. . . . Any girl who gets stewed in public, who frankly enjoys and tells shocking stories, who smokes constantly and makes the remark that she has 'kissed thousands of men and intends to kiss thousands more,' cannot be considered beyond reproach even if above it." Ultimately, he explained, "I love her and that's the beginning and end of everything."

In April, just one month after *This Side of Paradise* hit bookstores, Scott and Zelda married in a small, private ceremony at St. Patrick's Cathedral in New York.

"He's going to leave Zelda," predicted Scott's close friend Edmund Wilson, and "she will seize the opportunity to run away with the elevator boy."

So was inaugurated the most public marriage of the 1920s.

They were a perfect fit for the times: Young, handsome, exuberant, and risqué, they seemed to embody the confident spirit of the postwar era. Lillian Gish, the silent screen star, once claimed that the Fitzgeralds "didn't make the twenties; they were the twenties."

The country that Scott and Zelda took by storm was undergoing dynamic changes. Between 1921 and 1924, America's gross national product skyrocketed, aggregate wages rose steadily, and the United States, which entered World War I a debtor nation, emerged as Europe's largest creditor.

America was rich, and it showed. When a prominent Philadelphia banking family raised eyebrows for installing gold fixtures in its bathrooms, a spokesman for the clan shrugged off the criticism, explaining simply that "you don't have to polish them you know."

To be sure, most Americans weren't waking up to gold shower faucets. Much of the increase in national wealth was due to a fantastic jump in manufacturing productivity, the result of the widespread electrification and modernization of plants and factories. This meant that fewer workers were needed to prime the pump of America's industrial economy. As a result, employees were routinely laid off when there was slack demand for products and services or when factories were retooling.

This cycle bore down particularly hard on workers in seasonal industries, who could expect to be unemployed for several months each year. When the Lynds visited Muncie in 1924, only 38 percent of working-class men reported steady employment over the previous nine months. Altogether, the jobless rate probably hovered around 11 percent throughout the decade—a spectacularly high level for a seemingly flush era. In the days before unemployment insurance, this cycle of work and unemployment could translate to serious human misery.

If the nation was rich, shouldn't everyone have shared equally in the bounty? Not necessarily, the Brookings Institution discovered in 1929. Roughly 42 percent of American families lived at the minimum subsistence level for a family of five. Altogether, the income of the top 0.1 percent of families equaled the aggregate income of the bottom 42 percent. The United States in the 1920s might have been exceedingly wealthy, but its riches were distributed unevenly.

Yet even if there were glaring inequities in wealth and income, many ordinary Americans still shared in the general prosperity. By the mid-1920s, almost two-thirds of American households had electricity, a dramatic increase from the previous decade. This meant that the average family could replace hours of manual toil and primitive housekeeping with the satisfying hum of the electric vacuum cleaner, the electric refrigerator and freezer, and the automatic washing machine, all of which came into wide use during the twenties.

Americans living in the Jazz Age also experienced an information revolution on a par with the 1850s, when thousands of miles of telegraph lines and railroads had cut a swath through the midwestern prairies, and the 1950s, when television invaded the suburban living room. By the end of the 1920s, more than twelve million American households had acquired radio sets. It was the age of mass communication; Americans tuned in to hear Grantland Rice announce the World Series—*live*—and listened to Floyd Gibbons relate the day's news. All the while, the number of telephone lines almost doubled by 1930.

Wealth seemed to breed innovation. It took more than one hundred years for the U.S. Patent Office to issue its millionth patent in 1911; within fifteen years, it had issued its two-millionth. Scores of new factory products flooded the market, bearing soon familiar brand names like Scotch tape, Welch's grape juice, Listerine mouthwash, Wheaties cereal, Kleenex tissues, the Schick electric razor, and the lemonade Popsicle.

The country was eating better, too. "You just spent your summer canning in 1890," remarked a Muncie housewife, "but the canned goods you buy today are so good that it isn't worth your while to do so much." Before the perfection of commercial refrigeration and packaging, the long winters used to choke off supplies of vegetables and fruits, and "nearly everybody used to be sick because of the lack of green stuff to eat," one man recalled. Now, the year-round availability of spinach, lettuce, oranges, and carrots translated into balanced meals and better health.

Americans were also eating cheaper. Because the United States boasted enormous natural resources, Americans spent a much smaller portion of their wages on food than their European counterparts. This meant more money left over for nonessentials, such as phonographs, factory-made furniture, radios, electric appliances, automobiles, and—of course—"entertainment." By the mid-1920s, movie theaters were selling fifty million tickets *each week,* a sum equal to roughly half the U.S. population.

In effect, low prices and the availability of consumer credit—first introduced in the nineteenth century but made popular by automakers around 1915—helped democratize *consumption* in the twenties, even if the allocation of wages and wealth remained highly unbalanced. And Americans were clearly as tempted by credit then as now: By the mid-1920s, more than three-quarters of all furniture, phonographs, and washing machines were bought on credit.

These trends had been building for some time, but they converged in the 1920s to produce a sense of national triumph, wealth, and success. The whole country seemed given over to fads and frivolities that represented the gusto and confidence of the times.

At first it was mah-jongg, a Chinese board game that was "as intricate as an income tax blank," as a cultural critic wryly observed. Then it was flagpole sitting, a bizarre public spectacle that began in 1924, when Alvin "Shipwreck" Kelly, a professional daredevil, sat atop a flagpole in Los Angeles for thirteen hours and thirteen minutes. Nobody knew why he did it, and no one cared. Within weeks, hundreds of ordinary citizens were vying for their fifteen minutes of fame, decades before Andy Warhol found a way to characterize the popular pursuit of celebrity.

The 1920s also gave rise to a new cult of self-examination, a fashion that grew only more popular over the course of the century and went a long way in explaining the flapper's perpetual search for personal happiness and beauty. In the years immediately following World War I, psychology became a national obsession. Popular books of the day included *The Psychology of Golf, The Psychology of the Poet Shelley,* and *The Psychology of Selling Life Insurance.* Bookstores and mail-order houses peddled new titles like *Psychoanalysis by Mail, Psychoanalysis Self-Applied, Ten Thousand Dreams Interpreted,* and *Sex Problems Solved.*

Americans weren't simply intrigued by Sigmund Freud. They were drawn to a new ethic of self-improvement that celebrated the mastery of one's deepest impulses and thoughts. In a prosperous and winning nation, surely any man could be a success if only he tried hard enough. Or so many people believed. The Pelam Institute of America earned widespread acclaim for its method of "Scientific Mind Training," which "awakens the giant, the superman, within you; it enables you to *realize your true self,* to become the man or woman you have simply felt all along that you ought to be." And in 1923, millions of Americans eagerly followed the advice of French wonder guru Emile Coué and faithfully repeated the simple catechism "Every day, in every way, I am getting better and better."

In this environment, it would take a dynamic personality to achieve notice and acclaim. The Fitzgeralds were just that dynamic.

Free from Zelda's parents' watchful eyes, metaphorically drunk on Scott's success, and quite literally intoxicated by the steady stream of champagne and gin that they began pouring into their systems, the Fitzgeralds became the most celebrated couple of the Jazz Age. Hardly a week went by in the early twenties without some word of their antics.

When, after several days, they were evicted from the Biltmore Hotel for causing too much noise and too much damage, Scott and Zelda moved their honeymoon to the Commodore. They celebrated the change in itinerary by spinning around in the hotel's revolving door for more than a half hour and passing several delirious weeks drinking, attending rooftop parties, frequenting the theater, and generally burning through Scott's magazine royalties faster than they came in.

When Lawton Campbell strolled over to the Commodore one afternoon to meet the Fitzgeralds for lunch, he found that their "room was bedlam. Breakfast dishes were all about, the bed unmade, books and papers scattered here and there, trays filled with cigarette butts, liquor glasses from the night before."

Lillian Gish remembered first meeting them at a New York restaurant around this time with her sister, Dorothy Gish, also a movie starlet. "We were at a large round table. . . . They were both so beautiful, so blond, so clean and clear," she said, "—And drinking strait [sic] whiskey out of tall tumblers. . . . Zelda could do outlandish things—say anything. It was never offensive when Zelda did it, so you felt she couldn't help it, and was not doing it for effect."

In fact, she *was* doing it for effect. The Fitzgeralds basked in publicity. They arrived at parties with Zelda cheering from the roof of a taxicab and Scott perched on its hood. At a performance of the *George White's Scandals,* they were evicted from the midtown theater when Scott stood up in the orchestra section and shed his clothes along with the onstage talent. On slow news weeks, Zelda wasn't above diving into a park fountain fully clothed, and Scott was perfectly willing to stand on his head in a hotel lobby to impress nearby reporters and cameramen. Zelda arrived at other people's homes for parties and casually shucked her clothing to take long hot baths.

"The remarkable thing about the Fitzgeralds," observed Scott's close friend Edmund Wilson, "was their capacity for carrying things off and carrying people away by their spontaneity, charm, and good looks."

For three years Scott and Zelda crisscrossed the country, living in rented houses and hotel rooms in Westport, Connecticut; St. Paul; New York; Montgomery; and Great Neck, Long Island. Their refusal to buy a house reflected their refusal to grow up. At every destination, they brought chaos and excitement with them and left behind a trail of broken bottles and fantastic stories.

Dorothy Parker later observed that Scott and Zelda "looked as though they had just stepped out of the sun; their youth was striking. *Everyone* wanted to meet him."

Shortly after their marriage, the celebrity couple paid a visit to Princeton, where a university official with unspeakably bad judgment appointed them official chaperones at a weekend house party. Scott traumatized the impressionable undergraduates by introducing Zelda as his "mistress" and ended the sojourn badly hung over and with a black eye.

The following week, Zelda and Scott returned to Princeton to attend a banquet staged by the *Nassau Lit,* a student publication. Decked out in lyres and wreaths, they were denied entrance to the Cottage—Scott's old eating club—because of their deplorable conduct at the house party. Cottage members registered their disapproval by throwing Scott out of a first-floor window.

The Cottage Club eventually reconciled with its most prominent alum. It wasn't that Fitzgerald proved himself a changed man. On the contrary, the Club lowered its standards.

When Judge and Mrs. Sayre visited Westport for a summer weekend in 1920, they arrived to find two of Scott's friends passed out drunk in the front porch hammock. Later that evening, Zelda borrowed $20 from her mother—incredibly, but typically, she and Scott were dead broke—and husband and wife ballyhooed out for a night on the town. They returned at three a.m. with several friends and spent the daybreak hours in an orgy of gin and tomato juice before Zelda finally stumbled off to bed. When she climbed down the stairs the next morning, she found the kitchen littered with cigarette butts and empty glasses and Scott still half in the bag. She tried to liberate a half-filled gin bottle from his protective clutch, but Scott pushed her away reflexively, sending her back on her feet and smack into a swinging door. Cleaning the blood off her face and covering a swelling black-and-blue mark with foundation, Zelda managed to reassemble herself just as Judge Sayre descended to the kitchen for breakfast. His icy stare spoke volumes.

"Mama and Daddy are here this week," Zelda reported to Scott's Princeton friend and best man, Ludlow Fowler. ". . . At present, I'm hardly able to sit down owing to an injury sustained in the course of one of [the] parties in N.Y. I cut my tail on a broken bottle and can't possibly sit on the three stitches that are in it now— The bottle was bath salts—I was boiled— The place was a bathtub somewhere. None of us remember the exact locality."

Judge Sayre was even less pleased when Scott and Zelda paid an extended visit in Montgomery. There, decked out in a Hawaiian hula outfit, Zelda and several other local women performed in the annual Les Mystérieuses ball. A member of the audience remembered that "one masker was doing her dance more daring than the others. . . . Finally the dancer in question turned her back to the audience, lifted her grass skirt over her head for a quick view of her pantied posterior and gave it an extra wiggle for good measure." A dull murmur swept through the crowd. "That's Zelda!" the younger set whispered.

For the young, celebrity couple, it was all as confusing as it was exhilarating.

"Within a few months after our embarkation on the Metropolitan venture," Scott mused, "we scarcely knew any more who we were and we hadn't a notion what we were."

But they were having a good time. At the time, it seemed that was all that mattered.

Two young women at Chicago's White City amusement park, 1927.

6

I Prefer This Sort of Girl

I T WAS SCOTT and Zelda's good fortune to come of age in a country that was increasingly in the thrall of celebrity. The decade witnessed sensational murder trials like that of Nathan Leopold and Richard Loeb, two wealthy Chicago teenagers who killed a young boy just to see if they could get away with it, and Fatty Arbuckle, the portly Hollywood impresario who was tried twice—and finally acquitted—for the brutal rape and murder of a young actress. It gave rise to sports legends like Babe Ruth, who was just as renowned for his voracious culinary and carnal appetites as for his home run record, and Jack Dempsey, the heavyweight champion who by the mid-1920s had appeared in almost as many films as he did title fights.

In the decade following World War I, the average number of profiles that *The Saturday Evening Post* and *Collier's* published nearly doubled. Before 1920, most of these articles featured political and business leaders; now, more than half concerned key figures in entertainment and sports.

Scott and Zelda's general notoriety might have satisfied their burning drive for recognition. But Scott's continued success also hinged on the public's acknowledgment of his expertise on sex, youth, and the New Woman. To this end, both husband and wife encouraged the notion—probably true, anyway—that Zelda was the inspiration for many of Scott's female characters, including Rosalind, Amory Blaine's devastating crush in *This Side of Paradise*.

When asked how long it took him to pen that first novel, Scott answered slyly, "To write it, three months. To conceive it, three minutes. To collect the data in it, all my life"—a clear indication that the characters in the book, including Rosalind, were ripped straight from the pages of Scott's diary. More directly, in one of his many newspaper interviews on the subject of flappers, Fitzgerald confessed, "I prefer this sort of girl. Indeed, I married the heroine of my stories. I could not be interested in any other sort of woman."

Zelda drove home the same point when she told a Kentucky newspaper columnist, "I love Scott's books and heroines. I like the ones that are like me! That's why I love Rosalind in *This Side of Paradise*. . . . I like girls like that. I like their courage, their recklessness and spendthriftness. Rosalind was the original American flapper."

It wasn't long before people began clamoring for Zelda's wisdom on the topic of the New Woman. In early 1922, when Scott published his second novel, *The Beautiful and Damned*, Zelda wrote a syndicated review of the book for the *New-York Tribune*. Under the title "Friend Husband's Latest," she confided that "on one page I recognized a portion of an old diary of mine which mysteriously disappeared shortly after my marriage, and also scraps of letters which, though considerably edited, sound to me vaguely familiar. In fact, Mr. Fitzgerald—I believe that is how he spells his name—seems to believe that plagiarism begins at home."

Zelda wasn't exaggerating. Scott *had* lifted portions of her letters and diary for some of his work. She was pointing out what many people already assumed: that she was Scott's artistic muse and, by extension, the first American flapper. She recommended *The Beautiful and Damned* to readers, because "if enough people buy it . . . there is a platinum ring with a complete circlet" that she had her eye on.

Two years earlier, Fitzgerald had encouraged Max Perkins to incorporate Zelda's face in the book's promotional advertisements. "I'm deadly curious to see if Hill's picture looks like the real 'Rosalind,'" he wrote his editor in January 1920, referring to the sketch artist W. E. Hill contributed to the book's dust cover. Now, Fitzgerald fretted over the artwork for *The Beautiful and Damned*. "The girl is excellent of course—it looks somewhat like Zelda," he told Perkins, "but the man, I suspect, is a sort of debauched edition of me." In his scrapbooks, Fitzgerald pasted several photographs of Zelda beside the jacket of his new novel. The resemblance was striking.

Positioning Zelda as the inspiration for both Rosalind and Gloria, the lead woman in *The Beautiful and Damned,* was a clever trick.

Rosalind, the earlier flapper character, is a teenager, "one of those girls who need never make the slightest effort to have men fall in love with them," as Fitzgerald described her. "She is quite unprincipled; her philosophy is *carpe diem* for herself and *laissez-faire* for others." She revels in her sexual freedom, explaining casually that "there used to be two kinds of kisses. First when girls were kissed and deserted; second, when they were engaged. Now there's a third kind, where the man is deserted."

By contrast, Gloria, the central character in *The Beautiful and Damned,* is a different woman altogether. Already in her mid-twenties, she is "Mrs. Anthony Patch," one of the "younger marrieds" Scott now claimed as his cultural expertise. Newspapers and magazines went along happily with Scott's redefinition of the New Woman and agreed that "the flapper has grown up in F. Scott Fitzgerald's latest book." Acknowledging that a twentysomething wife could still be a flapper if she held to the right attitude, the *Columbus Dispatch* announced that "she is graduated from the bright, trivial, careless atmosphere of flapperdom, and, still wearing all the marks of flapperdom's charming vulgarity, is borne into an older world made unromantic by the super-sophistication of the people in it."

Newspapers accepted the notion that Zelda was the original model for both Gloria and Rosalind and noted casually that "Mrs. F. Scott Fitzgerald started the flapper movement in this country." At Scott's urging, Zelda slipped ever more assertively into her role as America's first flapper. During a brief sojourn in St. Paul, he even wrote a musical review, *Midnight Flappers,* for the Junior League's vaudeville night. Zelda was cast as one of the show's stars.

To promote Scott's work—and her own reputation—in mid-1922 Zelda penned a whimsical yet insightful article for *Metropolitan*

Magazine on the subject of young American women. Entitled "Eulogy on the Flapper," her commentary began with a deceptive claim that "the flapper is deceased."

Zelda didn't mean to suggest that flapperdom was out of fashion. On the contrary: Her article wasn't really so much a eulogy as it was a declaration of cultural conquest. "Now audacity and earrings and one-piece bathing suits have become fashionable," she explained, "and the first Flappers are so secure in their positions that their attitude toward themselves is scarcely distinguishable from that of their debutante sisters of ten years ago toward *themselves*. They have won their case. They are blasé."

Even as she celebrated the flapper for emerging triumphant in the 1920s, Zelda also believed that sexual liberation might ultimately exercise a salutary, domesticating effect on the New Woman. Critics blamed the flapper for a laundry list of social problems—divorce, mental illness, moral debauchery—but Zelda suspected that by "fully airing the desire for unadulterated gaiety, for romances that she knows will not last," a young, liberated woman might ultimately find herself "more inclined to favor the 'back to the fireside' movement than if she were repressed until she gives her those rights that only youth has the right to give. . . .

" 'Out with inhibitions,' gleefully shouts the Flapper," Zelda continued, "and elopes with the Arrow-collar boy that she had been thinking, for a week or two, might make a charming breakfast companion. The marriage is annulled by the proverbial irate parent and the Flapper comes home, none the worse for wear, to marry, years later, and live happily ever afterwards."

Zelda was effectively articulating an argument that would prove increasingly attractive to young women who asserted a right to personal autonomy and pleasure but weren't ultimately prepared to forsake more conventional dreams of motherhood and monogamous marriage.

On one level, Zelda's public musings on the flapper were designed, as always, to help turn the wheels of the Fitzgerald family publicity machine. But her "eulogy" also reflected Zelda's struggle to reconcile her role as a flapper spokeswoman with the realities of her marriage. With the birth of her daughter, Frances Scott Fitzgerald—known as Scottie—on October 26, 1921, Zelda graduated, at least in principle, from reckless youth to responsible adulthood.

Her article for *Metropolitan Magazine* was a valiant attempt to enlarge the definition of the flapper—to argue that there was nothing really incompatible about being a New Woman and a mother. By throwing off the shackles of Victorian restraint, Zelda claimed, young women like herself had actually prepared themselves to be *better* guardians of home and hearth than their mothers before them. Getting married, having children, becoming an adult—none of these steps necessitated an abandonment of the ethic of self-indulgence that was a staple of flapperdom and a central feature of 1920s culture.

Zelda was a product of this new culture. She belonged to the first generation of Americans who were raised on advertisements and amusements rather than religion and restraint. They rejected many Victorian-era values and redefined the pursuit of pleasure as a noble goal unto itself.

In nineteenth-century white America, men had largely defined their lives, politics, and identities around work. This was a world where a large proportion of citizens owned their own farms or shops. In a country flush with empty territory, even the growing population of wage earners could reasonably aspire to the dream of self-ownership.

When they spoke about the good life, most public authorities in the nineteenth century emphasized asceticism, self-control, and delayed gratification. These values made a great deal of sense in a world populated by independent farmers and shop owners who needed to internalize capitalist discipline. There were tangible rewards for self-control—not just in the next world, but in this one.

By the early twentieth century, the nature of work had changed, and the old, rock-ribbed values of the nineteenth century no longer made sense. Most men now worked for wages. Looking to expand their economies of scale, business owners turned to new forms of scientific management to speed up and increase production, and this meant the deskilling of work. In this environment, the typical worker found his or her job ever more monotonous and unfulfilling. It was a new world in which there was simply no evident reward for sobriety and asceticism.

Instead, many Americans began to define themselves not through their jobs, but by turning to other outlets like leisure and consumption. This required the creation of a new ethic, one that legitimated rather than scorned the pursuit of pleasure.

American businessmen and industrialists were happy to oblige. In the late nineteenth century, they had perfected new means of output and distribution and could now produce an enormous volume of glassware, jewelry, clothing, household items, and durable goods. But in order to *sell* these items, they needed to persuade a nation raised on the values of thrift and self-denial to complete a 180-degree turn and embrace the principles of pleasure and self-fulfillment.

In this new era, the apostles of good living were no longer ministers and schoolmasters, but advertising executives and public relations professionals who saturated American newspapers, magazines, movie theaters, and radio stations with a new gospel of indulgence. As an adman coolly explained, "The happiness of the [consumer] should be the real topic of every advertisement."

"Sell them their dreams," urged an advertising professional. "Sell them what they longed for and hoped for and almost despaired of having. Sell them hats by splashing sunlight across them. Sell them dreams—dreams of country clubs and proms and visions of what might happen if only. After all, people don't buy things to have them. . . . They buy hope—hope of what your merchandise might do for them."

Thus, Americans of Zelda Fitzgerald's generation were raised on a steady diet of bright and glitzy department store windows, advertisements and amusements, consumer products, and magazine articles—all urging them to let go, enjoy life, and seek out personal happiness.

"You find a *Road of Happiness* the day you drive a Buick," promised a typical 1920s advertisement. "The same old story of the nose to the grindstone," another ad scolded. "No time for play. No time for anything but work. And no time then to make a success of himself. Always too busy grinding—grinding. A slave to routine work."

The message was simple: To be a success in the modern world, it was essential to have *fun*. To have fun, you had to buy something.

Zelda Fitzgerald spoke for a generation of Americans who grew up believing that the pursuit of personal happiness was a noble goal. No wonder the motto beneath her high school yearbook picture read:

> *Why should all life be work, when we all can borrow.*
> *Let's only think of today, and not worry about tomorrow.*

And if it was good or even therapeutic to buy a new pair of shoes or a Buick in the pursuit of pleasure, couldn't the same be said of romance and even sex?

Margaret Sanger, the famous birth control advocate who endured repeated arrests for disseminating information on family planning, made much the same argument when, in the 1920s, she urged women to triumph over "repression" and chase "the greatest possible expression and fulfillment of their desires upon the highest possible plane." This, she explained, was "one of the great functions of contraceptives."

Sanger was an erstwhile socialist organizer who had once cavorted with the likes of such radical agitators as Emma Goldman, Mabel Dodge, Alexander Berkman, and "Big Bill" Haywood. When the militant International Workers of the World (IWW)—better known as "Wobblies"—struck the textiles mills at Lawrence, Massachusetts, in 1912, Sanger had helped evacuate the children of striking unionists. A year later, when the Wobblies called workers out of the mills at Paterson, New Jersey, Sanger had walked the picket line and helped plan a benefit pageant at New York's Madison Square Garden.

Sanger, a fiery propagandist who was a magnet for media attention, pegged her advocacy of family planning to a combination of feminist and socialist commitments. Borrowing—some would say stealing—from Emma Goldman's speeches on population control, Sanger called on working-class women to undertake a "birth strike" to deprive voracious capitalists of the surplus labor that kept wages pitifully low and working conditions both dangerous and backbreaking.

Whereas classical Marxists had urged the proletariat to be fruitful and multiply—all the better to raise an international army of workers who would overthrow capitalism—Sanger and Goldman begged poor women to embrace "voluntary motherhood." Only by limiting the size of their families would they stop producing "children who will become slaves to feed, fight and toil for the enemy—Capitalism."

By the 1920s, Sanger had switched tacks. After flirting briefly with the eugenicist movement, she came to stress the personal dimension of family planning. By eliminating the threat of unwanted pregnancy, she explained, birth control would help women to realize their "love demands" and "elevate sex into another sphere, whereby it may subserve and enhance the possibility of individual and human expression." Contraception wasn't "merely a question of population," she argued on another occasion. "Primarily it is the instrument of liberation and human development."

Margaret Sanger had found the right argument for the times, and certainly she wasn't the only Jazz Age apostle of self-realization and fulfillment.

In the beginning, Zelda told readers, the flapper "flirted because it was *fun* to flirt and wore a one-piece bathing suit because she had a good figure; she covered her face with powder and paint because she didn't need it and she refused to be bored chiefly because she wasn't boring. *She was conscious that the things she did were the things she had always wanted to do.*"

A young woman in Columbus, Ohio, echoed this logic when she claimed, "There is no air of ultra smartness surrounding us when we dance the collegiate, smoke cigarettes, and drink something stronger than a claret lemonade. The real enjoyment lies in the thrill we experience in these things."

If fun was the watchword of the younger generation, so was *choice*. Living in a world that was increasingly dominated by glossy magazine ads for makeup, furniture, and clothing, many Americans began applying the idea of the free market in surprising contexts. A news item dated August 1923 brilliantly captured the tensions that marketplace dogma could inspire. "This little town of Somerset [Pennsylvania] has been somersaulted into a style class war," reported *The New York Times,* "with the bobbed hair, lip-stick flappers arrayed on one side and their sisters of long tresses and silkless stockings on the other."

When the local high school PTA convened to endorse a new dress code that would bar silk stockings, short skirts, bobbed hair, and sleeveless dresses, the flapper contingent defiantly broke into the meeting and chanted:

> *I can show my shoulders,*
> *I can show my knees,*
> *I'm a free-born American,*
> *And can show what I please.*

These young, self-styled flappers weren't trying just to have fun, though fun was surely part of their agenda. They were asserting their right to make personal choices. Some forty years before prominent second-wave feminists declared that the "personal is political," many ordinary women in the 1920s had come to precisely the same conclusion.

"Personal liberty is a Democratic ideal," argued a 1920s marriage manual. "It is a woman's right to have children or not, just as she chooses." Americans had gone to war to make the world "safe for Democracy." Now, many seemed to believe that the essence of democracy wasn't just self-governance, but free choice in every realm of life.

Such was the idea behind the *Chicago Tribune*'s remark that "today's woman gets what she wants. The vote. Slim sheaths of silk to replace voluminous petticoats. Glassware in sapphire blue or glowing amber. The right to a career. Soap to match her bathroom's color scheme."

Here was where the modern culture could prove threatening to the Victorians. The ethos of the consumer market glorified not only self-indulgence and satisfaction, but also personal liberty and choice. It invited relativism in all matters ranging from color schemes and bath soap to religion, politics, sex, and morality. This is precisely what concerned the dean of women at Ohio State University when she complained that the younger generation exalted *"personal liberties and individual rights* to the point that they are beginning to spell lack of self-control and total irresponsibility in the matters of moral obligation to society."

Hers was not a lone voice in the wilderness. As a revolution in morals and manners swept across America in the early 1920s, the forces of reaction gathered in a last-ditch attempt to turn back the clock.

7

JTRAIGHTEN OUT PEOPLE

N OT BY CHANCE, the enemy of the flapper was often the enemy of change. No group brought this fact into sharper relief than the Ku Klux Klan, which enjoyed a brief but alarming resurgence in the 1920s.

Founded in 1866 by former Confederate officers, the original Ku Klux Klan bathed the southern countryside in blood throughout 1869 and 1870 in a half-successful attempt to roll back the gains African Americans had achieved during the early years of Reconstruction. Under the determined leadership of President Ulysses S. Grant, however, the federal government cracked down hard and drove the Klan out of business. By 1871, it was a relic of history.

Racial progress proved to be short-lived, and by the eve of World War I history was being written by the losers. For several decades, southern Democrats and their defenders had found strong allies in the northern intellectual community. The leading historian of the Civil War era, Columbia University's William Dunning, was training a generation of scholars to write and teach about Reconstruction as a dark episode in American history, marked by the cruel attempts of northern radicals to impose a harsh and unforgiving peace on the white South and to foist black equality on a proud Confederate nation.

Dunning's interpretation of Reconstruction was dead wrong, but it was conventional wisdom in the first decades of the twentieth century. It fit well with the country's diminishing goodwill toward

Thousands of Ku Klux Klan members take their protest against the modern age to Washington, D.C., in September 1926.

African Americans and its steady embrace of social Darwinism and scientific racism.

Even more popular among mainstream readers was a fictional trilogy by the southern writer Thomas Dixon. In *The Leopard's Spots* (1902), *The Clansman* (1905), and *The Traitor* (1907), Dixon held up the Ku Klux Klan as a savior of white society. The novels became instant best-sellers. Among their admirers was a young filmmaker, David Wark Griffith, who in the years leading up to World War I was laying designs to produce the industry's first ever feature-length movie.

Griffith needed new material—something stirring, something epic. The romance of the Ku Klux Klan was exactly the right fit. With the author's blessing, he adapted Dixon's trilogy into a new screenplay, *The Birth of a Nation*. Released in 1915, the film, which starred the Fitzgeralds' good friend Lillian Gish, caused a nationwide stir. Millions of viewers lined up to watch almost three hours of melodrama, replete with blackfaced actors portraying black slaves as alternatively dim-witted or predatory. In the climactic scene, white-robed Klansmen gallop into town and save white southern womanhood from the threat of racial miscegenation.

The film was America's first blockbuster success.

Among its many admirers was a motley group of Georgians who convened on Thanksgiving eve inside the stately lobby of Atlanta's Piedmont Hotel. They had been electrified by *The Birth of a Nation* and came with the express intention of reinaugurating America's most notorious and violent fraternity. After gathering together, the group climbed aboard a chartered bus and drove sixteen miles north of the city limits to a magnificent granite peak known locally as Stone Mountain. There, overlooking the distant lights of Atlanta, they fired up a tall wooden cross and set out to replicate the glory of the Invisible Empire. The Klan would ride again.

Unlike the original Klan, the new organization sought a national profile and identified several groups—not just African Americans—as alien threats to family and nation: Catholics, Jews, immigrants, New Women, bootleggers, and criminals. Above all, the Klan's five million members, including roughly five hundred thousand women, touted "one hundred percent Americanism" as an antidote to the social and cultural decay that seemed to be rotting away the core of American values.

In Texas, Klansmen beat a man from Timson who had separated from his wife and a lawyer from Houston who "annoyed" local girls. In Grove Creek, near Dallas, Klan riders broke into the home of a recently divorced woman who was convalescing from a recent illness; they dragged her from bed, chopped off her hair, and beat her male visitor senseless with a flail.

"Well," explained a Klan woman, "wasn't their original purpose to kind of straighten out people?"

Though the Klan particularly deplored "the revolting spectacle of a white woman clinging in the arms of a colored man," more humdrum violations of Victorian propriety also vexed members of the Hooded Empire. In Evansville, Indiana, William Wilson, the teenage son of the local Democratic congressman, remembered that Klan riders ruthlessly patrolled back roads in search of teenagers embroiled in wild petting parties or improper embraces. "They entered homes without search warrants" and "flogged errant husbands and wives. They tarred and feathered drunks. They caught couples in parked cars. . . ." One night, when Wilson was driving with his girlfriend on a backcountry road, a local farmer overtook him and warned, "If you kids know what is good for you, you'll move along. The Kluxers are patrolling this road tonight, and God knows what they'll do to you if they catch you here."

The Klan monitored movie theaters in order to police "moral conditions" among loose high school students and burned down dance halls frequented by teenagers, since "most of the cases of assault between the sexes have followed dances where they got the inspiration for rash and immoral acts." In an almost pornographic ceremony that was repeated dozens if not hundreds of times, Klan members hauled "fallen women" to remote locations, stripped them naked, and flogged them.

The Ku Klux Klan drew many—perhaps most—of its members from cities and metropolitan areas. Its rosters included a fairly even mix of small-business men, professionals, and manual workers.

Unlike the original Klan, which was a southern phenomenon, the new organization drew from a cross section of white Protestant America, and many of its members attended mainline churches. In effect, the Klan had broad appeal among different people who shared a profound sense of unease over social change and modernization.

The Klan was only one manifestation of cultural reaction in the 1920s. Like no other event of the 1920s, the Scopes "Monkey Trial" burned itself into the national imagination.

Throughout most of the nineteenth century, Americans remained firmly committed to evangelical Protestantism. They shared a general commitment to the doctrine of Christian salvation, personal conversion experience, and absolute biblical authority. Generations of public school pupils were raised on textbooks like *McGuffey's Readers,* which drove home the interconnected virtues of Sabbath observance, frugality, hard work, and Bible reading.

This evangelical consensus began to unravel in the late nineteenth century under the strains of scientific discovery. Scholars were simply discovering too much about matter, energy, and the cosmos to sanction literal readings of scripture. Such developments led Lyman Abbott, an outspoken modernist, to argue that "whether God made the animal man by a mechanical process in an hour or by a process of growth continuing through the centuries is quite immaterial to one who believes that into man God breathes a divine life."

Theologians like Abbott were raising the stakes high. If the Old Testament story of creation—of Adam and Eve and the Garden of Eden—was more allegory than straight history, then the entire Bible might very well be open to *individual* interpretation.

Who could say with certainty what was and wasn't the truth?

In the absence of absolute truth, how could humans avoid slipping into an endless cycle of moral relativism?

If biblical wisdom was fair game for interpretation, wasn't the same true of other time-tested values and social codes?

In 1910, traditionalists in the General Assembly of the Presbyterian Church identified five theological "fundamentals" that scientists and religious modernists could not challenge: absolute scriptural inerrancy, the virgin birth of Christ, personal salvation in Christ, Christ's resurrection, and the authenticity of Christ's earthly miracles. Other defenders of evangelical orthodoxy turned to the same language when they published *The Fundamentals,* a series of twelve paperback volumes that answered Christian modernists with a ringing defense of biblical literalism. In 1919, some of the more conservative members of the traditional camp formed the World Christian Fundamentals Association; and in 1920, journalists began lumping most conservative Christians together as "fundamentalists."

People who were uneasy about the unraveling of Victorian culture—those who were unnerved by the religious and ethnic diversity that accompanied mass immigration, who feared the modern world's celebration of personal choice and satisfaction, and who lamented the abandonment of old gender and sexual norms—tended to embrace fundamentalism as a bulwark against further social change.

The liberal-fundamentalist war came to a head in the summer of 1925, when a group of local boosters in Dayton, Tennessee, persuaded a young high school science teacher, John Scopes, to violate the state's antievolution law. They originally intended to draw attention to their economically depressed crossroads town. Instead, what followed was a sensational show trial that pitted the famous "lawyer for the damned," Clarence Darrow, a committed civil libertarian and almost fanatical atheist, against Williams Jennings Bryan, the famously eloquent Nebraskan who had thrice failed to attain the presidency but who remained a hero to rural fundamentalists in the South and Midwest.

The trial's climax came when Darrow unexpectedly called Bryan to the stand as a biblical expert. Darrow posed a series of questions designed to cage a biblical literalist like Bryan. How did Jonah survive inside a whale for three days? How did Joshua lengthen the day by making the *sun*—and not the earth—stand in place? These were not original inquiries. But, as Darrow later boasted, they forced "Bryan to choose between his crude beliefs and the common intelligence of modern times."

"You claim that everything in the Bible should be literally interpreted?" Darrow asked.

"I believe everything in the Bible should be accepted as it is given there," Bryan answered, though "some of the Bible is given illustratively. . . ."

Already, he was on shaky ground. If some of the Bible was "illustrative," could it be liberally construed? It was Bryan, after all, who had audaciously claimed that "one beauty about the Word of God is, it does not take an expert to understand it." Now he was admitting otherwise.

"But when you read that Jonah swallowed the whale, . . ." Darrow continued, "how do you literally interpret that?"

"I believe in a God who can make a whale and can make a man and make both of them do what he pleases."

Darrow was having the time of his life.

Did Bryan believe that in the book of Genesis "days" truly represented twenty-four-hour periods of time? "Have you any idea of the length of these periods?" Darrow asked.

"No; I don't."

"Do you think the sun was made on the fourth day?"

"Yes."

"And they had an evening and morning without sun?"

"I am simply saying it is a period."

Bryan had committed a fatal error. He had conceded the necessity of at least some interpretation in reading the Bible. It was a slight admission, and one that wouldn't have bothered a religious moderate. But it unnerved Bryan, who lost his composure. "I am simply trying to protect the Word of God against the greatest atheist or agnostic in the United States," he cried. "The only purpose Mr. Darrow has is to slur the Bible, but I will answer his questions."

Although Scopes was convicted and slapped with a small fine, liberals declared victory. Mark Sullivan, a popular journalist of the day, boldly concluded that the "Scopes trial marked the end of the age of *Amen* and the beginning of the age of *Oh Yeah!*"

In fact, the conservatives were far from licked. In the decades following the trial, they withdrew from the public eye and retrenched. Fundamentalists chartered missions, publishing houses, and radio stations; they founded seventy bible institutions; and they strengthened existing fortresses of traditional Evangelicalism like Riley's North-western Bible Training School in Minnesota and Moody Bible Institute in Illinois. In the 1940s, they began to reappear in public life, and by the 1980s, they once again assumed a prominent place in political and cultural debates.

Yet something important *did* change on the courthouse lawn in 1925. The contest over religion, much like the brief glory of the Ku Klux Klan, spoke to the profound sense of dislocation that accompanied the rise of modern America. By and by, Americans were becoming more comfortable with, or resigned to, modernity. But not without a struggle.

8

New York Sophistication

F the culture wars of the 1920s often seemed to pit city against country, it wasn't always the case. In 1922, Julia H. Kennedy, an official at the Illinois Department of Health, claimed that girls from small towns outside of Chicago and St. Louis were conducting themselves with even more reckless abandon than their big-city sisters. Among their other offenses, these small-town girls drank homemade concoctions like white mule and lemon extract from flasks that they tied around their necks. In Kearney, New Jersey, the local school board canceled all school dances after chaperones discovered cigarette butts, empty bottles, and semiclad teenagers in the nearby cloakrooms. Clearly, the flapper was every bit as much a small-town as a big-city phenomenon.

For every small-town flapper critic—like the eccentric businessman from Geneva, Illinois, who bankrolled a laboratory dedicated to studying the "flapper slouch" and set out to "give the world a warning of the evil effects of . . . such incorrect posture"—more tolerant voices cut against the grain. In response to a local uproar over the youth problem, preachers in Michigan City, Indiana, and Evanston, Illinois, rushed to the flapper's defense, arguing that "bobbed hair, short skirts and knickerbockers are not signs of sin, but a declaration of independence." Their sermons belied the notion that all of Middle America despised the flapper.

From left to right: Charlie Chaplin, Frank Crowninshield, Helen Sardeau, Lois Long, and Harry D'Arrast strike a pose at a Coney Island photo booth, 1924.

In Philadelphia, by comparison, upstanding citizens were scandalized to learn that Mrs. Anna Mesime, a middle-aged mother from Allentown, Pennsylvania, had been arrested for standing watch while her twenty-three-year-old daughter stole $150 worth of dresses, silk hose, and lingerie from a Market Street clothing store. In tears, Mrs. Mesime explained to the judge, "I had no money to buy the clothes my daughter wanted. Ida got the craze to be a flapper, and to get her the necessary clothing we decided to steal. I was afraid she would adopt a worse method of getting her finery, so intent was she upon being able to dress as well as other girls in the neighborhood."

And no wonder, too. Experts agreed that it would cost the average working girl at least $117—more than $1,200 in today's money—to affect the flapper look with passing success. Even then, "she must have good taste, practice self denial and steer away from the impractical garments."

Yet if the revolution in morals and manners was sweeping the entire country, in many people's minds she was a product of the best neighborhoods in New York and Chicago. This popular image of the flapper was owed in large part to the new prominence that middle-class urbanites came to enjoy in the 1920s. Flush with money and able to dominate the national conversation through newspapers, magazines, and radio, this new urban elite assumed broad license to teach Americans what to buy and how to dress. They self-consciously developed ideas about style, poise, and humor. And the rest of the country often followed suit.

As Zelda Fitzgerald remarked in her "Eulogy on the Flapper," fashions and manners could be counted on to circulate in a predictable chain reaction. The moment an urban sophisticate bored of her flapper attire, she shed her "outer accoutrements . . . to several hundred girls' schools throughout the country," which in turn bequeathed their own discarded wares "to several thousand big-town shop girls, always imitative of the several hundred girls' schools, and to several million small-town belles always imitative of the big-town shopgirls via the 'novelty stores' of their respective small towns."

The process took some time to run its course. In far-flung places like Butte, Montana, high school yearbooks didn't record a widespread popularity of signature flapper styles like bobbed hair until as late as 1924. The year before, seniors at Butte High School elected Mary Josephine McGrath as their prom queen. A "true Irish beauty," McGrath was popular because she wasn't "the flapper type." Her long, curly locks were imitative of those of Mary Pickford, not Louise Brooks.

The process of cultural transmission was subtle but continuous, and it often began in New York. There, in the long summer of 1925, when America's Jazz Age culture wars were just striking their apex, Herman Mankiewicz, assistant theater critic for *The New York Times,* strode into Harold Ross's ragtag offices on West Forty-fifth Street. Mankiewicz got straight to the point: He wanted Ross to hire one of his girlfriends. She didn't have much work experience, but she liked to drink, she loved to party, and she wasn't too bad a writer.

Mankiewicz had come to the right man. As founding editor of the upstart magazine *The New Yorker,* the Colorado-born Ross was quickly emerging as one of America's most influential arbiters of style and taste. And an unlikely one at that. One of Ross's more generous friends later remembered him as "a big-boned westerner . . . who talked in windy gusts that gave a sense of fresh weather to his conversation. His face was homely, with a pendant lower lip; his teeth were far apart." Stiff in demeanor and painfully awkward around women, Ross "wore his butternut-colored thick hair in a high, stiff pompadour, like some wild gamecock's crest [and] wore anachronistic, old-fashioned, high-laced shoes, because he thought Manhattan men dressed like what he called dudes."

Already in his early thirties by the time the twenties began to roar, Ross had spent most of his adult life as an editorial drifter. Boasting an education just shy of a high school diploma, he crisscrossed the continent before World War I and worked a series of dead-end writing jobs for second-rate newspapers in Brooklyn, New Jersey, Salt Lake City, Atlanta, New Orleans, Sacramento, and Panama. When World War I broke out, he joined the Eighteenth Engineering Regiment, shipped off to France, walked almost one hundred miles to Paris, and somehow managed to talk himself into an editorial post at *Stars and Stripes.* On the plus side, he got to see Europe, and he never heard a shot fired in anger. But when the army mustered him out in 1919, Ross faced an almost certain return to obscurity and mediocrity.

For the next five years or so, he kicked around New York, where he edited the house journal for the American Legion, a newly formed, archconservative veterans' outfit. It was an odd vocational choice for a man who would soon be known as the nation's leading arbiter of sophistication.

But New York was the nerve center of American arts and letters. From virtually every farm town in America, a stream of young, untested writers, artists, and muses was flooding the city: Sinclair Lewis . . . Edna St. Vincent Millay . . . John Dos Passos . . . Jean Toomer . . . Van Wyck Brooks . . . F. Scott Fitzgerald . . . Thomas Wolfe . . . Cole Porter . . . Al Jolson. If you were smart, if you were ambitious, if you could write, draw, paint, compose a tune, or spin a good story, New York was the place to be in 1919. Certainly, Harold Ross thought so. The city proved good to him.

In 1920, he married Jane Grant, a reporter and onetime vocalist. Together they bought side-by-side brownstones in Hell's Kitchen on West Forty-seventh Street, knocked down the adjoining wall, and began hosting all-night fetes that soon attracted some of New York's most celebrated purveyors of art and literature.

Part of the draw was surely their 625-square-foot living room— larger than some New York apartments and furnished with two working fireplaces and a piano on which George Gershwin publicly tested his composition "Rhapsody in Blue." More than that, Ross and Grant were popular with the rising smart set because they were exactly like so many other up-and-coming cultural leaders of the 1920s. They weren't city people by birth or even by temperament. They were from the hinterlands. They were outsiders looking in.

Soon enough, the soirees on West Forty-seventh began making the city's society pages. Ross's reputation really soared in 1920 when he and a group of other fledgling writers began lunching together regularly at the Algonquin Hotel. At the time, they had no idea that the weekly rendezvous would make them famous.

By the time Ross and his friends stumbled across the hotel's dining room—renowned for its Tokay grape salad, lemon layer cake, and cherry cobbler—the Algonquin was already a venerable New York institution. Booth Tarkington and Harry Leon Wilson had penned the last act of *The Man from Home* in one of its guest rooms; and celebrities as diverse as the Barrymores and Frank Craven were known to frequent its lobby.

Several times each week, Harold Ross and Jane Grant, along with a revolving cast of theater and literary figures, strolled through the Algonquin's famous antechamber and into one of its two dining rooms. Some members of the circle, like Alexander Woollcott, a popular writer for the *New-York Tribune,* and Franklin Adams, a columnist for the *New York World,* had worked with Ross on *Stars and Stripes.* Others, like Dorothy Parker, Robert Benchley, and Robert Sherwood, were editors for Condé Nast's *Vanity Fair.* Rounding off the new lunch clique were John Peter Toohey and Murdock Pemberton, two prominent New York "press agents"—a relatively new job category that presaged the modern-day entertainment industry publicist. In mid-1919, the hotel's manager moved the group to a circular table in the center of the Rose Room, and the famous "Algonquin Round Table" was born.

In later years, the Round Table was commonly remembered as a venue for highbrow discussions of highbrow ideas—the intellectual nerve center of 1920s America. It wasn't so. As Ross admitted to the notorious Baltimore wit H. L. Mencken, "I never heard any literary discussion or any discussion of any other art—just the usual personalities of some people getting together, and a lot of wisecracks, and quoting of further wisecracks."

Scott Fitzgerald's close friend from Princeton, Edmund Wilson, who began his distinguished literary career at Harold Ross's *New Yorker,* was dismissive of the Round Table. Its participants "all came from the suburbs and 'provinces,' and a sort of tone was set . . . deriving from the provincial upbringing of people who had been taught a certain kind of gentility, who had played the same games and who had read the same children's books—all of which they were now able to mock from a level of New York sophistication."

Wilson's dissent notwithstanding, the endless string of ripostes emanating from the Rose Room often *was* clever—especially those jibes popularly attributed to Dorothy Parker, who at age twenty-seven had just finished a stint as theater critic for *Vanity Fair* and was about to embark on a broader career as a poet, pundit, humorist, and essayist. Routinely, she slid into her seat at the Round Table, ordered a dish that she let go cold, and fired off an endless string of one-liners designed to dazzle her male colleagues. "If all those sweet young things present at the Yale prom were laid end to end," went one of her famous quips, "I wouldn't be at all surprised."

Clever friends telling clever—and self-referential—jokes over lunch would never have caught fire had not the key players all been connected in some way or another to the press. New York in the 1920s was at the center of a nationwide information revolution. It was home to Madison Avenue, the advertising industry's informal headquarters; it boasted twelve daily newspapers and dozens of magazines that reached regional as well as national audiences; it had just recently displaced Boston as the capital of American publishing and was home to every major literary house from Doubleday, Harper, and Scribner's to Knopf and Viking. By the end of the decade, it would also surface as the hub of American radio broadcasting.

In such a thoroughly wired city, any journalist with enough cunning and the right contacts could bend America's news cycle to his own will. Which was exactly what the Algonquin Round Table did. Fame didn't find them per se. They hunted it down.

Ross and his friends were skilled promoters. Within a few weeks of their first lunch, Adams and Woollcott began reporting the Round Table's wit in their own gossip columns; Toohey and Pemberton fed still more tales, particularly of Dorothy Parker's quick repartee, to friends in various editorial departments. Frank Case, the Algonquin's manager and part owner, quietly paid off city columnists to publish "overheard" witticisms from within the cavernous reach of his own hotel.

This almost shameless promotional collaboration quickly transformed the Round Table participants into parlor-set headliners. By the mid-1920s, tourists were dropping by the Algonquin around lunchtime just to steal a glimpse of New York's allegedly sharpest minds.

Ross and Grant understood how capricious and fleeting was their fame. Building on their reputation, in 1924 they raised $45,000 to start a new magazine, *The New Yorker*. Their advertising prospectus announced that the *New Yorker*'s "general tenor will be one of gaiety, wit and satire"—similar to the climate of the Round Table. "It will not be what is commonly called highbrow or radical," the pamphlet continued, setting the magazine apart from venerable publications like *Harper's* and *The Nation* but placing it within the broader currents of 1920s culture. "It will be what is commonly called sophisticated, in that it will assume a reasonable degree of enlightenment on the part of the reader." Above all, *"The New Yorker* will be the magazine which is not edited for the old lady in Dubuque. It will not be concerned in what she is thinking about. This is not meant in any disrespect, but *The New Yorker* is a magazine avowedly published for a metropolitan audience. . . ."

In February 1925, the first issue of Ross's bold new magazine hit the stands. By the summer, with advertising sales plummeting and circulation figures at a standstill, the magazine came close to folding. It was around that time that Herman Mankiewicz told Ross about Lois Long.

9

Miss Jazz Age

ois Long was just twenty-three years old and barely three
years out of Vassar when Harold Ross called her up to arrange
a job interview. She was from the placid suburb of Stanford,
Connecticut, the daughter of a Congregationalist minister who
moonlighted as a lithographer. Long grew up in a quiet neighborhood
where fathers caught the seven o'clock train into the city and the six
thirty-five back each night and mothers clipped articles from *Good
Housekeeping.*

Despite her quiet upbringing, nothing about Lois Long was
domesticated. Peering over the heaps of copy that were strewn over
Ross's desk at the frenzied office on West Forty-fifth Street, she could
only break into a sly grin when the famously misogynistic editor
asked, with no small measure of condescension, "What can you do for
this magazine?"

Ross might have been a male chauvinist, but he was also a brilliant
judge of talent. It didn't take him more than a few minutes to realize
that Lois Long was an asset. She could give *The New Yorker* a pulse.

Brendan Gill, who served on the magazine's editorial staff for
many years, remembered her as "the most dashing figure on *The New
Yorker* in the early days. Ross was often uncertain of what he wanted
the magazine to be . . . but [he] never doubted that the ideal *New
Yorker* writer, to say nothing of the ideal *New Yorker* reader, would be
someone as like Lois Long as possible. He felt himself an outsider in

One of her colleagues wrote that Lois Long was "the most dashing figure on The New Yorker *in the early days."*

New York and something of a hayseed, and in his eyes Miss Long was the embodiment of the glamorous insider."

The year before, following a brief stint as a low-level copywriter at *Vogue* and several failed stabs at a stage career, Long had stumbled her way into Dorothy Parker's old job as theater critic at *Vanity Fair*. But she was better known as a girl about town. Living in a cramped apartment on Manhattan's fashionable East Side, Long and her roommate, the actress Kay Francis, threw exclusive soirees and passed their evenings gliding from one smart nightclub to another.

What she had to offer Ross's magazine was her lifestyle. Like tens of thousands of other single young women in Manhattan, she was living high in the Jazz Age. Unlike most of those women, she was armed with a keen eye for detail, a wicked sense of humor, and razor-sharp prose.

A contemporary described Long as "exceptionally well-constructed, tall, and dark-haired. She had striking features embellished by violet-gray eyes. . . . She had energy in abundance. Her movements and her conversation were supercharged. She could have modeled for Miss Jazz Age." In an Edward Steichen photograph snapped sometime in the early 1920s, Long struck a fetching pose, with jet black hair bobbed to perfection just above her ears, a thin strand of pearls dangling from her neck, the corners of her mouth turned upward to reveal a wide, toothy grin, a pencil pushed gently to her lips. She smoked; she drank; she stayed out all night. She worked for her own money and made no apologies for her lifestyle. She was the very embodiment of the New Woman. Or so *The New Yorker* would claim.

Long had been earning $35 a week at *Vanity Fair*. Ross hired her away at $50—later raised to $75—to pen a regular column on New York nightlife. Essentially, Long would be the magazine's resident flapper journalist. Writing under the pseudonym "Lipstick," she continued her long nights of drinking, dining, and dancing—all on the magazine's expense account—and regaled her captive readers with weekly tales of her adventures on the town. She became one of America's most insightful chroniclers of the new, middle-class woman who seemed to embody the flapper's spirit and style.

On a typical evening, just as the late-night crowd began crawling out of the midtown theaters and restaurants, amid the glow of electric streetlights and the steady din of car horns and subway rumbles, Long and her friends would catch a taxicab, "start at '21,' and go on to Tony's after '21' closed." Both venues were tucked away on West Fifty-second Street, just minutes from the *New Yorker*'s offices. Occupying an entire mansion, Jack Kriendler and Charlie Berns's "21" skirted the city's strict curfew laws, which mandated a two a.m. closing time, by incorporating itself as a "private club," complete with rooms specially fitted for pedestrian delights like Ping-Pong, mahjongg, and backgammon.

In reality, anyone with the right connections or calling card could breeze past the winding row of live porters and black lawn-jockey statues that stood guard before the heavy, brass-studded doors of "21." The club advertised "luncheon at twelve" and "tea at four and until closing." Lois Long and her friends didn't go for the tea. "Drinks were a dollar twenty-five," she explained years later. "We thought brandy was the only safe thing to drink, because, we were told, a bootlegger couldn't fake the smell and taste of cognac."

Like most other club owners, Jack and Charlie paid a small fortune in protection money to the police, but for contingency purposes—in case an overzealous city commissioner decided it was time to crack down on vice just before a round of municipal elections—the club's rich stock of wine, champagne, and hard liquor was well hidden behind a faux brick wall that sprang open when the owners inserted a specially fitted wire into a certain crack in the mortar.

After cavorting at "21," Long and her friends often made their way uptown to Harlem, the storied center of black cultural life in 1920s New York, which was also a popular nighttime draw among middle-class white New Yorkers. Often, Long and her entourage would arrive uptown after three a.m. and stumble home well after the stock exchange bell sounded the opening of business.

Incredibly, she stuck to this routine almost every night. And she developed a titanium tolerance for liquor. "If you could make it to the ladies' room before throwing up," she chortled, you were "thought to be good at holding your liquor. . . . It was customary to give two dollars to the cab driver if you threw up in his cab." Which happened from time to time.

At the *New Yorker*'s ragtag headquarters, with papers, magazines, and metal filing cabinets strewn about as if at random, where writers were always coming and going, where confusion reigned supreme, and where staff members habitually pilfered one another's desks, typewriters, and office supplies, Long quickly emerged as a commanding presence. She wasn't above sauntering into work at three or four in the morning when, remarkably, even at that late (or early) hour there were always editors still laboring away over their manuscripts.

Fresh from a night on the town, dressed to the nines, and flush from hours of heavy drinking, Long managed consistently to leave the key to her enclosed cubicle at home and amused her colleagues by kicking off her heels, climbing in stocking feet onto the doorknob of her workstation, and hoisting herself over the demipartition wall. In hot weather, she'd casually strip down to her slip and clack away at her typewriter.

Because its offices were interspersed among several levels of a building owned by Raoul Fleischmann, Ross's wealthy friend and founding publisher of *The New Yorker,* Long and her assistant were initially installed at opposite ends of the floor. After weeks of collaborating by telephone, to the amusement of everyone but Harold Ross, they donned roller skates and whirled back and forth between their desks, bobbing and weaving between overstuffed trash cans, abandoned cigarette stubs, and small mounds of stray pencil shavings. Finally, out of pure exasperation, Ross moved them both to a vacant restroom.

Many years later, another staff member evoked a disparaging image of Lois Long, seated before her typewriter "in her Lilly Daché hats, with a cigarette dangling from her mouth, laughing at her own jokes as she banged them out for her column." The problem with this picture—one that probably held as true for 1925 as for 1968, when Long was closing her lengthy career at *The New Yorker*—is that her writing *was* funny.

"I always miss all the real excitement," she typically complained, "and it isn't fair. Here I go plodding around, in my conscientious, girlish way, to all kinds of places at all hours of the night with escorts only reasonably adept at the art of bar-room fighting, and nothing ever happens to me. . . . I was at the Owl on Saturday and on Tuesday, and what did the nasty gunmen do but hold the place up on Monday night. It simply isn't fair. . . . All in all, I feel very badly about the whole thing."

Laced with precisely this sort of dry humor, the typical installment of "Tables for Two," Long's weekly column, brilliantly captured the distinctive sound and feel of the Jazz Age in all its frivolity, bluster, and melodrama.

"Just before staging a complete collapse, with definite indications of rigor mortis, galloping Charleston, and the chronic mirages of a home in the country," Long wrote in one of her early columns, "I wish to go on record as saying that, everything considered, this HAS been a week!"

From attending the debut of County Fair—a popular theme club on East Ninth Street, decorated in gold and scarlet and featuring authentic grandstand boxes doubling for booths, a dance floor encircled by a white picket fence, and kiddie cars drawn straight from an honest-to-God state fairgrounds—to the opening on election night of the Nineteenth Hole Club—another theme venue, fashioned after a golf course—to afternoon tea dancing at the Lorraine Grill—an old standard, but a disappointment, as "the old place is not the same," too many "middle-aged businessmen amusing themselves between leaving the office and catching the 6:35 for New Rochelle"—Lipstick gave her readers a bird's-eye view of a week in the life of the New Woman.

Or did she? As a magazine writer earning upward of $3,900 per year, Long fell comfortably in the upper middle class and belonged to an elite 14 percent of women workers who were professionals. Hers was an uncommon experience.

Most working women in the 1920s toiled at less glamorous and remunerative jobs—nearly a third as domestic servants, the rest as clerical workers, factory workers, store clerks, and farmers. They sweated behind department store counters, typewriters, and sewing machines; they earned lower wages than men who did the same work (saleswomen earned less than half of what salesmen brought home); and they faced grim prospects for career advancement.

Yet by the end of the 1920s, almost four of every ten working women qualified as white-collar. Their jobs demanded that they dress fashionably, groom themselves carefully, and stay abreast of aesthetic and cultural trends. At ornate department stores, downtown law firms, advertising agencies, and government offices, they brushed shoulders with professional men (and some professional women) and learned to identify as middle class, even when the cost of a middle-class lifestyle far outstripped their salaries.

In short, though few women in the 1920s lived like Lois Long, increasing numbers of them encountered her image every day at the office, in magazine advertisements, and on the silver screen. Flapper-dom was every bit as much an expression of class aspirations as it was a statement of personal freedom.

Americans in the 1920s found creative ways to circumvent Prohibition.

10

GIRLISH DELIGHT IN BARROOMS

I F LOIS LONG's charmed life in Manhattan was at once iconic and unusual, by mid-decade Zelda and Scott Fitzgerald were leading an astonishing existence.

In 1923, Scott earned the whopping sum of $28,754.78—equal to about $300,000 in today's money—but still managed to over-spend by $7,000 (roughly $75,000 in twenty-first-century dollars). Despite the high fees he earned for articles like "Why Blame It on the Poor Kiss If the Girl Veteran of Many Petting Parties Is Prone to Affairs After Marriage?" and "Does a Moment of Revolt Come Some Time to Every Married Man?" Scott and Zelda simply couldn't keep pace with their insatiable appetite for good food, good liquor, and good times.

In a moment of financial desperation and self-deprecation, Scott even resorted to writing a satirical piece for *The Saturday Evening Post* entitled "How to Live on $36,000 a Year."

"Our garage is a large bare room whither I now retired with pen-cil, paper, and oil stove," he reported, "emerging the next afternoon at five o'clock with a 7,000-word story. That was something; it would pay the rent and last month's overdue bills. It took twelve hours a day for five weeks to rise from abject poverty back into the middle class, but within that time we had paid back our debts, and the cause for immediate worry was over."

Scott was only half in jest. In a decade that witnessed a virtual explosion in consumer credit and spending, the Fitzgeralds were poster children for material excess and indulgence.

They didn't seem too embarrassed by it, either. "I wanted to find out where the $36,000 had gone," Scott told readers. "Thirty-six thousand is not very wealthy—not yacht-and-Palm-Beach wealthy—but it sounds to me as though it should buy a roomy house full of furniture, a trip to Europe once a year, and a bond or two besides. But our $36,000 had bought nothing at all."

In fact, Scott knew exactly where the money had gone, since he kept meticulous household budgets. A typical month's expenses included $80 for "house liquor" and $100 for "wild parties"—together equivalent to almost $2,000 in today's money—and $276 in "miscellaneous cash."

Perhaps out of economic necessity, and surely craving the adventure of a foreign excursion, in the summer of 1924 Scott and Zelda set sail for the French Riviera.

However high they had climbed the social ladder in the United States, the Fitzgeralds were relative provincials among the more seasoned American expats who converged on France in the interwar years. During their first week in Paris, they accidentally bathed young Scottie in the bidet and got her violently ill on a gin fizz, thinking it was lemonade.

Though he and Zelda would spend the better part of five years in France, Scott never bothered to learn anything beyond rudimentary restaurant French and made a point of frequenting American cafés on the Right Bank. When he ate at Voisin, a renowned Parisian bistro, he ordered club sandwiches, much to the disgust of the white-jacketed waiters. Largely apathetic about the explosion of experimental art and music that swept the European continent, Scott slaked his literary thirst at Sylvia Beach's English-language bookstore, Shakespeare & Company, read mostly American novelists, and sought out English-language translations whenever he bothered to read French writers like Marcel Proust.

The Fitzgeralds weren't sojourning in Europe out of a profound sense of alienation with American culture. They were just looking for the cheapest way to live well. Hauling along seventeen pieces of luggage and a complete set of *Encyclopaedia Britannica,* they hoped to profit from France's deep postwar economic slump. Since the franc had plummeted to an all-time low against the dollar, a good meal with wine could be bought for less than 20 cents. Surely even the Fitzgeralds could survive in such discounted circumstances.

Upon arriving in Valescure, Scott and Zelda purchased a used Renault for $750 and rented an enormous stone villa that was studded with balconies of blue and white Moorish tiles and surrounded by a fragrant orchard of lemon, olive, and palm trees that gave way to a long gravel road—the only passageway out of their Mediterranean castle. An additional $55 per month provided the services of an English nanny for young Scottie and a proper French cook and maid.

While Scott labored away on his new novel, a short but powerful work he would eventually entitle *The Great Gatsby,* Zelda found herself courted by a dashing French naval aviator, Edouard Jozan, who lived nearby. Jozan turned aerial stunts above the Fitzgeralds' villa and lavished considerable attention upon Zelda. It was like 1918 all over again.

By July, America's most celebrated couple was mired deep in crisis. Zelda fell in love with Jozan and asked Scott for a divorce.

The record of events is murky, but sometime after July 13 Scott demanded a meeting with Jozan. The Frenchman opted instead to salvage Zelda's honor—and perhaps his own scalp—by leaving town. "That September 1924," Scott wrote after tempers had cooled, "I knew something had happened that could never be repaired."

Seeking solace, and of a mood simply to forget the sting of Zelda's betrayal, Scott rededicated himself to the novel, reading drafts of the work in progress to John Dos Passos, Donald Ogden Stewart, Maxwell Struthers Burt, and other prominent American literati who stopped by to visit and pass some time on the warm, coarse beaches of southern France. Within the space of a few months, with the novel well on its way to completion and the wound of infidelity on the way to healing, Scott could report back to his stateside correspondents that all was well—or, at least, better—in

France. "Zelda and I sometimes indulge in terrible four-day rows that always start with a drinking party but we're still enormously in love and about the only truly happily married couple I know."

While the Fitzgeralds passed the days bronzing themselves in the late afternoon sun of the Riviera and patched up their sporadically rocky marriage, Lois Long carried their torch back in New York, traipsing from one watering hole and feeding spot to the next.

For staid occasions, there was her favorite standby, the Colony, at Sixty-first Street and Madison Avenue. It was distinctly "the restaurant of the cosmopolite and the connoisseur," a tourist guide warned. "The rendezvous of the social registrite; the retreat of the Four Hundred rather than the Four Million which emulate them. It is to the Manor born. . . . Here you'll find no gold ceilings, no glittering grandeur, no novelties for the nouveau riche. The Colony is quiet, exclusive, expensive, and wholly disinterested in the newest wrinkles in interior decoration. . . ."

For more whimsical occasions, there were theme clubs like the Pirate's Den, owned by Don Dickerman, the flamboyant nightclub impresario who also gave New Yorkers the County Fair. At the Pirate's Den, clientele like Lipstick could enjoy a variety of escapism and voyeurism oddly similar to—but much more expensive than—the Great Chicago Fire or San Francisco Earthquake rides at Coney Island.

"It is a rather boyish night club," a patron noted with amusement. "All the waiters are disguised as pirates of the 18th century, and except for their mild eyes and blameless mouths are a fearsome looking crowd." As customers sipped cider from battered copper mugs and feasted on a variety of fresh seafood in Dickerman's dimly lit cavern, costumed wait staff performed mock sword fights and ship brawls. To round out the effect, the walls were lined with maps, toy ships, fish skeletons, and seafaring trinkets from Coney Island.

It was a weird sort of venue, but a popular one among urban folks who had money to spend and an itch for something more spectacular than their own workaday lives. Decades before American suburbanites began flocking to Las Vegas in search of simulated reality, there were the nightclubs of Manhattan, ready to satisfy the same yearnings of the city's rising middle class.

As a rule, *The New Yorker* didn't include photographs or sketches, so Long and her colleagues had to develop a deft hand at descriptive narrative. After visiting Chez Fysher, Lipstick reported that "the crowd there (and it is a crowd!)" thoroughly enjoyed a house act that included "a very tiny little chanteuse, who sang perched up on a high table and later danced a tango; a savage young woman who glowered and sang songs of the Russias; a young ventriloquist who, by painting eyes, nose, and mouth on his clenched fist, and adding to it a dummy about two feet high, managed to create a hilarious little being who kept everybody as amused as if they were at the Palace." Finally, there was "Yvonne, who is too wonderful to describe."

Neither her fans nor New York's many nightclub owners and restaurateurs knew who she was or what she looked like. And that was half the fun. As her column caught on, any number of impostors were spotted around town claiming to be Lipstick, hoping to buck a reservation list or score a better table. Long only encouraged the sense of intrigue, variously claiming to be "a short, squat maiden of forty who wears steel-rimmed spectacles, makes her son pay her dinner checks, and habitually carries a straw suitcase filled with Aquizone" or closing her column as "the kindly, old, bearded gentleman who signs himself—LIPSTICK."

Readers knew only that Lipstick was probably young and that she was a woman. At least so they would have discerned when she complained in late 1925 that her "escort's snappy little roadster sobbed gently and died in the middle of Park Avenue. . . . There was a lot of rushing around in the rain to find a taxi, and more scurrying in search of a garage, and then just as we started again toward the Century cellar"—a popular East Side nightspot—"one of the taxi windows fell out and smashed sweetly on the pavement, and the deluge finished off what was left of a perfectly good evening dress."

But such clues were few and far between. Lipstick's devotees were free to imagine her as they wished—as a blonde, a brunette, or a redhead, as tall or short, as the girl next door or a glamorous big-screen starlet. And Long indulged them, playing to the public's fascination with that new species of woman who seemed wholly in command of her life and fortune.

Long also used her column to flaunt the drinking habits and adventures of young women like herself who no longer felt bound by Victorian notions of feminine propriety. What reader could forget the week she stayed out until dawn, realized that her copy was due at *The New Yorker* by noon, rushed to the office still decked out in a backless evening dress, "threw up a few times" in the bathroom, and still managed to bang out her column before the deadline?

Her position on Prohibition was nothing short of heretical. "About the spectacular dry raids of last week," she once wrote, "there is nothing special to be said except that a number of naughty cabaret owners just won't be allowed to sell liquor any more. And, by the time you read this fifty or more clubs will be on the verge of closing, and fifty-seven others will be on the verge of opening." All in all, it was a hollow victory for the "cause of Enforcement," even if it was likely to drive up cover charges at the city's many notorious watering holes.

Of course, few if any restaurant and speakeasy owners knew that the young, raven-haired flapper clutching the brandy snifter was actually Lipstick, the influential columnist for *The New Yorker*. So "it was nothing out of the ordinary to get thrown out of those clubs," she later recalled. "People were frequently brawling, and the proprietor usually made an arbitrary decision to put out a chronic offender from time to time just to show the other patrons that there was an intention of good order, even if it didn't in fact exist."

All of this was a source of endless concern for Harold Ross, who by the late 1920s could claim to edit one of America's most cosmopolitan magazines but never quite prevailed over his old-fashioned notions of propriety. So, like a distressed parent who realizes that the kids are going to drink no matter what, Ross opened his own *New Yorker* bar—open only to editors and contributors—in the basement of one of Fleischmann's buildings. As Long understood it, "He hoped we could drink and stimulate one another to come up with good ideas for the magazine. He thought if the magazine had its own speakeasy it would be safer for us and that the same general decorum could be kept that Mrs. White"—Katharine White, the *New Yorker's* fiction editor and unofficial chief of staff—"inspired at the office."

But Long's job was to prowl the streets, not to cloister herself in the magazine's offices. Her lifestyle was outrageous and frivolous, and she knew it. "I shall not write about restaurants," she began one column, "because I haven't been to any and I am tired about writing about eating anyway. I shall write about drinking, because it is high time that somebody approached this subject in a specific, constructive way."

With her trademark flair for satire, Long blamed the "Youth of America" for the nation's drinking dilemma. Prohibition would never have been a necessity, Lipstick claimed, had young people learned "to drink with aplomb" rather than excessive debauchery. "The answer," she proposed, "lies in the nursery and the classroom. . . . We will teach the young to drink. There would not be so many embarrassing incidents of young men falling asleep under the nearest potted palm or playing ping-pong with Ming china if little Johnny, at the age of six, had been kept in regularly at recess to make up his work because he had failed to manage his pint in Scotch class. . . .

"Besides all this," Long concluded, "we should have a new type of baccalaureate sermon."

Whether to acknowledge her flamboyant disdain for Prohibition, or in general recognition of her libertine sensibilities, the noted New York City socialite Barney Gallant invented a new cocktail, "the Lipstick," popularly advertised as "sweet but with a wallop." Long's signature combination called for two parts champagne, one part gin, one part orange juice, a dash of grapefruit juice, and a trickle of cherry brandy.

Lipstick lived up to her reputation, ever ready with useful advice about which speakeasy to visit or what brand of drinking paraphernalia to procure. "[As] an accompaniment to grown-up sport of any kind," she recommended "the following drinking accessories" by Abercrombie and Fitch: "a quart cocktail shaker, four glasses, a bottle opener and corkscrew, strainer and squeezer, all fitting into a suede bag $4\frac{1}{2}$ × 3 inches in size." As any self-respecting subscriber to *The New Yorker* surely knew, the Volstead Act penalized the manufacture, sale, and distribution of liquor—but not its purchase or consumption.

Lipstick also provided instruction on the upkeep and maintenance of drinking kits. "Remedy for a dented flask, demonstrated to me when I expressed incredulity," she wrote under the subheading "Little Hostess Department." "Fill a flask with ginger ale or carbonated water, put the stopper in, and shake. Really! All right, try it yourself. Flasks, like humans, become better and more beautiful when filled with innocuous beverages." The following week: "Two infuriated experimenters report that their flasks split in half when they tried my dent remedy of filling them with ginger ale and shaking them. Go easy."

On another occasion, Long expressed shock and dismay that, "incredible as it may seem—there are still many people who are completely at a loss before a tightly corked bottle without a corkscrew in sight." The solution, Lipstick informed readers, was certainly not to drive a rusty penknife into the cork in vain hopes of liberating the bottle. "The answer, of course, is to pound the bottle against a padding (bath towel, napkin, odd pieces of lingerie, or what have you?) against the wall. The cork, honestly, emerges slowly and surely to a point where you can simply lift it out with the fingers." Or so she had heard.

"My girlish delight in barrooms . . . which serve the best beefsteaks in New York," she opened an early column, "received a serious setback a week or so ago in a place which shall, not to say should, be nameless. The cause was a good, old-fashioned raid." Writing in the heyday of Prohibition, Long made the event seem almost common, informing her loyal fans that "it wasn't one of those refined, modern things, where gentlemen in evening dress arise suavely from ringside tables and depart, arm in arm, with head waiters no less correctly clad, towards the waiting patrol wagons. It was one of those movie affairs, where burly cops kick down the doors, and women fall fainting on the tables, and strong men crawl under them and waiters shriek and start throwing bottles out of windows."

Lipstick reported that the entire event was "very exciting" until a "big Irish cop regarded me with a sad eye and remarked, 'Kid, you're too good for this dump,' and politely opened a window leading to the fire escape. I made a graceful exit."

It was vintage Lois Long. And her readers loved every word of it.

First-wave feminists marching for women's suffrage in New York City, May 6, 1912.

11

THEJE MODERN WOMEN

I RONICALLY, the 1920s flapper sustained some of her fiercest criticism not from the Christian moralists or spokesmen for the older generation, not from politically conservative men, but from hard-line feminists. Whereas once the women's rights movement had mobilized millions of activists around important issues like suffrage, occupational health and safety, income equality, and legal rights, the New Woman of the 1920s—women like Lois Long and Zelda Fitzgerald—struck many veteran feminists as an apolitical creature interested only in romantic and sexual frivolities.

Charlotte Perkins Gilman, the celebrated author and activist, scored younger women for their "licentiousness." And Lillian Symes, another old hand in the women's movement, found that her "own generation of feminists in the pre-war days had as little in common with the flat-heeled, unpowdered, pioneer suffragette" of the nineteenth century "as it has with the post-war, spike-heeled, over-rouged flapper of to-day. We grew up before the post-war disillusionment engulfed the youth of the land and created futilitarian literature, gin parties, and jazz babies."

Symes's generation of feminists—women who came of age just before World War I—weren't prudes. They were "determined to have both, to try for everything life would offer of love, happiness, and freedom—just like men." This didn't entail a rejection of femininity. The key notion was balance.

"If in those younger days we believed didactically in our right to smoke and drink, we considered over-indulgence in either 'rather sloppy' if not anti-social," she wrote. "If we talked about free love and if a few even practiced it 'as a matter of principle,' we should have been thoroughly revolted by the promiscuous pawing and petting permitted by so many technically virtuous younger women today. . . . If all this makes us sound like prigs, I can assure you we were not. We made ourselves as attractive as we knew how to be, we were particular about our clothes, and few of us ever 'sat out' dances."

Many prewar activists agreed that "sex rights"—"the right of women to a frank enjoyment of the sensuous side of the sex-relation"—deserved an important place in the feminist agenda. Like their flapper successors, they also sought new meaning and fulfillment in romance.

In 1926, Freda Kirchwey, editor of the liberal journal *The Nation,* solicited autobiographical essays from a group of seventeen feminist leaders, most of them middle-aged women who grew up before the war. All but three were or had been married at some time during their lives. Their stories, which ran under the banner "These Modern Women," revealed an almost uniform desire to balance career and family and to stake out a new and satisfying kind of "companionate marriage" in which husbands and wives interacted as friends and equals in their relationships.

Most of these women were also social activists. Their feminism combined a concern for the personal *and* the political.

In the prewar years, prominent radical women in New York had even founded a group called Heterodoxy, which convened regularly at a Greenwich Village restaurant to discuss sex, romance, politics, and culture. Some of the participants practiced heterosexual free love, others were involved in long-term monogamous relationships with men; some were lesbians, and some were celibate. Heterodoxy celebrated the idea of free choice and personal fulfillment.

As Lillian Symes noted, prewar feminists had matched their burning desire for personal fulfillment with an intense engagement in the world around them. "While we were not all political radicals," she maintained, "we were examining our socio-economic order and our sex mores with an inquisitive and skeptical eye."

But the Jazz Age flapper? She was another matter entirely. Disengaged from politics, more interested in shopping than picketing, drunk on the ethic of sexual freedom and romance, the flapper struck many feminists as misguided at best. At worst, a sellout.

The ferocity of these attacks betrayed some of the deep political fissures that ran through feminist circles after World War I. Having won the vote in 1920, women's rights activists now faced the daunting challenge of reconciling sharply divergent ideologies and priorities that threatened to rend the movement in two just as it graduated into the mainstream of American life. With feminists now engaged in a hot contest over just what "feminism" really meant, the flapper became a convenient whipping girl who could unite competing factions in universal condemnation and scorn.

American women had certainly traveled a long road from rural Seneca Falls, in upstate New York, where one hundred people convened on July 19, 1848, to sign a "Declaration of Sentiments" drafted by Elizabeth Cady Stanton. Borrowing directly from the Declaration of Independence, these early activists boldly averred that "all men and women are created equal; that they are endowed by their Creator with certain inalienable rights: that among these are life, liberty and the pursuit of happiness."

The generation of women's rights activists who lent their names to this creed had cut their political teeth on radical abolitionism. Stirred by William Lloyd Garrison's cry for an immediate and unconditional end to chattel slavery, crusaders like Lucy Stone, Susan B. Anthony, Elizabeth Cady Stanton, and Lucretia Mott built a strong argument for women's emancipation on the very same natural rights foundation that informed the abolitionist movement. If all men were equal—unlike most of the country, abolitionists believed passionately that this was the case—weren't men and women also equal to each other? If it was wrong to hold humans in bondage, wasn't it also wrong to deny women the right to vote, hold property, sit on juries, enter the professions, and enjoy equal treatment in divorce and custody proceedings? The founders of the women's movement thought so, as did many of their male abolitionist supporters like Garrison, Bronson Alcott, Wendell Phillips, Gerrit Smith, Theodore Parker, and Frederick Douglass.

But times changed, and so did the women's rights movement.

Over the next seventy-five years, no one could have appreciated better the strange trajectory of American protofeminism than Charlotte Woodward, a nineteen-year-old farmer's daughter who traveled all day by horse-drawn cart to attend the Seneca Falls convention. Woodward, who dreamed of being a typesetter (and, in the words of a perceptive historian, "might as well have aspired to fly to the moon"), was the only signer of the Declaration of Sentiments who lived to see the Nineteenth Amendment ratified in 1920.

In Woodward's youth, crusaders for women's rights rested their argument on the logic of absolute equality. Elizabeth Cady Stanton, one of Charlotte's early heroes, acknowledged that men and women were not "the same and identical"—either by nature or nurture, women were more moral and kind, men more aggressive and dogmatic. But the *"rights* of every human being are the same and identical."

By the turn of the century, as Charlotte Woodward edged toward middle age and august pioneers like Elizabeth Cady Stanton and Susan B. Anthony passed from the scene, a new generation of women's leaders shifted the emphasis of the suffrage argument. Out of expediency, they accepted at face value the predominant Victorian belief that women and men were inexorably different and maybe just a little unequal.

According to prevailing wisdom, it was a woman's natural role to provide a stable, soothing home life for her husband and to confer an ethical education on her children. Left to their own devices, men were easily given over to excess and decadence. The same emerging industrial economy that demanded sober, self-controlled employees to staff its factories and offices needed wives and mothers to exert a civilizing influence at home. In the absence of that civilizing influence, men would never learn to master their impulses and lead the kinds of sturdy, disciplined lives that would make them good employees in a new, industrial order.

This was always a false ideal. Middle-class Americans could comfortably espouse the virtues of separate spheres, but for millions of women in the textile mills of New England and the Piedmont, the garment factories of Chicago and New York, and the cotton fields of Mississippi and Alabama, the grind of poverty demanded that sons and daughters share equally in the punishing routine of wage labor.

To many second-generation suffragists, most of whom hailed from comfortable, middle-class backgrounds, whether or not the Victorian gender system actually mirrored reality was entirely beside the point. It was popular and enjoyed wide support, especially among men of influence. Rather than fight the gender code, suffragists used it to their advantage. In a rapidly industrializing and urban nation where the line between public and private was often blurred, they claimed, a woman could not fulfill her duty to safeguard the domestic sphere unless she was granted political rights.

"Women who live in the country sweep their own dooryards and . . . either feed the refuse of the table to a flock of chickens or allow it innocently to decay in the open air and sunshine," wrote the distinguished settlement house founder Jane Addams in an article entitled "Why Women Should Vote." But in "a crowded city quarter . . . if the street is not cleaned by the city authorities no amount of private sweeping will keep the tenement free from grime; if the garbage is not properly collected and destroyed a tenement house mother may see her children sicken and die of diseases. . . ."

The modern world was too complex to sustain rigid divisions between public and domestic spheres, Addams explained. People now lived in closer quarters, bought most of their food and household items from stores, and came into daily contact with urban blight and vice. In short, "If woman would keep on with her old business of caring for her house and rearing her children she will have to have some conscience in regard to public affairs lying outside of her immediate household."

"Women's place is Home," Rheta Childe Dorr affirmed in 1910. "But home is not contained within the four walls of an individual house. Home is community. The city full of people is the Family. The public school is the real Nursery. And badly do Home and Family need their mother."

This rationale for equal suffrage resonated with many Americans who were prepared to grant women a role in politics but weren't ready to reject Victorian notions about gender difference. So in the years before World War I, at thousands of dramatic torchlight parades and petition drives, mainstream suffragists softened the potentially radical implications of their cause by insisting that women wanted the vote primarily to be better wives and mothers—not to engage in a power grab or to press unorthodox ideas on an unwilling nation. It proved a winning formula.

But in the wake of their stunning constitutional victory in 1920, former allies in the suffrage cause found themselves torn over the implications of this argument.

Over the preceding decade, even as it pressed for equal suffrage, the women's lobby had also pressured states into enacting maximum work hours for women. By 1925, all but four states bent to political pressure and set anywhere between eight-hour and ten-hour work-days for women. Other states even banned women from working at night or set minimum wages for women workers. The women's lobby had also campaigned for health and safety measures that would shield women from the ruinous effects of industrial work. In an era when few Americans enjoyed any real protection against the whims of their employers, these statutes succeeded in alleviating some of the most egregious conditions for women who toiled in textile factories in Paterson, New Jersey, or fruit canneries in Los Angeles.

But in order to justify these laws—in order to get the legislatures to pass them and the courts to uphold them—feminists had to concede that women needed special shelter from mental, emotional, and bodily harm. If women were naturally weaker than men—and this is precisely what future Supreme Court justice Louis Brandeis famously argued in the 1908 case *Muller v. Oregon,* which established a legal precedent for women's labor laws—then the state had a compelling public interest in extending them special protection.

It wasn't necessarily hypocritical to press for *equal* voting rights and *special* labor legislation. After all, mainstream suffrage groups based their demand for enfranchisement on the premise that women were different from men—physically weaker, morally stronger—but nevertheless in need of the vote.

By the 1920s, not all feminists agreed on this point.

On one side of the divide stood so-called social feminists, many of them members of reform groups like the National Women's Trade Union League, the National Consumer's League, and the League of Women Voters (the successor to the National American Woman Suffrage Association). Even as they celebrated their achievement of equal voting rights, social feminists continued to argue that women were a more delicate sex, in need of special protective legislation.

This tack didn't sit well with members of the National Woman's Party (NWP). Led by the fiery young Quaker activist Alice Paul, the NWP wholly rejected the maternalist argument for women's enfranchisement and called for an Equal Rights Amendment (ERA) to the Constitution—a measure that would ban all policy distinctions between men and women.

It wasn't that Alice Paul was totally unsympathetic to working women. "Personally, I do not believe in special protective labor legislation for women," she said. "It seems to me that protective labor legislation should be enacted for women and men alike . . . and not along sex lines." Another member of the NWP warned, "If women can be segregated as a class for special legislation, the same classification can be used for special restrictions along any other line which may, at any time, appeal to the caprice or prejudice of our legislatures."

To the NWP, feminism could not afford to compromise on the *idea* of equality, even if such a position might temporarily set back the cause of working women. If women wanted to share equally in life's pleasures, they couldn't claim special immunities from life's trouble.

Social feminists hit back hard. A member of the League of Women Voters asserted it was obvious that "the most important function of woman in the world is motherhood, that the welfare of the child should be the first consideration, and that because of their maternal functions women should be protected against undue strains." Many social feminists were middle-class reformers who genuinely felt concerned for "the tired and haggard faces of young waitresses, who spend seventy hours a week of hard work in exchange for a few dollars to pay for food and clothing." It was all well and good to invoke abstract doctrines of legal and social equality, but ultimately the ERA wing of the feminist movement would only "free women from the rule of men . . . to make them greater slaves to the machines of industry."

These issues would take years to resolve. In the meantime, if they could agree on little else, feminists across the divide found most young women in the 1920s sorely lacking in the kind of ideological rigor and political commitment that their own generation of activists had exhibited on such a grand scale. Much as veteran second-wave feminists of the 1990s would lament the seemingly apolitical posture of Gen-X women, flappers simply didn't strike first-wave feminists in the 1920s as concerned one way or the other about the weightier issues of the day. None of this seemed to augur well for the future of feminism.

When conservatives denounced feminists for betraying a "flapper attitude," they were missing the point entirely. Most committed feminists were also chagrined by American flapperdom.

There were a few exceptions. Dorothy Dunbar Bromley, a noted liberal writer, defended the "modern young woman" who viewed feminism as "a term of opprobrium." The problem wasn't the lipstick-wielding flapper, Bromley wrote, but the "old school of fighting feminists who wore flat heels and had little feminine charm" and their successors—self-styled feminists of the 1920s who "antagonize men with their constant clamor about maiden names, equal rights, women's place in the world, and many another causes . . . *ad infinitum.*"

Young women weren't frivolous or apolitical, Bromley argued. They weren't trading politics for pleasure. Rather, they were "feminists—New Style—truly modern" Americans who "admit that a full life calls for marriage and children" but *"at the same time . . . are moved by an inescapable inner compulsion to be individuals in their own right."*

The young woman of the 1920s, Bromley concluded, "knows that it is her American, her twentieth-century birthright to emerge from a creature of instinct into a full-fledged *individual* who is capable of molding her own life. And in this respect she holds that she is becoming man's equal."

In condemning the flapper for her turn inward, first-wave feminists may have betrayed a lack of imagination. Perhaps the trick wasn't to combine the personal and the political. Maybe the personal *was* political. Maybe the flapper was pioneering a distinct brand of individualist feminism.

Illustrator John Held Jr. captured the spirit of the Jazz Age.

12

THE LINGERIE SHORTAGE

IN THIS COUNTRY

VERYWHERE ONE TURNED in the mid-1920s, sex was on the brain. When Americans weren't having it, they were thinking about it or reading about it.

Magazine aficionados consumed real-life glossies like *True Confessions, Telling Tales, True Story,* and *Flapper Experiences,* which ran stories with such lurid titles as "Indolent Kisses" and "The Primitive Lover" ("She wanted a caveman husband"). Dish detergent advertisements featuring scantily dressed Egyptian women guaranteed the "beauty secret of Cleopatra hidden in every cake" of Palmolive. Popular songs of the era included "Hot Lips," "I Need Lovin'," and "Nursing Kisses."

Movie posters for films like *The Cowboy and the Flapper*—"See What Happens When the Cowboy and the Flapper Meet. William Fairbanks and Dorothy Revier do their stuff in a way that raises this picture into the ranks of really dramatic production"—testified to the new level of sexual candor that permeated mass culture.

Though her columns appeared to suggest that Lois Long was dating half the eligible bachelors in Manhattan—and maybe a few of the ineligible ones, too—sometime around 1926 she became romantically involved with the *New Yorker's* swank but mercurial staff artist, Peter Arno, who pioneered the magazine's distinctive cartoon humor. He was, as *The New York Times* would later write, "tall, urbane, impeccably dressed, with the kind of firm-jawed good looks popularized in old Arrow collar ads."

The scion of a prominent New York family (his father was a state supreme court justice), Arno—né Curtis Arnoux Peters—was raised with the best people and attended the best schools (Hotchkiss, Yale). Yet he did everything he could to cast off the shackles of Victorian respectability. At Yale, he dabbled in music and art rather than business or law. Upon graduation, he moved to Greenwich Village rather than the Upper East Side. He changed his name. He changed his friends. But he could never change the way he talked—that upper-crust accent common to Hotchkiss boys—or the way he walked. And he couldn't change that winning smile.

In many respects, he was a perfect match for Long. He was no prude. In a legendary *New Yorker* moment, Arno penned a cartoon depicting a young couple who appear before a motorcycle cop carrying a removable automobile seat. The caption reads: "We want to report a stolen car." Harold Ross thought the cartoon was a side splitter and immediately gave it his approval. A week later, when it was already too late to change the edition, he finally got the joke. He took Arno out for a drink a few days after the magazine hit the stands.

"So you put something over on me?" he asked with a forlorn expression. Arno shrugged, sipped his cocktail, and asked why Ross had approved a cartoon he didn't even understand. "Goddamn, I thought it had a kind of Alice in Wonderland quality," Ross replied. "It would have had the same effect on me if the guy had been holding a steering wheel instead of the back seat!"

With the exception of Harold Ross, James Thurber quipped, "the cartoon was surely understood by everybody else between the ages of fifteen and seventy-five."

Long and Arno carried on an affair for a year or so before marrying in 1927. Neither courtship nor marriage seemed to have domesticated either partner. Once, they passed out after a long night of drinking at the *New Yorker*'s staff club. The next morning, according to Long, managing editor Ralph Ingersoll found them "stretched out nude on the sofa and Ross closed the place down. I think he was afraid Mrs. White would hear about it. Arno and I may have been married to one another by then; I can't remember. Maybe we began drinking and forgot that we were married and had an apartment to go to."

On another occasion, after lending the celebrity couple his town house for the weekend, Harold Ross fired off a terse note to Long. "I just learned that you . . . copped a lamp from my house that I was going to send back to Wanamaker's," he opened. "All right, you can have it—as a bridal gift, with my compliments."

Especially when clothed, they struck a handsome couple. "She had been a sort of Zelda Fitzgerald figure," a staff member explained many years later. "She was beautiful and witty and [Arno] was handsome and worldly. They had been . . . the most glamorous couple in New York."

Their marriage announcement in the society columns was typically irreverent but also too clever by half, as it effectively blew Lipstick's cover. "Lois Long, who writes under the name 'Lipstick,' married Peter Arno, creator of the Whoops sisters, last Friday," read the notice. "The bride wore some things the department stores give her from time to time, and Mr. Arno wore whatever remained after his having given all his dirty clothes to a man who posed as a laundry driver last week. . . . Immediately after the wedding the couple left for 25 West 45th Street, where they will spend their honeymoon trying to earn enough money to pay for Mr. Arno's little automobile."

Arno had bought the car, a Packard, on the understanding it could reach one hundred miles per hour on the open road. The newlyweds tested it for four thousand miles, couldn't achieve the promised speed, and sued the automobile company for breach of contract.

No, Lois Long's lifestyle was anything but ordinary. As she later summed it up, "All we were saying was, 'Tomorrow we may die, so let's get drunk and make love.' "

Most young women simply never lived as wildly and recklessly as she. For starters, though the urban flapper was popularly known to flout the rules of Prohibition, in fact nationwide alcohol consumption plunged in the 1920s. If many young people—particularly city dwellers—found plenty of ways around the law, still, on the whole, the Eighteenth Amendment accomplished just what it set out to do.

What's more, though about half of all college-educated women in the 1920s had lost their virginity before the eve of their weddings, most had slept only with their future husbands. To be sure, the younger generation regarded premarital sex and foreplay with a far more liberal eye than their parents. In one study, three-quarters of all college-age men expressed their willingness to marry women with previous sexual experience. But most of these Jazz Age youths viewed sex as an appropriate and fulfilling act between two people who loved each other and intended to marry. Although this was a revolutionary view in its time, it paled in comparison with the further unraveling of social customs in the 1950s and 1960s.

In some ways, the personal feminism of the flapper era even *narrowed* the romantic and sexual possibilities available to women.

In the Victorian era, before the latter-day revolution in courtship and dating, women and men had inhabited a world largely segregated by gender. Men worked, women ideally stayed at home. Men socialized at the saloon, the private club, or the fraternal society; women passed their free hours at one another's homes. In an environment where men and women rarely enjoyed meaningful relationships outside of their families, many women—especially middle-class teenagers who attended finishing schools and colleges—developed intense emotional and physical bonds with one another.

This was true of Mary Hallock Foote, known as Molly, and Helena DeKay, two young women who met in 1868 as students at the Cooper Union Institution of Design.

"Imagine yourself kissed a dozen times my darling," read one of Molly's typical dispatches. "You might find my thanks so expressed rather overpowering. I have that delightful feeling that it doesn't matter much what I say or how I say it, since we shall meet so soon and forget in that moment that we were ever separated."

On another occasion, even as both women looked forward to their imminent marriages, Molly confided that "I wanted to put my arms round my girl of all the girls of the world and tell her . . . I love her as wives do love their husbands, as *friends* who have taken each other for life—and believe in her as I believe in my God. . . ."

Whether Molly and Helena ever sexually consummated their love for each other is unknown and beside the point. Theirs was a typical homosocial relationship in the nineteenth century, the sort that was actually encouraged from the pulpit, in etiquette books, and in medical tracts. In a world where women and men were expected to occupy separate spheres, it was acceptable and even preferable that unmarried women should enjoy close bonds. It was expected that they would kiss, hug, and even sleep together in the same bed.

Many female college students found themselves "smashed" on other women. "When a Vassar girl takes a shine to another," explained a student in 1873, "she straightaway enters upon a regular course of bouquet sendings, interspersed with tinted notes, mysterious packages of 'Ridley's Mixed Candies,' locks of hair perhaps, and many other tender tokens, until at last the object of her attentions is captured, the two become inseparable, and the aggressor is considered by her circle of acquaintances as—*smashed*."

For young people like Molly and Helena, marriage and child rearing could interrupt, if not destroy, long-standing emotional and physical relationships. Others simply couldn't bring themselves to accept this new order of things. From the 1870s to the 1920s, roughly half of all female college graduates opted out of marriage entirely, compared with only a tenth of American women on the whole.

Many of these educated women surely rejected matrimony because they weren't interested in sacrificing their careers. But others might have been reluctant to forfeit the deep-felt bonds they forged with other women. In these years, it was common for educated middle-class women, particularly professionals and social activists, to forge so-called Boston marriages—long-term domestic partnerships that were acknowledged openly but lacked any real legal standing. Such was the case for the settlement house founder Jane Addams and her life partner, Mary Rozet Smith; Mary Woolley, president of Mount Holyoke College, and her former student Jeanette Marks; and Vida Scudder and Florence Converse, both professors at Wellesley College.

The Victorians didn't feel particularly threatened by these domestic partnerships or by more casual romantic ties between unmarried women. For one, few medical or scientific experts envisioned rigid distinctions like homosexuality and heterosexuality until the late nineteenth century—the age of eugenics, social Darwinism, scientific management, and taxonomy—when all the natural world suddenly seemed fodder for rigorous study and classification. More important, unmarried women forming close bonds with other unmarried women didn't pose a fundamental threat to the Victorian gender code; married women in the workplace did.

The same forces that revolutionized sex, romance, and courtship in the early twentieth century shattered this Victorian world in which women could openly nurture emotional and physical ties with one another. By the 1920s, it was completely normal for girls and boys to disappear with each other in the dark recesses of parked cars and movie theater balconies. It had become *abnormal* for two women to do these things together.

Social scientists, physicians, and political leaders suddenly discovered the "problem" of female homosexuality. Many of these professionals, like England's noted sexologist Havelock Ellis, thought of themselves as distinctly progressive for their advocacy of a more candid and open approach to sexual pleasure. But their tolerance knew limits. Lesbians—women who didn't need men, who bucked the larger system of heterosexual romance and intimacy—were an open threat to new social arrangements like modern dating and companionate marriage. In a world that was "hip on Freud," as one of Scott Fitzgerald's characters boasted, but where most people fundamentally misinterpreted Freudian theory as a mandate for unleashing repressed sexual desire, it just didn't make sense for women to reject the pleasures of heterosexual intimacy.

Institutions that allegedly encouraged lesbian relationships, like women's colleges, came in for a terrific drubbing by the 1920s, and for one reason or another, most women—particularly those middle-class collegians who had once been likely to reject heterosexual partnerships—seemed to internalize the new order. Whereas more than half of all women who graduated from Bryn Mawr College between 1889 and 1908 remained single, by 1918 roughly two-thirds eventually married. Overall, the marriage rate in the United States rose in the 1910s and 1920s, while the average age of married couples continued to plummet. Whereas women in 1890 married at the average age of 22 years, by 1920 that average had dropped to 21.3.

Maybe young women took up marriage because it was no longer quite as shocking to juggle a career with family. Maybe they did so because the new sexual and romantic climate encouraged and even fostered relationships between men and women. Or perhaps they embraced heterosexuality because same-sex intimacy was no longer regarded as a legitimate outlet for romance and desire. Either way, the new sexual freedom of the 1920s came with a price. It meant that women could no longer turn to one another as freely for sexual and romantic intimacy.

For men, things might have been somewhat different. Although male homosexuality was widely regarded as deviant, gay men subtly profited from the steady maturation of an urban economy where the family farm or business was no longer a cornerstone of the economy. In this new setting, wage earners lived alone and negotiated the workplace as individuals rather than continuing to live in the bosom of their families. This made it possible and even acceptable for men to live outside traditional households and to forge relationships that weren't oriented toward the time-honored pattern of courtship, matrimony, and procreation. New opportunities arose for closer romantic and physical bonds between unmarried, unattached men.

It's little coincidence that the early decades of the twentieth century saw the emergence of subterranean gay subcultures in big cities like New York, Washington, D.C., and St. Louis, but also in smaller urban centers like Worcester, Massachusetts; Des Moines, Iowa; and Columbia, South Carolina.

Not so for those women who harbored romantic or sexual longings for other women. They wouldn't enjoy an equal degree of social freedom until their earnings kept pace with men's. For the typical working girl, living outside the bounds of heterosexual institutions was a luxury she simply couldn't afford.

If there were real limits to the first sexual revolution—particularly for women—many Americans found the changing social landscape jarring. In speaking of Harold Ross, who was hardly an old-guard

Victorian, Lois Long remembered that "he was one of those Protestant Westerners who was certain no woman who drank, smoked and cursed could be truly respectable. One night I took him with me on my nightclub tour and he never got over the shock. You never knew what you were drinking and who you'd wake up with, and in Ross's Western outlook if you slept with a girl you compromised her, and ought to marry her. There was an *obligation*."

On other occasions, Long seemed to relish her capacity to offend guardians of feminine virtue and chasteness. "Once, I found myself drinking beside a priest who gave me the blazing-eye treatment and tried to convert me." She chuckled. "I promised him I'd slash my wrists before I had the chance to die a natural death."

With Harold Ross at its helm, *The New Yorker* was neither quite so bold nor so tasteless as to print that caliber of story. But Long had a keen eye for cultural currents and an acid tongue. In living and recording the adventures of the New Woman, she brought a gust of candor and lighthearted wit to the popular discussion about sexuality.

In her report on the opening of the Nineteenth Hole, a new theme club, Long noted with delight the "informality achieved by tricky putting greens [situated] on either side of the dance floor. What with the girls' skirts short as they are nowadays, and the additional uplift contingent upon the position required for putting, the evening was not without humor. Really and truly," she ribbed, "something ought to be done about the lingerie shortage in this country."

"Turn about is fair play," she acknowledged on another occasion, "and the only way I could persuade a particularly adventurous youth to take me to Phil Baker's Rue de la Paix after the theatre was by a solemn promise I would accompany him downtown afterwards to gaze on the wonder of the Club Caravan, for reasons which he did not disclose at the time." It soon became clear to Lipstick that her escort was motivated chiefly by "an artistic mission to investigate first-night reports of a young woman strolling about clad in a single red rose— a real one!" And only a red rose. Whether out of legal concerns or to avoid giving customers too much of a good thing, "what had they gone and done but draped her in a green chiffon by the time we got there!" Her young date was "so upset by his tardiness in seeing the sights of the town that it completely ruined his evening. You might have thought *I* had dragged him there, the way he carried on."

As Lois Long, creator of the droll and devil-may-care Lipstick, well knew, the "flapper" was always a caricature—one part fiction, one part reality, with a splash of melodrama for good measure. Much like her cultural heirs—the teenybopper, the sweater girl, the hippie chick, the Valley girl, the punk girl, the queen bee—she was a broad and sometimes overdrawn social category. People who were in the know, like Lois Long, often objected to being labeled flappers, if only to avoid being rigidly compartmentalized.

Long's literary persona, Lipstick, certainly demurred on this question, though never too strenuously. While she detested downtown Manhattan during the summertime, "if you must be a sightseer or a flapper, whatever the cost," she informed her readers, "the perennial Greenwich Village Inn, at Sheridan Square, and the Blue Horse are about the safest bets in warm weather." On other occasions, she might preface a remark, "Without being flapper about it . . ."

Her columns suggested an important point: Most Americans could recognize a flapper. But why? Clearly the flapper could be recognized by her style, not just her behavior.

Just months after joining *The New Yorker,* Lois Long sailed for France, where she chronicled the work of a small number of fashion elites who were redefining how the world thought about feminine beauty and form. She saw at once that the American flapper was no isolated phenomenon. Now that clothing and cosmetics could be mass-marketed, the lines were suddenly blurred among people of different regions and classes. The flapper was a role that every young woman could play.

That story begins in a small couturier's shop in Paris.

PART TWO

Coco Chanel, ca. 1926, outfitted the New Woman for the modern age.

13

A Mind Full of Fabulations

ITTING IN HER rambling town house on the rue du Faubourg
St.-Honoré, with its army of uniformed footmen, maids, and
chefs, its grand piano, striking geometric furniture, and haute
epoque chairs draped in a fine, beige-colored satin, Coco Chanel had
considerable cause to celebrate. Queen of Paris couture, supreme
architect of the feminine form, artisan of jersey and tweed and rayon,
creator of Chanel No. 5 and the "little black dress," she had overcome
the disadvantages of an unfortunate childhood spent deep in the wilderness of rural France. Her admirers naturally wanted to know how
she did it—how she had landed on top having started so low down.

Though she would always prove strangely reticent about her past,
journalists pried at least this much from the tight-lipped Mademoiselle Chanel:

She was born in 1893 to a poor but upstanding family of traveling
merchants. Her mother, a frail woman only thirty-two years of age,
contracted pneumonia and died when Coco was a child. Her father,
an affable but unreliable drifter, couldn't own up to the responsibility
of raising three young daughters and two sons. He did what any good
wanderer would do: He abandoned them and sailed for fortune and
freedom in America, leaving his family destitute and at the mercy of
private charity.

The boys, Alphonse and Lucien, were packed off to a work farm.
Her sisters, Julia and Antoinette, went to live with distant relatives.

And little Coco, all of six years old, was taken in by two aging spinster aunts in Auvergne.

Living "at the farthest corner of that backward province," young Coco—her real name was Gabrielle—was provided for but not loved. Later in life, she told an acquaintance, "My aunts were good people, but absolutely without tenderness. . . . I got no affection. Children suffer from such things."

Coco didn't have many friends—in fact, she didn't have any. Her afternoons were spent in melancholy play at a long-forgotten cemetery near her aunts' farmhouse. There, with a bitter autumn wind whistling in the trees, amid the crackling of dead leaves and overgrown weeds, she positioned her rag dolls over the headstones and tried to communicate with all the departed souls. "I told myself that the dead are not dead as long as people think about them," she later confided to a friend.

Those bleak country winters would remain etched in her memory. From late fall until early spring, snowdrifts as high as a grown man's waist blanketed the thick woods in a sea of unending white. Ice crystals clung to the branches of the tall chestnut trees that ringed the town. The house grew cold and dark. Coco stayed mostly indoors. She remembered thinking of herself as a "little prisoner."

From the small alcove where she slept, young Coco devoured popular romance novels—especially those by the popular writer Pierre Decourcelle—and allowed her imagination free rein. Lying on her plain cot, with one arm behind her head and the other propping up the latest newspaper serial, she learned to block out the sounds of the old women who gathered each afternoon in her aunts' kitchen to confer in hushed tones about the financial burdens of raising someone else's child.

Every year on her birthday, her grandfather sent her five francs. And every year she used a small portion of the money—just one franc—to buy a handful of mint candies at a local market stall. She squirreled the rest away in a piggy bank, until one year her pious aunts forced her to tithe all of her savings at a church charity drive. She never forgot the rage that consumed her. It taught her an early lesson about the distinction between avarice and autonomy.

"I have never been interested in money," she said of the incident, "but I was concerned with independence."

It's easy to understand why her admirers were spellbound by Coco's tale of a lonely Auvergne childhood. Hers was a classic story of triumph over adversity.

And almost every word of it was untrue.

Coco Chanel lied about it all. She lied about her aunts, who never existed. She lied about her father, who never went to America. She even lied about her age and hired someone to doctor her birth records at the city hall at Samaur. She was born in 1883—not 1893.

Some of the details of Coco's fictional childhood were torn directly from the pages of Pierre Decourcelle's romance novels. She borrowed other story lines from her friends, who either didn't notice or didn't care that she was appropriating their memories. Certainly she never pretended to be even remotely forthright about her roots. When a close companion proposed that she consult a psychotherapist, Coco laughed off the suggestion. "I—who never told the truth to my priest?"

Chanel's early life—or the little that is known about it—was even lonelier than she chose to remember in public. Her mother succumbed to pneumonia when Coco was twelve years old—not six, as she claimed—and her father abandoned the family shortly thereafter, though not for adventures in America. Coco's brothers were sent off to a work farm; she and her two sisters went to live at a church-run orphanage at Auberzine, a grim, densely wooded backcountry town that lay on high terrain above the Corrèze River.

The orphanage was a converted twelfth-century monastery bounded by towering stone walls that kept out the sun. Coco and the other girls wore identical black skirts and white blouses, lived in unadorned rooms with black-painted doors and whitewashed walls, and spent six days a week learning practical homemaking skills like sewing and needlepoint. What little academic work they accomplished was taught by rote: the kings and departments of France, the alphabet, the multiplication tables.

In later years, Coco never acknowledged this part of her life. In nineteenth-century France, poverty and orphanhood were marks of shame. Anything—*anything*—was better than admitting she had been penniless and unwanted. Even a made-up story about two spinster aunts.

As it stood, her only solace came during school vacations, when the Chanel sisters went to stay with relatives in a small town just outside the provincial capital of Moulins, where her grandparents still lived. Her female relatives taught Coco how to sew with more skill and flourish than the nuns at the orphanage were able to demonstrate. It was probably during these cherished escapes that she discovered Pierre Decourcelle's novels, whose plotlines and characters she blended effortlessly into her own life story.

When Coco turned eighteen, she left the orphanage. "Nobody can live with low horizons," she later said. "A narrow outlook will choke you. All I had when I left my Auvergne"—she stuck tenaciously to her story about the spinster aunts—"was a summer dress in glossy, wiry black woolen fabric with cotton wrap and for winter a suit in Scottish tweed and a sheepskin, but my mind was full of fabulations."

After a brief stay at the Notre Dame boarding school in Moulins, where she was admitted as a charity case, Coco took a job as shopgirl with a local milliner. On weekends, she picked up extra money by working for a tailor. It was there on a slow Sunday morning that a rich playboy walked in and asked for a last-minute alteration on his riding suit. He changed Coco's life.

Whoever invented the term *prodigal son* might well have had Etienne Balsan in mind. The youngest heir of a wealthy textile baron, he spent his teenage years at a posh boarding school in England, where he developed all the affectations associated with the Edwardian gentry, including a lifelong adoration of horse breeding. Balsan's parents died when he was eighteen, leaving him a vast fortune and little incentive to work. Instead, he raced Thoroughbreds. All day. All week. All the time.

Etienne bought a sprawling twelfth-century castle called Royallieu, where he kept dozens of horses and staged lavish parties and outings for his old friends from the cavalry, many of whom spent weeks on end at the pleasure and hospitality of their rich, twenty-four-year-old host.

As if his retreat from the family business weren't adequate cause for offense, Etienne scandalized his older brothers by keeping a well-known courtesan, Emilienne d'Alençon, at his grand chalet.

The crowd of men and women that Etienne gathered around him at Royallieu was unusual—sons of wealthy industrialists who shirked their family callings in favor of fast horses and expensive wine; famous Parisian courtesans; daughters of the rising bourgeoisie who rejected their parents' manners and morals; Oxbridge graduates who fled England and empire for the more permissive atmosphere of pre-war France.

They all gravitated to Etienne. And Coco fit in with ease. She was twenty-one years old when she went to live at Royallieu, though she would later claim to have been sixteen. Tall, long necked, and angular, with dark olive skin and pitch black eyes that shone flecks of gold when the light touched her face at just the right angle, Coco was no ordinary beauty. But she was striking in her own fashion. If it bothered her that Etienne already had a mistress, she never complained. In turn, Emilienne welcomed Coco to the fray and helped her make the leap from a childhood of minimal comfort to the lifestyle of the landed elite.

Coco was unaccustomed to the art of high living, but she was a discerning student. On one of her first trips to Paris with Etienne, from their lavish suite at the Hotel Ritz, Coco discreetly ordered several dozen oysters to the room. She had never so much as tasted one but knew she would have to develop a liking for—or at least a tolerance of—the cold, slimy delicacy that was featured so prominently at many of the Royallieu dinner parties.

"I invited the chambermaid to share them with me." Coco laughed. "She didn't want any. I told her: 'make an effort. You're young, you're pretty, one day perhaps you'll have to eat oysters.' "

Coco's role at Royallieu defied classification. Along with Emilienne, she was one of Etienne's resident mistresses. This much was certain. But she was less a coquette than a resident personality, and she soon became part of the maverick culture that Balsan endeavored to establish at his refuge for wayward gentlemen. "She would lie in bed until noon, drinking coffee and milk and reading cheap novels," he recalled. But she was ready in a flash to join the men in the most unfeminine of amusements.

Leaving the bustles and crinolines and lace and feathers to Emilienne, Coco opted instead for jodhpurs, men's collars and ties, pigtails, and bowler hats. She raced Thoroughbreds with the boys, attended the races decked out boldly in masculine attire, trudged through the mud in her high riding boots, and galloped astride her horse without the slightest care when the mire and manure splattered and caked on her pants.

She even studied breeding and training with the jockeys.

"I just didn't know anything," she once admitted. "I understood in the broadest sense, but I had to teach myself. The boys with whom I was living didn't want me to change. They played with me, and had a great time. They had found a person who was straightforward. They were wealthy men who had no idea who this girl was who came into their lives."

It was fun for a while, but Coco knew there was a limit to how long she could act as part-time mistress to Etienne Balsan and part-time play pal to his friends. Almost by accident, she discovered that she had a talent that was begging to be cashed in. Whether out of boredom or pent-up creativity, she began decorating simple straw and felt hats that she bought on the cheap at Galeries Lafayette in Paris. Her unusual designs caught the notice of other women who attended the horse races at Longchamps, especially after a well-known stage actress began sporting them around the countryside. Soon enough, the wives and mistresses of the racing set were beseeching her to custom-design headpieces to complement their afternoon attire.

Coco had an exit strategy.

But Etienne wouldn't hear of it. When she asked for a loan to fund her own millinery shop, he brushed off the idea and reminded her that she knew nothing about running a business.

So Coco continued to bide her time.

Then she met Boy Capel. It was 1907, and Coco was twenty-four years old.

Arthur "Boy" Capel was Etienne's close friend and opposite in every possible way. An Englishman of modest wealth and impeccable style, he could match the Thoroughbred set on horseback and vanquish them on the polo grounds without so much as breaking a sweat. His French was near perfect, his woolen suits *were* perfect, and unlike Etienne, he didn't think it was a crime to work. He planned to multiply his wealth rather than spend it.

Coco and Etienne met up with Boy Capel in Pau, where all three were vacationing at a thirteenth-century château that overlooked the vast, snow-capped Pyrenees mountains. There were extravagant dinners, stallions and Arabian horses for racing, and bloodhounds for foxhunting.

Etienne was so consumed by the local equestrian splendors that he scarcely noticed when Boy and Coco started lingering by candlelight each night in the mirror-lined manor hall. There, sipping from generous tumblers of pale red cognac, and by daylight, when they took long rides through the lush meadows encircling the château, they found a spark that neither could have expected. It didn't hurt matters at all that Capel endorsed Coco's plans to open a millinery shop. He was the first person in her life who took her seriously.

Boy Capel returned to Paris at the end of the week, and Coco went with him.

"Forgive me," she wrote to Etienne, "but I love him."

Coco had been ready to make the break for some time. "I had just spent two years in Compiègne, riding horses," she said—actually more like four years, but when it came to Coco, who was counting?— "[and] I couldn't earn a livelihood with that. And, now that I loved someone else, I had to move to Paris."

Had theirs been a conventional story, Coco and Boy would have ridden off into the night, severing all ties to Etienne Balsan. But these weren't conventional people. Balsan's ego was probably bruised, but he tried not to let on. "Like every good Frenchman," Coco later remarked, "like all men in general, Etienne Balsan began to love me again because I'd left him for someone else."

The year 1908 found Coco living with Boy Capel at his apartment on rue Gabriel—and sometimes in a furnished suite at the Hotel Ritz—and running her upstart millinery out of Etienne's apartment on the boulevard Malesherbes, an elegant, tree-lined thoroughfare bordered by expensive shops, banking houses, and private apartment buildings. With both men now invested in Coco's success—Etienne had put up the real estate, and Boy had lent her starting capital—the three friends became almost inseparable. "I was just a kid," she later explained. "I had no money. I lived at the Ritz and everything was paid for me. It was an incredible situation. Parisian society talked about it. I didn't know Parisian society. I still didn't know anybody."

But her objective was independence. "It was very complicated," she admitted. "The cocettes were paid. I knew that, I'd been taught that. I said to myself, 'Are you going to become like them? A kept woman? But this is appalling!' I didn't want it." Etienne and Boy agreed. "You have no idea how amusing it was," Coco recalled with a smile, "that three-sided discussion that started up fresh every day."

Coco didn't have to wait long for success to beckon. Headquartered just blocks from the Greek Revival columns of the Madeleine, Chanel found that her quirky style might be out of pace with old Paris, but it was right in step with the modernist sensibility that was taking hold among the fashion-conscious New Women of France, England, and America. Within months, the business was booming.

It was the beginning of the House of Chanel.

Years later, when asked how she emerged from obscurity to become the world's most important designer of women's clothes, Chanel said it was simple.

"Two gentlemen were outbidding each other over my hot little body."

14

An Athletic Kind of Girl

THE FEMININE AESTHETIC that Coco Chanel set out to revolutionize from her small shop on the boulevard Malesherbes had stayed remarkably consistent over the better part of the preceding one hundred years.

To be sure, the long nineteenth century—stretching from the French Revolution in 1789 to the Guns of August in 1914—had borne witness to a multitude of fashion cycles. At the dawn of the century, the typical well-heeled woman on either side of the Atlantic would have favored the Empire dress, a tapered, one-piece affair with an artificially high waistline that fell just below her breasts and drawstrings that met at the small of her back. Featuring a high, ruff-collared neckline for daylight hours and a more tantalizing décolletage at night—one that formed a perfect line across the top of her breasts—the Empire style recalled the toga of ancient Greece and was trimmed with puffs, scallops, and other three-dimensional frills.

By the 1830s, the Empire dress gave way to a new mode whose slightly lower waistline and leg-of-mutton sleeves—fitted forearms with puffed upper sections—presented a more top-heavy silhouette.

This style yielded in turn to a new midcentury aesthetic favoring enormous bell-shaped skirts that trailed around women's feet and asymmetrical "pagoda sleeves" that widened toward the wrist.

This pattern was superseded in the 1870s by wide, triangular

Three young women in Chicago, 1924, proving that sports and competition were not just a man's game.

skirts that culminated in a bustle——layers of material gathered at a woman's back that resembled a large, decorative drapery.

The bustle fell out of vogue in the early 1870s, then came back into fashion in the 1880s.

The 1890s saw the popular rise of the two-piece dress suit whose starched white shirtwaist, tight jacket, leg-of-mutton sleeves, and belted midriff gave the impression of a tall hourglass.

Yet despite this constant evolution in fashion, a single, overriding theme remained the same: *control*. By painfully disciplining women's bodies, clothing helped impose the political and social subordination of America's daughters and wives and enforced the rigid separation between the masculine public sphere and the feminine domestic sphere.

Consider the daily torment experienced by a typical woman just in getting dressed each morning. Whether the year was 1800 or 1900, whether she was fifteen years old or sixty, rich or in the middle class, married or unmarried, the representative American woman kicked off her ensemble with a one-piece foundation garment combining drawers and an undershirt, complete with a built-in "trapdoor"; then a tightly bound corset with drawstrings or metal clasps to contort the waist and midriff; next, restrictive silk pads that slipped in above the hips and in the underarms to provide the illusion of more dramatic curves; then several layers of petticoats or a steel-and-wood-frame crinoline to hold the skirt in proper shape; then a long-sleeved chemise; then underpants; then silk stockings and garters that fastened to the corset; and, finally, the dress or skirt itself.

This wasn't just an exercise in extreme pageantry. It was about social control.

The tight-lacing of corsets, which was considered essential until the early twentieth century, artificially reduced women's waists to as little as seventeen or eighteen inches. By constricting the rib cage just below the sternum, the corset amplified the hips and bust and shrank the waist, bending the feminine form into the idealized "steel engraved lady" whose unreal shape——stick thin in the middle and ample in the bosom, with a protruding rear end——suggested fragility, delicacy, and sexual availability all at once.

It also restricted oxygen intake, crushed the internal organs, caused chronic fatigue and headaches, and created serious long-term medical complications.

An English magazine correspondent—a proponent of women's dress reform—shared with readers the story of her daughter, who left for boarding school (uncorseted) a "merry, romping girl" and returned (corseted) a "tall pale lady" who had to strain just to "languidly embrace me." The daughter told her mother "how the merciless system of tight-lacing was the rule of the establishment, and how she and her forty or fifty fellow-pupils had been daily imprisoned in vices [sic] of whalebone drawn tight by the muscular arms of sturdy waiting-maids, till the fashionable standard was attained. The torture at first was, she declared, intolerable; but all entreaties were vain, as no relaxation of the cruel laces was allowed during the day under any pretext except decided illness."

By the time her daughter returned home, "her muscles [had] been, so to speak, murdered."

A study of fifty women conducted in 1887 revealed that the corset forcibly contracted their waists by anywhere between two and a half and six inches. The pressure it applied to women's bodies averaged twenty-one pounds but could reach as high as eighty-eight pounds. Tight-lacing was thus akin to crushing oneself slowly from all sides. As a harsh critic of the corset noted, "It is evident, physiologically, that air is the pabulum of life, and that the effects of a tight cord round the neck and of tight-lacing only differ in degree . . . for the strangulations are both fatal. To wear tight stays is in many cases to wither, to waste and to die."

Not only did these devices force women's bodies to conform to popular standards of beauty. They helped police the "weaker sex." This was no conspiracy theory drummed up by protofeminists and dress reformers. The loudest defenders of the corset routinely used words like "discipline," "confinement," "submission," and "bondage" and spoke favorably of "training the figure" with a degree of pain "rigidly inflicted and unflinchingly imposed." A Victorian man admitted that "half the charm in a small waist comes not in spite of, but on account of, its being tight-laced."

"The corset is an ever present monitor," argued yet another man, "indirectly bidding its wearer to exercise self-restraint: it is evidence of a well-disciplined mind and well-regulated feelings."

The corset was only one of many clothing features that reinforced women's subordination to men. The design of women's sleeves and silk pads made it impossible for them to raise their arms to shoulder height. Both bell dresses, which were popular in the antebellum period, and barrel-shaped "hobble skirts"—which narrowed at the ankles and came into wide fashion in the early twentieth century— severely restricted women's ability to walk. Running was simply out of the question.

"No one but a woman," wrote one fashion critic, "knows how her dress twists about her knees, doubles her fatigue, and arrests her locomotive powers."

If layers of clothing choked off women's ability to move and breathe, crinolines kept them in a literal state of captivity. Built out of flexible steel, whalebone, or wood, these contraptions were little more than hooped cages that gave full definition and body to women's dresses while simultaneously confining their subjects within an intricate enclosure. Sometimes as much as five yards in circumference, crinolines visually and physically reinforced a political order that denied most women the right to hold property, vote, file for divorce, or sit as jurors in criminal and civil courts.

To add injury to insult, wooden crinolines commonly ignited when women stepped too close to a fireplace or caught their dresses on a loose ember. "Take what precautions we may against fire," wrote one Victorian woman, "so long as the hoop is worn, life is never safe . . . all are living under a sentence of death which may occur unexpectedly in the most appalling form."

With women so tightly bound, layered, and caged, it's little wonder that the typical Victorian wife experienced fainting spells, headaches, exhaustion, and "neurasthenia"—a fictive nervous disease that supposedly befell women who wasted their energy reserves on strenuous endeavors like a college education or sensual experiences like masturbation.

Of course, there is no such thing as neurasthenia. Women suffered physical and nervous attacks because they were laced with twenty pounds of weight and trapped beneath layers of hot, cumbersome petticoats. But doctors didn't know that in the 1890s. Viewing the feminine body as a fragile, closed system that contained a fixed amount of energy, the finest minds of the nineteenth century agreed that a woman's natural condition—dictated by birth and nature—required protection from the harsh realities of the world and a supreme imposition of control—from both within and without.

Clothing was just one piece of the larger puzzle.

There were lots of other ways to impose masculine authority over women.

Take medicine. With pronounced enthusiasm, American medical experts in the mid–nineteenth century embraced the groundbreaking efforts of J. Marion Sims, a country doctor from Alabama who pioneered the field of gynecological surgery. Unaware of recent developments in anesthesia, Sims subjected helpless black slaves to four years of brutal, experimental study. One of his subjects endured thirty gynecological "operations," all in the name of unlocking the mysteries of the female reproductive system.

Based on his research, Sims passionately believed—and convinced most of the American medical establishment—that the only legitimate function of women's reproductive organs was to procreate. He frowned upon "too frequent sexual impulse" and maintained that female arousal was an extraneous, even counterproductive, phenomenon. "It is only necessary to get the semen into the proper place at the proper time," he wrote. "It makes no difference whether the copulative act be performed with great vigour and intense erethism." In other words, the male orgasm was vital and useful; the female orgasm, not.

Sims invented surgical instruments like the "uterine guillotine" and taught adoring medical students how to amputate ovaries and clitorises. By the late 1800s, his techniques were commonly used on women whose physical or nervous conditions seemed to derive from an overexcited libido. What these women needed, the theory went, was management, discipline, and control.

Most women (and many men) didn't necessarily see or understand the socially and politically proscriptive function of either uterine guillotines or corsets. Some dress reformers even blamed women themselves for internalizing male definitions of beauty and thereby submitting to their own captivity.

"The corset-curse among women is more insidious than the drink-curse among men," declared one such critic in 1892. "A woman can no more be trusted with a corset than a drunkard with a glass of whiskey."

In the 1850s, feminists like Amelia Bloomer and Elizabeth Cady Stanton flamboyantly rejected women's fashion and donned loose-fitting Turkish trousers and sack skirts that rose to just four or five inches below the knee. Dubbed "bloomers," these comfortable outfits represented an abrupt break with prevailing styles. Stanton put the matter in sharp relief when she asked, "How can you . . . ever compete with man for equal place and pay with garments of such frail fabrics and so cumbersomely fashioned, and how can you ever hope to enjoy the same health and vigor as men, so long as the waist is pressed into the smallest compass, pounds of clothing hung on the hips, the limbs cramped with skirts . . . ?"

Amelia Bloomer was equally blunt, if somewhat less political, about the question. "We only wore it because we found it comfortable," she said many years later. "[We] had no thought of introducing a fashion."

Although its appeal was limited to a small number of political iconoclasts, the bloomer provoked a firestorm of controversy. Journalists reported that "ladies of irreproachable character, walking in the streets of New York, accompanied by their husbands and brothers [were] hissed and hooted," while prominent moralists complained that "if a gentleman . . . were to promenade Broadway in a bonnet or petticoat, he would very justly meet with general attention. Why should the ladies expect to commit similar departures from custom with greater impunity?"

Dress reformers—many of them forward-thinking doctors and nurses—answered these criticisms with dire warnings against the dangers of tight-lacing and crinolines. If they didn't necessarily rush to embrace the bloomer, they repeatedly stressed the importance of less restrictive clothing.

But it was at the grassroots level that change first occurred. The caged, tight-laced lady—delicate, trim, and buxom all at the same time—was simply an impossible ideal for the millions of women who were forced, or chose, to enter the world of work. A country in which women increasingly worked in factories and lived in cities—where they participated in a revolution in sexuality, morals, and manners—also saw profound changes in feminine attire.

Beginning in the 1890s, working women turned to less burdensome, though still conservative, styles of dress, usually featuring long, tailored skirts that fell to the floor, mass-produced blouses (then called "shirtwaists"), and long-sleeved jackets. These outfits offered the advantage of increased mobility.

Equally vital to the reform of women's fashion was the popular rise of sports in the late nineteenth and early twentieth centuries. All across the United States, ordinary Americans were rushing to embrace a more vigorous life. College football emerged from obscurity in the 1880s to become a major phenomenon by 1899, when the legendary coach Walter Camp selected the first all-American team. Basketball grew up in the 1890s, too, when a YMCA athletics instructor formalized its rules and created a national mania for indoor leagues. Boxing aficionados donned padded gloves and imitated the magic moves of "Gentleman Jim" Corbett. Would-be musclemen rushed to buy the latest edition of *Physical Culture,* a serial whose banner said it all: WEAKNESS IS A CRIME.

There was a lot at stake. As working-class Americans fell into the drudgery of assembly-line labor, and as middle-class Americans found themselves filling monotonous office jobs, there arose a popular longing for the vigor and strength of yesteryear. Slaves to the time clock, which made its first appearance in offices and factories sometime around 1890, servants to a new managerial elite who told them what to do and how to do it, increasingly divorced from the natural world—from the farm, from the food chain, from dirt and grime and physical exertion—ordinary Americans longed for an outlet to vent their frustrations with the machine age.

When future president Theodore Roosevelt—author of *The Strenuous Life*—warned his countrymen against the "soft spirit of the cloistered life" and implored them to "boldly face the life of strife . . . for it is only through strife, through hard and dangerous endeavor, that we shall ultimately win the goal of true national greatness," he struck a resonant chord.

Americans in the 1890s bought dime novels like Ralph Connor's *Black Rock* and Owen Wister's *The Virginian* and forsook romantic verse and poetry for the heavy bass line of marching songs and ragtime. "Ta-ra-ra Boom-der-e," a new anthem for a new age, made its debut in 1891 and sounded a death knell for the nineteenth-century waltz. Gentility was out. Muscle was in.

It wasn't just men who jumped on the bandwagon. Women, too, were inclined to prove their mettle. By 1901, books like *The Power and Beauty of Superb Womanhood* no longer attracted scorn for claiming that vigorous exercise would "enable a woman to develop in every instance muscular strength almost to an equal degree with man."

"Running, jumping, and natation, navigation, ambulation," began a popular poem, "So she seeks for recreation in a whirl. She's a highly energetic, undissuadable, magnetic, Peripatetic, athletic kind of girl!"

Changing times demanded a change in attire. The same two-wheel craze that challenged American sexual mores—ten million people were riding bicycles by the dawn of the twentieth century—created a quiet revolution in women's clothing.

"To men, rich and poor," wrote a female correspondent for *Cosmopolitan,* "the bicycle is an unmixed blessing, but to women it is deliverance, revolution, salvation. It is . . . impossible to overestimate the potentialities of this exercise in the curing of . . . ills of womankind, both physical and mental, or to calculate the far-reaching effects of its influence in matters of dress and dress reform."

The rise of women's colleges and coeducational universities in the decades following the Civil War also helped usher in a new era of athleticism for American women. College coeds were breaking with long-established conventional wisdom that held "a girl could study and learn but she could not do all this and retain uninjured health," as Dr. Edward Clarke, a Harvard medical school professor, argued in 1873.

In order to beat back these charges—to prove to the critics that college women were strong and sturdy specimens—administrators at all-women's institutions like Smith College introduced mandatory gymnastics classes during the winter months and outdoor sports for the fall and spring semesters. Students played basketball, volleyball, baseball, and tennis. They skied and ice-skated and took long bike rides around the town of Northampton, Massachusetts. In a letter to her parents, one student described a typical bike course of sixteen miles as just a "day's tramp."

Intramural sporting events like the annual freshman-sophomore class basketball game were the cause of great exhilaration. Ella Emerson reported home that "we got our tickets yesterday for the big basket-ball game next Saturday. They say it is always a terrible time. The girls cannot gather until two o'clock and then there is a dreadful crowd. Girls get knocked down and hurt."

A week later, she informed her family that the game provided "the biggest day for excitement. I got so excited, I just couldn't stand still but hopped up and down with the other girls and yelled. What a day!"

Although women's athletics at coeducational universities took longer to develop—at Cornell, for instance, they didn't come into their own until the 1920s—as early as the 1880s most female students were required to take gym class and participate in at least some outdoor sports. Obviously, these women couldn't don corsets, crinolines, and hobble skirts on the basketball court. At colleges like Smith, administrators set out guidelines for gym outfits that broke with long-standing fashion conventions.

"This year there are to be no skirts at all," Josephine Wilkin wrote home to her mother in 1891. ". . . The trousers are Turkish; pleated into a band, which buttons on the waist. Each leg is 80 inches wide! They are sewed up from the bottom about a foot & then in the center between the legs is a square piece about 8 inches square to give them better shape."

The irony probably didn't escape Josephine's mother. Her daughter's gym outfit was a bloomer. The problem was, of course, that for all its importance and innovation, the bloomer was ugly. Perhaps it was all right for gym class. But it carried too much political baggage to enjoy wide use. Someone was going to have to devise a better solution.

Paris had an answer to the problem.

The silhouette of the 1920s flapper emphasized grace and slenderness.

15

LET GO OF THE WAISTLINE

OVER THE COURSE of a long and active life, Paul Poiret was accused of many things. Modesty was not one of them.

"I know that you consider me a King of Fashion," he told a group of women gathered in New York. "It is thus that your newspapers entitle me, and it is thus that I am received everywhere, surrounded with honors, and fêted by vast gatherings. It is a treatment that flatters me, and of which I cannot complain."

Tall and robust, equipped with wide hands and a thick torso, Poiret had a piercing gaze, a long, angular nose, prominent cheekbones, and a dark, neatly trimmed beard. Attired as he typically was in a flowing camel cloak, white linen jacket, and white silk gloves, Poiret exuded the supreme confidence and ostentation that one might expect of a fashion king.

And justly so. He was a leading member of the generation of Parisian couturiers who revolutionized women's clothing in the early twentieth century. His upbringing couldn't have been more different from Coco Chanel's.

The son of a conservative and well-to-do cloth merchant, Poiret was born in 1879 and raised in the heart of the city—the First Arrondissement, just a stone's throw from the great courtyards of the Louvre, Les Halles, and the Palais Royal.

"I am a Parisian of Paris," he later boasted. It was central to his identity.

Poiret's earliest memories were of long strolls along the Seine with his mother. Ducking in and out of the winding side streets that laced through the quai de Louvre, he marveled at the clothing shops "whose mingled smell of dust and perfume I loved" and took great "delight" in listening to "the chat and commonplaces of the ladies, while giving the impression that I was busy playing at something quite else."

Yes, young Paul was a Beau Brummel in miniature and something of a mama's boy at that. Years later, he could still summon up vivid images of the black velvet suit and the gold ring encrusted with turquoise flowers that his mother bought for him when he was a child.

As a student at a private boarding school, Poiret suffered frequent bouts of homesickness and depression. Unlike most boys, he didn't dream of battlefield glory or romantic conquest. He dreamed of "stuffs and chiffons."

"Women and their toilettes drew me passionately," he admitted without embarrassment. "I went through catalogues and magazines burning for everything appertaining to fashion; I was very much of a dandy, and if I sometimes forgot to wash, I never forgot to change my collar."

Poiret glided through school without making much of a mark. When he graduated, his father, a stern and unforgiving character who believed passionately in God and work—and not necessarily in that order—forced him to take a job as shop assistant to an umbrella manufacturer.

"Listen," the elder Poiret told Paul's new boss, "he is a boy who has a well developed *amour propre*. He might easily become over-proud; we must break him of that, I want him to learn everything from the beginning."

So young Paul set to work sweeping floors and delivering umbrellas to customers. "The point of this breaking-in," he understood, was to "smash my pride."

If that was indeed the objective, his father miscalculated badly. Paul didn't get humble. He got ambitious. Armed with bundles of silk and muslin, he spent every night holed up in his bedroom, designing innovative women's wear with the assistance of a sixteen-inch mannequin that his sisters gave him as a gift. It wasn't long before Poiret was committing his patterns to paper and hawking them to the different fashion houses in Paris. His keen eye for color and knack for experimental shapes and forms caught the attention of the city's leading couturiers.

When the renowned designer Jacques Doucet invited him to join his firm, Poiret jumped at the chance. Poiret learned his craft from the master, and the product in these early years was decidedly conventional. His first model was a red cloak with cloth lining around the neck, a lapel made of crepe de chine, and six enamel buttons that lined up along the side. Not too flashy, but with enough pizzazz to capture the imagination of customers. Four hundred copies sold within just a few weeks.

In an eerie foreshadowing of his future rivalry with Coco Chanel, one of Poiret's early clients was Emilienne d'Alençon.

Between 1897 and 1900, Poiret churned out dozens of new models for the House of Doucet. Consisting mostly of jacket-and-skirt combinations, his designs were perfectly in step with the currents of the day. "The women wore them over corsets that were real corselets, sheaths in which they were imprisoned from the throat to the knees," he wrote. "Thence the skirts fell to the ground in a number of pans."

These were happy days for Paul Poiret. Doucet was a congenial personality—very much like Charles Dickens's character Mr. Fezziwig, who cheerfully prods his young employee Ebenezer Scrooge to lighten up from time to time. Doucet paid his brooding young protégé a handsome salary and encouraged him to go to the theater, take in an occasional show at Moulin Rouge—even find a girlfriend. But Poiret rarely took the advice. He was driven by a singular goal—to dominate the competitive world of women's fashion.

His career was interrupted by an unhappy year of compulsory military service sometime around 1900. Upon his discharge, he returned to the fashion world as a designer for the House of Worth, the venerable firm established in the mid–nineteenth century by the Englishman Charles Worth. The old man, who had more or less invented couture, was long dead, but his label lived on under the able direction of his two sons, Gaston and Jean.

From the start, the brothers made crystal-clear their expectations of Poiret's employment. "Young man, you know the Maison Worth . . . has always dressed the Courts of the whole world," Gaston began. "It possesses the most exalted and richest clientele, but today that clientele does not dress exclusively in robes of State. Sometimes Princesses take the omnibus, and go on foot in the streets. My brother Jean has always refused to make a certain order of dresses, for which he feels no inclination: simple and practical dresses which, none the less, we are asked for. We are like a great restaurant, which would refuse to serve aught but truffles. It is, therefore, necessary for us to create a department for fried potatoes."

Poiret took to the idea instantly. He believed that the modern woman needed a modern frock, and he instantly set about creating simple models that appealed to well-to-do Parisians who had money to spend on his bold and unusually minimalist creations.

Predictably, Jean Worth hated his designs. "You call that a dress?" he scoffed. "It is a louse." Maybe so, Poiret answered. But it was a louse that sold. And anyway, he had been brought on board to cook up fried potatoes.

In 1904, tired of being caught in the middle of the Worth brothers' unremitting feud over the artistic direction of their firm, Paul Poiret opened his own house. Capitalizing on his reputation for simple but elegant designs, he set about revolutionizing women's fashion. His clothing for the New Woman featured a high waistline, a long, straight silhouette, V-shaped necklines, and, in the place of those lackluster dark shades that dominated Victorian-era fashion, a bold palette of red, gold, and yellow that betrayed the influence of Eastern themes— particularly Serge Diaghilev's Ballets Russes, which took Paris by storm in 1909. Above all, Poiret's "look" banished the dreaded corset from women's wardrobes. Starting in 1906, his designs consciously rejected the S-curve—bust pushed out, waist sucked in, derriere jammed back—that had dominated women's fashion since the 1890s.

"I waged war upon it," he said of the corset. "It divided its wearer into two distinct masses: on one side there was the bust and bosom, on the other, the whole behindward aspect, so that the lady looked as if she was hauling a trailer."

In true character, Poiret was extraordinarily modest about his accomplishment. "Like all great revolutions," he opined, his triumph over the S-curve "had been made in the name of Liberty. . . . I proclaimed the fall of the corset and the adoption of the brassiere which, since then, has won the day."

He may have been overstating the case just a little. Like many great men, Poiret was a complicated personality. True, he "liberated" women from the agony of tight-lacing—or, at the very least, he made that liberation trendy and chic. But he wasn't exactly a poster boy for modern feminism.

"Yes, I freed the bust," he crowed many years later, "but I shackled the legs."

Poiret was referring to the hobble skirt, his original design that narrowed toward the ankles and made it exceedingly difficult for women to walk in anything more ambitious than baby steps.

"You will remember the tears, the cries, the gnashings of teeth caused by this ukase of fashion," he sneered. "Women complained of being no longer able to walk, not get into a carriage. All their jeremiads pleaded in favor of my innovation. Are their protestations still heard? Did they not utter the same groans when they returned to fullness? Have their complaints or grumblings ever arrested the movement of fashion, or have they not rather, on the contrary, helped it by advertising it?"

Indeed, for all his inconsistent braggadocio, Poiret didn't banish the corset in order to promote women's health, safety, or equality. He did it to shake things up. Fashions changed constantly, he argued. This was the very *definition* of fashion. Like the good "King of Fashion" he advertised himself as—it was a claim he made to the ladies of New York, Chicago, Los Angeles, and more or less every city he visited— Poiret enjoyed testing the loyalty of his subjects.

The "despotism of fashion," he told a group of Chicago women, placed everyone "at its mercy, for you evolve unconsciously, and you come to the point of wishing the same thing as fashion wishes, but in truth you have no free will and it is fashion which, like some astral influence, sets its impress upon you, and commands and controls your decisions, a tyrant doubly despotic since it orders women, who direct the actions of men."

In Poiret's mind, fashion was a mystic force that demanded constant change and innovation. People were in its service, not the other way around.

This wasn't a particularly usable definition for the New Woman. In fact, it wasn't even clear that Poiret *liked* the New Women who wore his designs. One of the first couturiers to use live "mannequins" (or models), he spoke with supreme derision of those tall, arresting beauties. One of them was "as stupid as a goose, but as beautiful as a peacock." Another had a "voice like a penny whistle. Fortunately her duties did not oblige her to speak." His favorite of the whole bunch, Paulette, was a "vaporous blonde" with pale blue eyes beneath which "there was hidden a malice, perhaps a viciousness, whose depths I never learned."

No, Paul Poiret wasn't the New Woman's best friend. He was in the game for reasons entirely his own.

It would be left to someone else to offer women a shot at self-definition and freedom through their clothes. And who better to meet this challenge than someone already accustomed to wearing men's jersey and tweed, who rode horses for sport, whose adult life was a study in vigor and athleticism? Coco Chanel was the ideal architect of this new fashion—the right woman, at the right time, in the right place.

From Etienne Balsan's apartment on the boulevard Malesherbes, Coco opened her millinery operation, Chanel Modes, around 1909. Within less than two years, she earned enough money to lease her own shop at 21, rue Cambon, a narrow lane that bordered the Ministry of Justice.

The back door of the Hotel Ritz, where Scott Fitzgerald, living in Paris, would later spend many a weekday afternoon getting plastered with his old Princeton chums, opened virtually onto the doorstep of Chanel's new workshop. In fact, the great writer and the great couturiere almost certainly brushed shoulders in the lobby from time to time, since Coco kept a private set of rooms at the hotel.

Coco's relationship with Boy Capel grew stronger even as Coco's millinery operation demanded more of her time and attention. "We were made for each other," she remarked many years later. "That he was there and that he loved me, and that he knew I loved him was all that mattered."

It might even have been Boy who suggested that Coco branch out and venture into the world of couture. In 1913, the couple rented an exquisite suite of rooms at the Normandy Hotel in Deauville, a popular resort town where many of their friends gathered each summer for weeks of quiet repose along the choppy, deep blue waters of the English Channel. Possibly at Boy's instigation, and certainly with his financial backing, Coco opened a boutique on rue Gontaut-Biron. Situated between the shore and the casino and set against a sharp horizon of imposing granite cliffs and Norman-style brick-and-stone houses, Coco's shop welcomed wealthy patrons with a striped awning that boldly announced: CHANEL.

The new operation offered a perfect opportunity for Coco to break into the exclusive world of high-end dresses, skirts, chemises, and accessories—in effect, to offer up clothing designs for the New Woman whose day now combined work, sport, and public leisure.

That summer, Chanel made a small fortune selling original models that blurred the line between masculine and feminine. Her store did a brisk business in navy blue blazers and turtleneck sweaters of the variety that English sailors wore, as well as other loose-fitting concoctions of knit and flannel materials. She proved especially deft at crafting models out of jersey, a heavy material that no dressmaker had ever dared to enlist in the cause of haute couture. This was the fabric of school uniforms and work clothes—maybe even golf outfits and tennis pants—but Chanel made it chic for all occasions.

All of this was peculiar and innovative, but, if Coco was to be believed, the rough silhouette of flapper fashion was born more of chance than design. "One day I put on a man's sweater," she told an interviewer, ". . . because I was cold. It was in Deauville. I tied it with a handkerchief at the waist." The fellow vacationers she met socially on the beach and at the polo grounds accosted her for information. "Where did you find that dress," they asked her. "If you like it," she replied, "I'll sell it to you." Ten dresses later, the signature Chanel frock was born.

If Paul Poiret had unloosed women from the tight grasp of the corset, Chanel drove the revolution forward in leaps and bounds, eliminating altogether the frills and excesses of women's couture in favor of styles that offered comfort, maneuverability, and practical use. In place of the three-dimensional ruffles, edges, and leg-of-mutton sleeves, she used complicated beadwork and colored swirls that evoked some of the trends in modern art then very much in favor in Paris.

It was a style that took hold quickly. Though World War I proved the undoing of many Parisian designers, including Paul Poiret, who closed down his firm to join the war effort and never quite figured out how to jump-start it after the armistice of 1918, Chanel thrived. She expanded her operations in Paris and Deauville and added a larger work space and store at Biarritz, a resort town in the south of France.

The war accelerated precisely those trends that made Coco's signature style so appealing. As hundreds of thousands of American, British, and French women entered the workforce to help sustain war production—these were the unsung heroines whose daughters would earn greater renown during World War II as "Rosie the Riveter"—they needed more practical clothes. They couldn't build munitions or man typewriters and telephone lines while wearing crinolines and corsets. Strict wartime rationing of raw materials like silk and cotton also inspired a move toward minimalism and simplicity. Out with the pagoda hips and tapered hems and in with the slender, elegant outline that was favored at the House of Chanel.

In her personal life, Coco had been dressing for sport and maneuverability since her earliest days with Etienne Balsan. She knew exactly how to clothe the New Woman of 1914 because she *was* that woman.

Coco's wartime designs featured hems that rose a few inches above the ankles and a long, sleek outline—all the more comfortable for the hospital volunteer or war production worker. By eliminating once and for all the corset and achieving continuity between the torso and chest, Chanel "let go of the waistline"—in her own words—"and came up with a new silhouette. To get into it, and with the war's connivance, all my clients lost weight, to 'become skinny like Coco.' "

Chanel was hardly alone in embracing these designs. But she was at the front of the pack—so much so that by 1915, *Harper's Bazaar* had announced that "the woman who hasn't at least one Chanel is hopelessly out of the running in fashion." Even as far away as New York, couture aficionados learned from *The New York Times* that the firm of Chanel was "leading the way" in the field of women's fashion.

By the following year, Coco was fully out of debt to Boy Capel and employed three hundred women at her various factories and stores. By the early 1920s, that figure grew to upward of three thousand workers. She was well poised to dominate feminine fashion for the coming decade.

Coco proved a demanding, sometimes autocratic boss. Moderately talented as a seamstress and completely unschooled in standard draftsmanship, she was nevertheless a master artist and perfectionist. She worked with live mannequins rather than paper patterns and often required as many as thirty fittings—each lasting hours on end—to complete just one muslin design. Then it was left to her small army of workers to replicate her model with total precision.

Marie-Louise Deray was twenty-one years old when Coco tapped her to be chief seamstress for her fashion house. "We worked with jersey, a fabric that no one had used before to make dresses," she remembered. "The 'diagonals' went every which way and we had to start over again several times. Mademoiselle was very demanding. If a fitting went wrong she exploded. She loved to pester people. I cried a lot, believe me. She was tough, unrelenting with the staff. But what she came up with was sensational, both chic and exceedingly simple, so different from Poiret. . . ."

Coco paid her mannequins the paltry sum of 100 francs per month, scarcely enough to live on and certainly a mere fraction of what it cost wealthy clients to purchase just one Chanel dress. When associates urged her to pay a living wage, Coco just shrugged. "They're beautiful girls. Let them take lovers."

Arriving at work each day in a chauffeured Rolls-Royce, she conducted most of her business from a lavishly decorated private apartment above her couture house and adamantly refused to make appearances even for the wealthiest of customers. It was a calculated trick that the narcissistic Paul Poiret could never have pulled off, but it worked for Coco. Her inaccessibility lent an aura of mystique to the whole Chanel operation. The dresses kept selling.

Chanel's signature style culminated sometime around 1923 in what commentators called the "garçonne look"—a nod to the 1921 best-selling novel *La Garçonne,* about a young woman who rebels against prevailing feminine roles to strike out on her own and earn an independent living. The book was so scandalous that its author was stripped of his *Légion d'honneur.*

The garçonne look—called simply the "flapper look" in England and America—dominated women's fashion for the better part of the decade. It featured tubular dresses with dropped or invisible waistlines, high hemlines that crawled up toward the knees, tank tops, straight vertical lines, and intricate decorative beading, topped off with bell-shaped cloche hats. Though its color schemes changed from year to year, and though it gradually incorporated new fabrics like tweed and new design elements like geometric patterns, the flapper style remained fairly constant throughout the decade—so much so that Bruce Bliven, editor of *The New Republic,* felt confident in speaking of a quintessential "flapper uniform"—"the style, Summer of 1925, Eastern Seaboard."

Lois Long, who expanded her coverage for *The New Yorker* to include fashion as well as nightlife in 1925, summed up Chanel's lasting imprint on women's wear in 1926 by observing that "when sports clothes first came into vogue for every type of day wear, a few years ago, the general opinion was that England, land of the hearty sportswoman, would provide fashions in this line, and that Paris would continue content with her supremacy over afternoon and evening frocks. Such was not the case."

On the contrary, designers like Chanel "got busy, immediately feminized tweeds and flannels." The New Woman, Long observed, now enjoyed a selection of comfortable, durable, yet elegant clothing that carried the added bonus of being "suitable for participation in all, save the very strenuous, sports, such as mountain climbing, lion hunting, and the exploration of the arctic."

Those who knew Coco before she became world famous would

easily have recognized the masculine influences in her clothing line. Her jerseys, sweaters, and dresses incorporated subtle elements of sailors' uniforms, stonemasons' handkerchiefs, reefer jackets, and mechanics' dungarees. Paul Poiret scoffed at her designs and called them *misérabilisme de luxe*—poverty of luxury. A somewhat more impartial observer noted that "women no longer exist; all that's left are the boys created by Chanel."

The androgyny in Chanel's design—and its physical redefinition of feminine sexuality—suggested that men's and women's roles were bleeding into each other. A Parisian law student underscored this point well when he asked, "Can one define *la jeune fille moderne*? No, no more than the waist on the dress she wears. These beings—without breasts, without hips, without 'underwear,' who smoke, work, argue, and fight exactly like boys, and who, during the night at the Bois de Boulogne, with their heads swimming under several cocktails, seek out savory and acrobatic pleasures on the plush seats of 5 horsepower Citroëns—these aren't young girls! There aren't any more young girls! No more women either!"

Androgyny didn't go hand in hand with asexuality. Quite the contrary. Flapper fashion regularly incorporated "Oriental" or "primitive" themes drawn from sub-Saharan and Asian civilizations, like skullcaps adorned with Egyptian textiles; hat designs by the French milliner Agnès that were "suggested by an African Head-Dress"; wooden-and-gold bangles, "slave collars," and "slave bracelets"; and an "exotic toque from Alex," "trimmed with cross in tête de nègre." In the context of the 1920s, to borrow "Oriental" themes was to suffuse one's designs with raw sexual power.

This borrowing from other cultures reflected the greater contact that Americans and Europeans enjoyed with non-Western peoples in the late nineteenth and early twentieth centuries, courtesy of imperialism and global trade. When white Europeans wrote, talked about, and analyzed these people—tasks to which they devoted considerable time and effort—they often contrasted their own state of over-civilization with the alleged raw, primitive instinct of the "Orient." In "Thoughts for the Times on War and Death," Sigmund Freud concluded in 1915 that "white nations" enforced a "renunciation of instinctual satisfactions," whereas nonwhite societies encouraged the realization of human urges.

Popular and pseudoscientific tracts on the raw sexuality of "primitive" peoples—volumes like Ernest Crawley's *Studies of Savages and Sex* (1929) and Bronislaw Malinowski's *The Sexual Life of Savages* (1929)—drove home precisely this point. The white American journalist Ray Stannard Baker best summed up prevailing ideas about exoticism when he explained, "If civilization means anything, it means self-restraint; casting away self-restraint the white man becomes as savage as the negro."

In weaving so-called primitive or Oriental themes into their wares, leading couture houses were assigning the modern woman a new, unspoken sexual power popularly associated with darker, non-Western peoples. It was an idea that worked in concert with other features of flapper design.

The most familiar ingredient of flapper fashion was the creeping hemline, which culminated sometime in 1925 or 1926 with skirts that fell fourteen inches above the ground. " 'The hemline moveth slowly up and nowhere doth abide,' " reported the *Washington Post*'s fashion critic in 1925. Two years later, *The New York Times* marveled at the new spring lineup from Paris. DISPLAY OF SPRING FASHIONS SHOWS THEM BARELY LONG ENOUGH TO COVER KNEES, readers learned.

The trend scandalized defenders of the old order, who were particularly alarmed by the sight of bare legs—a result of the preference for sheer stockings that quickly became a feature of the garçonne look. A Baptist pastor offered the following object lesson to his congregates:

> *Mary had a little skirt,*
> *The latest style no doubt,*
> *But every time she got inside,*
> *She was more than halfway out.*

Others took it all in stride. Even the conservative *Ladies' Home Journal* remarked that "as American women are noted for their pretty feet and ankles, it is pleasant to learn that skirts are going to be short . . . though one must adjust length to becomingness."

Coco wasn't the only designer in Paris to raise her hemlines or to make an imprint on flapper fashion. Whereas Chanel's sleek, boyish models enforced the appearance of a trim and linear figure—often achieved with the help of a breast flattener that deaccentuated all traces of feminine lines—Madeleine Vionnet, one of her chief rivals in women's couture, pioneered bias-cut designs that emphasized women's natural curves. By cutting material against the grain—an exceedingly difficult process involving great patience and skill—she was able to create an altogether new effect in dresses and skirts. The bias cut clung to the body and assumed the shape of its subject rather than the other way around.

Though Vionnet adopted many of the conventions of Chanel's flapper look, a discerning eye could tell one woman's imprint from the other. And in the twenties, many women were developing that eye for fashion. Still, by sheer force or personality, it was Coco who dominated the world of couture in the twenties.

In one of her first fashion columns for *The New Yorker*, Lois Long mocked other journalists for their "yearly cry" that "bobbed hair is going out; that big hats are to be *de rigueur;* that skirts are to be longer; and that waistlines are to be reestablished. This time, they pin one of their stories on the fact that Mrs. Reginald Vanderbilt insists upon long skirts. They forget that Mrs. Vanderbilt has always worn them." Ultimately, Long claimed, "what Mrs. Vanderbilt wears and what manufacturers want has no more effect on fashion than Dancing Teachers' conventions on night clubs."

Short skirts, dropped waistlines, and straight silhouettes were here to stay. For that, the world could largely thank Coco Chanel.

Standing outside the Rainbow Fashion Show in Chicago, 1926, two flappers enjoy the democratizing effects of the ready-to-wear revolution.

16

INTO THE STREETS

I T WAS ONE thing for Coco Chanel and a select group of Parisian couturiers to revolutionize the clothing of those fortunate few women in France and America who could afford to drop hundreds of dollars on an evening gown. But what of the millions more who couldn't? After all, rich people throughout the ages had slavishly embraced new fads and styles without influencing the purchasing habits of their economic and social inferiors. Why should the 1920s have been any different?

"The whole position of women in Western civilization," wrote Madge Garland, a prominent 1920s fashion critic, "her struggle for equality and her success, is reflected in the garments she has worn." In earlier years, this struggle for autonomy and self-definition was limited to those privileged women who could afford to carve out their identities by following the currents of style. Now, with the advent of ready-to-wear clothing, the development of cheaper fabrics and synthetics, and more take-home pay in the pocket of the average working woman, "fashions [became] democratic."

By the time Coco made her name in the world of high couture, it took startlingly little time for the latest designs unveiled at rue Cambon to filter their way down to midrange department stores in Muncie, Indiana. More striking still, it took only a short while longer for Chanel's signature to work its way into the vast American countryside, courtesy of Sears, Roebuck and other mail-order catalogs that brought city fashions right to the doorsteps of American farm families.

In effect, the flapper look that Chanel helped pioneer wasn't just for the rich Parisian. It belonged to every woman who wished to claim it as her own. This was a radical concept.

Until the early twentieth century, most American women made their own clothing. The mass-made, ready-to-wear garments that we take for granted today simply didn't exist.

This had been the case for a long time. In 1791, when Secretary of the Treasury Alexander Hamilton prepared a report on American manufacturers, some "two-thirds, three-fourths, and even four-fifths of all the clothing of the inhabitants" of the United States were "made by themselves." Twenty years later, the government commissioned yet another study that found more than two-thirds of all American clothes were homemade. The rest were hand crafted by dressmakers and tailors who designed and sewed their wares for wealthy patrons who could afford to enlist their services.

The status quo changed slowly over the course of the nineteenth century. Technological advances like the flying shuttle (1733), which wove broad pieces of material at a quickened pace, the spinning jenny (1764), which improved thread and yarn production, and the power loom, which rendered the old weaving frame obsolete, made it easier to mass-produce fabric. Later developments like the sewing machine—first patented in the United States in 1846—made it possible to assemble precut cloth into finished garments with less time and greater precision.

But technology was only one engine driving the ready-to-wear revolution. As the American economy matured throughout the nineteenth century, there arose new demand for prefab clothing. Working-class men who lived apart from their families—sailors, miners, lumbermen, railroad crewmen, and soldiers, for example—couldn't turn to their nonexistent wives or absent sisters for a steady supply of homemade wares. Instead, they began patronizing so-called slop shops that offered crude, ready-made pants and shirts at reasonable prices. Usually situated near docks and work camps, these establishments were the first in America to produce clothes in standard form and variable sizes. A few of the pioneer slop shops like Brooks Brothers, which opened its doors around 1818, had evolved into high-end men's clothiers by the time Coco Chanel arrived on the scene a hundred years later.

Oddly enough, the ready-to-wear revolution that many observers would later credit with democratizing fashion also had its earliest roots in that most undemocratic of American institutions. Southern planters had better use for their slaves than to let them spend time sewing their own clothing. Instead, they bought coarse garments in bulk from slop shops that sprang up in New York, Cincinnati, and New Orleans especially for the purpose of creating "cheap clothing to supply farmhands and Negro slaves."

In the 1860s, when a majority of northerners finally decided that the country couldn't endure half-slave and half-free, the Civil War ensued, creating an unprecedented demand for soldiers' uniforms and providing government contractors with a strong motive to perfect methods of sizing their prefabricated coats, pants, shirts, and hats.

In the years after the Civil War, as America left the age of iron for the age of steel, increasing numbers of American men moved off the self-sufficient farm and into the factory or office. The ready-to-wear industry evolved with the times. By the turn of the century, most men were buying their clothes off the rack. American women would have to wait a bit longer for their own ready-to-wear revolution; most still sewed or commissioned their dresses as late as 1900.

Nevertheless, standardization was creeping into the market. In the 1850s, an American named Ellen Curtis Demorest—known professionally as Mme. Demorest—invented the paper dress pattern. Demorest made a small fortune with her line of simple but elegant blueprints, and within a short space of time, popular women's journals like *Godey's Lady's Book* and *Ladies' Home Journal* were offering middle-class readers similar opportunities to re-create haute fashion at cut-rate prices.

"A sketch is given of a little French dress that any artful woman can copy with her own needle," began a typical article. A writer for *Good Housekeeping* advised mothers to "begin to teach early the little girls to do their own mending and to help with the easiest parts of the sewing."

These same magazines routinely published instructions on how to revamp old outfits to keep them from looking worn or outdated. Women were urged to convert material from one dress into flounces that concealed the wear and tear on the hemline of another dress. They were taught to let out the bouffant skirt draperies that were in vogue one year in order to create a longer, flowing foundation skirt for the next season. Virtually every woman was at least minimally skilled in the art of sewing.

But not everyone had the time to devote to *Godey's Lady's Book*. Just as slop shops answered workingmen's need for unpretentious, ready-made clothing, a new line of entrepreneurs emerged in the late nineteenth century to outfit working women who couldn't put in twelve-hour shifts at the factory, cook and clean for their families, *and* sew their own outfits from scratch. At least a few wholesalers and department stores offered working women the opportunity to buy some of the simpler components of their everyday outfits—shirt-waists, long black skirts, hats, cloaks, and shawls.

Still, women's fashion was far more complex than the simple, broad-shouldered, box-suit style preferred by most American men of the era, and this complexity made it next to impossible to reproduce fashionable women's wear in bulk.

This state of affairs was obviously bound to change. The same trends that simplified women's fashion and ushered Paul Poiret and Coco Chanel into global prominence made it possible to mass-produce women's clothes. It was far easier to replicate a Chanel-style jersey than a Victorian-era dress, with its silk and lace flounces, its high bustle, and its layers of petticoats and supporting garments.

It was also cheaper to produce the new styles en masse. In 1884, a typical dress required over six yards of forty-eight-inch fabric. By 1924, with hemlines creeping up and necklines drifting down, a standard outfit demanded just under three yards of fifty-four-inch wool. For the enterprising factory owner, the profit margin was too good to resist. The boom in ready-to-wear women's clothing had arrived.

One result was that a word that previously didn't get much play began to creep into everyday conversation: *"fashion."*

With her discerning eye for detail and trademark wit, Lois Long helped readers of *The New Yorker* grasp the dynamic new cycle that came increasingly to dominate ordinary women's lives in the Jazz Age. It began in Paris. "The winter openings of the great couturiers are over," Long reported in August 1926, "and the American buyers, those lucky devils who get a trip to Europe for nothing, are returning to their more or less native land for a good rest in the office."

Long walked her readers through the "great pomp" of the typical Paris fashion show. Beginning around nine at night, "in stream the representatives of the newspapers and magazines—modish as to their evening attire, their pearls, coiffures, and genteel voices," and situate themselves around "a series of chastely paneled rooms, with gilt tables placed socially about, laden with bonbons and cigarettes and vases full of roses." From nearby corridors drift the faint sounds of a jazz ensemble, barely audible over the steady hum of voices and the shuffling of handbags and click of shoes against the marble and wood floors.

"In due course of time, when everybody is comfortable, the music softens and becomes soulful, and the first of the mannequins makes her appearance simultaneously with that of several gentlemen in livery bearing large trays of champagne, wine and cocktails."

With each round of drinks, the audience's applause grows more pronounced. The models "burst through the curtains, shoulders back, swinging the hips out of line with each step," and boldly display the next season's wears for the throng of admiring journalists, buyers, and hangers-on. By eleven-thirty, amid a "final burst of applause, a babble of conversation, many congratulations all around, and considerable politeness being shown as to the real opinions of the guests about the excellence and significance of the presentation," the evening was complete.

Early the next morning, Long explained, hordes of buyers for American and British department stores assemble outside the doors of the major fashion houses and "battle madly to gain entrance, some waving cards over their heads, others hoping to bluff their way in." By two in the afternoon, a crowd of seven hundred prospective clients is crammed into a room with only three hundred chairs. The main doors to the couture house are closed, leaving "Mr. Ginsberg, the most lavish buyer in America . . . left raging on the sidewalk."

At four o'clock, the mannequins reappear. "Bored and furious," and looking somewhat more haggard than the night before, they mingle among the buyers and repeat "their numbers over and over again . . . being stopped every other step by the clutching hands of gentlemen who want to feel the goods. Nobody has yet ascertained how many telephone numbers are obtained by this simple, businesslike process."

Agreements are made. Deals are cut. Representatives of the major department stores scramble for the telegraph office to convey the day's business to London and New York. "The press is reverent. Buyers are reverent. The mannequins, who understand English, become more and more annoyed as jests about their ankles, morals, and size are bandied about amidst merry laughter. And at six, everybody storms out, making appointments for final selections as he goes, and silence settles over the house, until the next day. Thus, my children, a Mode is born."

Actually, Lois Long, the New Yorker's normally perceptive fashion and society columnist, just missed the mark. This was the story of how a fashion was conceived—not born.

"Fashion does not exist until it goes into the streets," Coco Chanel observed. "The fashion that remains in the salons has no more significance than a fashion ball."

Long should have deferred on this question to her friend Elizabeth Hawes. Hawes was a young expatriate who overlapped briefly with Long at Vassar College and was moonlighting as a Paris stringer for The New Yorker, covering the fashion scene on those occasions when Long (aka Lipstick) was stuck in Manhattan, tearing up the town and writing "Tables for Two."

Hawes also worked for Madame Doret, one of the hundreds of copy artists who supplied moderately priced replicas of Parisian couture. Collaborating with individual customers who could afford to buy one or two authentic dresses each season, Hawes would slip Chanel originals under her coat and dash over to Madame Doret's workrooms, where a team of professional dressmakers worked fever-ishly to copy the designs. Hours later, Hawes would return the origi-nals to their owners. In exchange for loaning Madame Doret a Chanel original, a customer would receive copies of another client's designer goods.

Doret's representatives also attended the fashion shows and stealthily sketched the latest line of clothes they saw on the runway. Working behind locked bathroom doors and in dark passageways out-side the main hall, they could deliver a reasonably accurate rendering of a new model within hours of its official premiere.

Elizabeth Hawes and her associates were aiding and abetting the high-end duplication of couture. But other intermediaries quickly emerged to supply Americans with low-cost versions of Paris origi-nals. While Madame Doret's operatives enjoyed direct exposure to Chanel dresses and copied them faithfully to the smallest detail, a less exclusive copy house might simply replicate Doret's replicas. Other entrepreneurs catering to women on strict budgets availed them-selves of the advertising sketches in popular magazines. The end effect was a wide and swift dissemination of Parisian fashion.

Magazines and catalogs were flooded with ads for "60 Exquisite 'Chanel' Rhinestone Bags" (priced at $15.95 each) and "copies of Patou, Vionnet, Agnès, Chanel, Le Bouvier, in gorgeous gowns of satin, crepe Elizabeth, Canon crepe, luminous velvet, lace, transpar-ent velvet, chiffon, metal lame and brocade." Department stores like Macy's and bargain shops like Broadway Basement, Best, and Mimi's offered copies of "Paris hats . . . so exact that only the labels and prices tell the story."

When *The New York Times* observed in 1926 that even farm girls had access to high fashion, the Old Gray Lady was on to something.

True, farm prices plummeted in the aftermath of World War I and widened the already pronounced gulf between America's comfort-able, electrified towns and cities and its primitive, unelectrified, and chronically impoverished countryside. But in the decade before the war, farm income in regions like the upper South climbed by almost half. If millions of the nation's farmers were caught in a vicious cycle of tenancy, debt, and deprivation, many others were able to devote small amounts of money to buying Kodak cameras, table lamps or china sets, and the occasional piece of factory-produced clothing.

Rural free delivery and parcel post, two services introduced in 1896 and 1912, respectively, by the U.S. Postal Service, made it possible for farm families to participate in the burgeoning consumer culture without traveling to far-off market towns and cities. Mail-order catalogs like Montgomery Ward and Sears, Roebuck became so popular that rural schools used them to teach children about the latest scientific and cultural achievements of the growing nation. Men and women alike looked to the monthly catalogs for information on urban styles and fashions.

If a farmer's wife couldn't afford the price of a new dress, no problem. Most of the leading mail-order companies introduced credit offices by the 1920s and allowed customers to buy items "on time."

Throughout the 1920s, it took only twelve to twenty-four months for the latest in couture to travel from the pages of *Vogue* to the pages of the Sears catalog. For as little as $8.98 a young farm girl living miles outside Duluth, Minnesota, could purchase a silk flat crepe skirt and chemise of the latest flapper style; another 95 cents bought her a real "Clara Bow hat" to match.

America was becoming a more standardized country. Just as the advent of mail-order catalogs and national advertising eliminated regional variations in dialect and vocabulary—the "sling-bam" or "sling-blade," as it was popularly known by southern farmers, was soon known far and wide as a "weed cutter"—so too was fashion partly democratized and the chasm between rural and urban bridged by a new, common sensibility.

Just as it was easy to come by a convincing, durable Chanel knock-off on Main Street, American women also enjoyed access to cheap costume jewelry. In 1868, two brothers from Albany, New York—John Wesley Hyatt and Isaiah Hyatt—invented "celluloid," a synthetic substance they used to manufacture cheap alternatives to ivory billiard balls. It didn't take long before someone realized that the new material was also handy for making buttons and buckles.

Over the next fifty years, the plastics industry kicked into high gear as ingenious minds found new ways to imitate precious minerals like

amber, horn, tortoise, mother-of-pearl, coral, jade, ivory, and diamond. By the eve of World War I, women who worked on farms and
in factories could drape themselves in as much cheap imitation jewelry
as they could afford, thanks to country stores and mail-order catalogs.

But there was still a sharp distinction between women who wore
real pearls and women who wore fake ones—until the rise of Coco
Chanel.

Coco embraced fake jewelry and made it "costume jewelry." Her
couture house churned out colorful necklaces, bracelets, lapel pins,
and earrings crafted from glass beads and plastic gemstone look-
alikes. These weren't new items. Fashion-conscious women of modest means had been wearing them for years. But Coco made it chic to
don fake jewelry and to admit to it freely. Wealthy women were now
buying essentially the same synthetic trinkets at Saks Fifth Avenue
that blue-collar women were ordering by catalog on the cheap. The
end result was a dramatic leveling of the social playing field.

"Now that Woolworth's has gotten out its own version of the plain
gold or silver necklet," joked Lois Long, young working women no
longer had to "mourn that the tin rings around Heinz pickle jars are
not bigger."

"Today," wrote one observer, "both the parlor maid and the debutante wear ornaments which may be classified roughly as 'attention
getters' or what the professional buyers call 'conversation pieces,'
designed to bridge the first awkward seconds in a momentous
encounter."

Indeed, by the mid-1920s, it was hard to tell what was or was not
authentic and what constituted a fair price. Long doubted whether
there were any French designs that could be seen "at one big shop
exclusively" and even suggested that "the copies you buy in regulation
sizes probably will be better made and fit better than any bought at
the original Paris shop."

"It is most annoying," Long quipped on another occasion, "after
having spent a large sum for a particularly smart frock, to find that
the tiny hole-in-the-wall next door happens to know the same whole-
saler patronized by your specialty shop, and is able to sell it for half
the price you paid. Ho-hum, what it is to be exclusive!"

She was on to something. It wasn't just that imitation blurred the distinction among different qualities of clothing and jewelry. It blurred the distinction among different qualities of *people*. "I used to be able to tell something about the background of a girl applying for a job as stenographer by her clothes," remarked a businessman in Muncie, Indiana, "but today I often have to wait till she speaks, shows a gold tooth, or otherwise gives me a second clue."

Stuart Chase, a prominent 1920s social critic, marveled at the democratizing influence of fashion. "Only a connoisseur can distinguish Miss Astorbilt on Fifth Avenue from her father's stenographer or secretary," he wrote in 1929. "An immigrant arriving on the Avenue from the Polish plain described all American women as countesses. So eager are the lower income groups to dress as well in style, if not in quality, as their economic superiors, that class distinctions have all but disappeared. To the casual observer all American women dress alike." As another writer observed, "Nowadays no one can tell . . . whether a given person lives on Riverside Drive or East 4th Street."

This might have been a slight overstatement of the truth. A discerning eye could still separate people by their clothes. Jane Addams, the legendary Chicago settlement house founder, noticed that working-class women—many of them immigrants or the children of immigrants—"imitate, sometimes in more showy and often in more trying colors, in cheap and flimsy materials, in poor shoes and flippant hats, the extreme fashions of the well-to-do."

Nevertheless, something was changing, and Coco Chanel understood this better than most. Though she issued a pro forma ban on copy-house sketch artists at her runway shows, Coco was far more permissive than her fellow couturiers when it came to imitation. "Let them copy," she said. "I am on the side of women, not the fashion houses." Coco believed that all of the imitation "accessories I've made fashionable—the chains, the necklaces, the stones, the broaches, all the things that have enriched women so much and so cheaply," helped level the social and political playing field. "Thanks to me," she boasted, working women "can walk around like millionaires."

There was irony in all of this. For all their glitter and fascination, the 1920s were years of profound inequality. Rarely in American history had power, wealth, and income been concentrated so singularly in the hands of a relatively small elite. Labor unions were anemic. Workers wouldn't enjoy federal unemployment insurance, disability benefits, or Social Security until the late 1930s. Few Americans could afford decent health care.

All the while, a powerful combination of mass disenfranchisement in the South (courtesy of poll taxes, literacy tests, and state-sanctioned violence) and gerrymandering in the North (small towns often sent the same number of legislators to the state capital as did large cities) made it exceedingly difficult for ordinary people to exercise meaningful political sovereignty.

But as working men and women lost control over their political and economic lives, they flexed their muscles in the purchase of shiny new things, an activity that seemed to hold out the promise of a new brand of "democratic" citizenship. Upward mobility was redefined as the right to dress like the Rockefellers rather than earn like the Rockefellers; the ownership of commodities replaced the ownership of labor as a mark of social achievement. More and more, the personal became political.

In effect, Americans embraced a new definition of freedom that hinged on participation in a burgeoning consumer economy. How "democratic" this new order—and how "free" the average consumer—really was was open to debate. A social critic for *The Atlantic Monthly* worried that "individuality, in the sense of a man's distinct personality, in the material domain, is becoming an increasingly rare phenomenon. We are forced to a common standard. Even those of us who have not material objectives cannot be non-conformers. For the few are powerless to escape the brand of eighty millions. We are socialized into an average."

Such protestations could barely be heard against the general din. A powerful group of cultural mediators made material things seem like the stuff of human liberty.

In the late 1920s, George W. Hill, owner of American Tobacco, hired America's leading public relations guru, Edward Bernays, to design a new advertising initiative. The problem was simple: Despite a decade's worth of movies, magazine photos, and F. Scott Fitzgerald stories, many Americans still regarded women smokers as "hussies." Working on behalf of his new, prize client, Bernays hired a prominent psychoanalyst, A. A. Brill, to see what might be done to eliminate once and forever the negative connotations associated with cigarette-wielding women.

"Some women regard cigarettes as symbols of freedom," Brill advised. "Smoking is a sublimation of oral eroticism: holding a cigarette in the mouth excites the oral zone. It is perfectly normal for women to want to smoke cigarettes. Further, the first women who smoked probably had an excess of masculine components and adopted the habit as a masculine act. But today the emancipation of women has suppressed many of the feminine desires. More women now do the same work as men do. . . . Cigarettes, which are equated with men, become torches of freedom."

Torches of freedom. The idea *leaped* out from the page at Edward Bernays. "I found a way to help break the taboo against women smoking in public," he later boasted. "Why not a parade of women lighting torches of freedom—smoking cigarettes."

Bernays contacted Ruth Hale, "a leading feminist," and arranged to have "ten young women lighting 'torches of freedom' " at the 1929 Easter parade on Fifth Avenue. Newspapers carried front-page items marveling at this "bold protest against women's inequality." And American Tobacco had itself a new market segment.

"The man with the proper imagination is able to conceive of any commodity in such a way that it becomes an object of emotion," wrote a prominent advertising guru in 1911, ". . . and hence creates desire rather than a mere feeling or thought." In the 1920s, the man who could create desire was the new apostle of American freedom.

17

WITHOUT IMAGINATION, NO WANTS

I N LATE NOVEMBER 1928, with the winter holiday season in high gear, millions of American magazine readers opened the latest edition of *The Saturday Evening Post* and saw a familiar, illustrated icon staring past them. Tall and angular, young and chic, outfitted stylishly in distinctive flapper wear, the "Fisher Body Girl" seemed, at first glance, to be selling clothes, or makeup, or shoes. On closer consideration, she was selling automobiles. "Of all those who express motor car body preference," announced the advertisement, "95% Prefer 'Body by Fisher.' " The message couldn't have been clearer: Buy a GM model—be it a Pontiac, Cadillac, Oldsmobile, Chevrolet, or Buick—and this body was yours.

The idea of using sex and fashion to sell cars wouldn't have made a great deal of sense to the prewar generation. But it was well in line with the ethos of the Jazz Age. By the 1920s, a powerful group of advertising specialists, headquartered along Madison Avenue in New York City, had perfected ways of using the flapper to sell consumer items and using consumer items to define the flapper.

One of the more curious publishing phenomena of 1925 was a sparsely written biography of Jesus Christ authored by a leading New York advertising executive, Bruce Barton. Almost as quickly as it hit bookstores, *The Man Nobody Knows* climbed to the top of the best-seller list, where it remained for more than two years and through twenty-seven different printings. The half-million readers who

A typical John Held flapper in a moment of deep contemplation.

thumbed through Barton's slim volume learned that Christ was, above all, "the founder of modern business" and a sage for all times who "picked up twelve men from the bottom ranks of business and forged them into an organization that conquered the world." It was a wholly unusual take on Jesus Christ, but it seemed to strike a chord.

The son of a prominent Congregational minister, Bruce Barton was born in 1886 and grew up in Oak Park, Illinois. After a successful undergraduate career at Amherst, he scrapped plans to pursue a PhD in history and instead found his way to New York City, where he earned personal fortune and popular acclaim as a magazine writer and advertising executive. His firm, Batten, Barton, Durstine, and Osborn, grew into one of Madison Avenue's premier agencies—so much so that by the 1920s, Barton could afford to divide his attention among various political, literary, and business endeavors.

Living in the shadow of his father, a distinguished liberal clergyman and amateur biographer of Abraham Lincoln, the younger Barton struggled to reconcile his role as an apostle of American consumer culture with his deeply felt sense of Christian faith. Hawking new products for his clients demanded that Barton argue against the ethos of rectitude and thrift that pervaded the Protestant Midwest of his youth. Ordinary Americans wouldn't spend money on luxuries, he believed, unless they were disabused of long-held ideas that privileged a life of self-denial over a life of indulgence.

Barton turned to precisely this question when, in a short profile of the automobile magnate Henry Ford, he urged readers of the *American Magazine* to discard "the old fashioned notion that the chief end in life is a steadily growing savings account, and that one must eliminate all pleasures from his vigorous years in order to prepare for possible want in old age." In a new era of mass production and consumption, he argued, "life is meant to live and enjoy as you go along. . . . If self-denial is necessary, I'll practice some of it when I'm old and not try to do all of it now. For who knows? I may never be old."

This ethic of self-indulgence didn't square with the rock-ribbed values that many Americans had imbibed as children. The challenge was to find a way to invoke 1920s vernacular in a manner that gave consumer culture a stamp of approval from none other than Jesus

Christ. Which was exactly what Barton accomplished in *The Man Nobody Knows*. In a twist on the well-worn question "What would Jesus do?" Barton implicitly invited readers to ask what Jesus might have thought about 1920s American capitalism. The answer, of course, was that Christ would have approved wholeheartedly of the new culture of consumption.

In Barton's rendering, Christ was a born salesman who "recognized the basic principle that all good advertising is news" and who catered scrupulously to the "marketplace." "Few of his sermons were delivered in synagogues," Barton asserted. "For the most part he was in the crowded places, the Temple Court, the city squares, the centers where goods were bought and sold."

Whereas in Christ's time the marketplace was, quite literally, a town square where people gathered to buy and sell their wares, "the present day market-place is the newspaper and the magazine. Printed columns are the modern thoroughfares; published advertisements are the cross-roads where the sellers and the buyers meet. Any issue of a national magazine is a world's fair, a bazaar filled with the products of the new world's work. Clothes and clocks and candle sticks; soup and soap and cigarettes; lingerie and limousines—the best of all of them are there, proclaimed by their makers in persuasive tones."

Would Jesus disapprove? Not at all. "He would be a national advertiser today, I am sure, as he was the great advertiser of his own day."

As a leading ad executive, Bruce Barton represented a new cadre of elite men and women who enjoyed unprecedented influence over the ways in which Americans envisioned and understood the world around them. They would play a central role in disseminating flapper fashion and style and, even more important, in shaping the contours of femininity, sexuality, and physique in the 1920s.

As recently as the 1890s, advertising agents had served as little more than freelance brokers who purchased newspaper ad space in bulk and sold it back to local businesses at a marginal profit. Ads were tucked away discreetly in the back pages of magazines and serials, used small print, and contained only the most essential information. No pictures, no catchphrases, no extra draw. Just the facts.

This status quo couldn't last. In the several decades following the Civil War, American industry expanded in leaps and bounds, resulting in warehouses virtually overflowing with unsold consumer goods. Businessmen now faced an unforeseen embarrassment of riches. They could produce the goods, but they couldn't always unload them.

On paper, at least, America seemed ripe for the development of a national market. Since the mid–nineteenth century, armies of itinerant workers had laid down thousands of miles of railroad tracks, half of which were still less than twenty-five years old on the eve of World War I. Telegraph services and telephone lines facilitated an instant flow of information from coast to coast. The potential was there to move ideas, business orders, raw materials, and finished products across vast amounts of space over relatively little time.

Indeed, "the goods must be moved," cried a merchant in 1912. But how? People first needed to be taught how to consume.

It became increasingly popular to view the problem as one of underconsumption rather than overproduction. Though a few left-wing voices like that of Edward Bellamy called on the government to guarantee a minimum income to every family in America—in effect, to impose a massive downward transfer of wealth that would allow the working poor, who were barely scraping by, to enjoy more of the fruits of American prosperity—more conservative voices won the day.

"We are not concerned with the ability to pay," wrote an early proponent of advertising, "but with the ability to want and choose." Americans could and would empty the warehouses of their surplus goods, if only they were given the "imagination and emotion to desire." *"Without imagination, no wants,"* explained another advertising guru in 1899. "Without wants, no demand to have them supplied."

The idea that advertisers should produce desire rather than simply provide information about specific products gained currency in the early years of the twentieth century. "It is all very well to get the sales of things that people want to buy," argued a speaker at the Nashville Ad Club in 1916, "but that is too small in volume. We must make people want many other things, in order to get a big increase in business."

Between 1900 and 1920, the nature of advertising changed markedly. Leading firms no longer acted as mere brokers but now designed arresting ad copy and artwork that championed new brands. They suggested with varying degrees of subtlety that consumer items were not just luxuries, but *necessities*.

Whereas a typical advertising expert in the 1890s claimed that "pictures are merely adjuncts to the ad. . . . When they dominate the ad they weaken it," within the space of just a few years, industry professionals agreed that "the advertising of the future will be illustrated. There can hardly be a question about that."

By the early 1920s, the visual focus of ads had moved away from the product itself and toward the image of people enjoying the product. New Age admen weren't selling soap, automobiles, and clothing. They were selling the happiness and exhilaration that came from buying soap, automobiles, and clothing. Hence, advertisements for Arrow shirts that featured a handsome, sharply chiseled man clad in elegant evening wear, descending a gilded staircase with a tall blonde at his side. Or the 1926 ad for Chesterfields featuring an attractive young couple seated by a secluded oceanfront horizon. The focus wasn't on the product; it was on the dream that the product held out for its consumers.

The smartest admen understood that in a world where ordinary people were increasingly beholden to the time clock and the company foreman, and where powerful and inaccessible bureaucracies— banks, government agencies, national corporations—enjoyed a disproportionate share of political and economic power, buying an Arrow shirt or a pack of Chesterfields offered the prospect of balance and compensation.

"To those who cannot change their whole lives or occupation," argued Helen Woodward, a successful ad copywriter in the 1920s, "even a new line in dress is often a relief. The woman who is tired of her husband or her home or her job feels some lifting of the weight of life from seeing a straight line change into a bouffant, or a gray pass into a beige."

It was a short step from longing for the latest dress to compensate for a sense of lost autonomy to using that dress to satisfy a desire for authenticity. In a world where indoor plumbing, centralized heating, canned foods, carpeting, home insulation, and electric lights removed ordinary people from the dirt, grime, smells, exertion, and discomforts of everyday life, people seemed to crave direct experience, and advertisers turned this yearning to their advantage. As G. Stanley Hall, a leading turn-of-the-century psychologist, argued, "Everyone, especially those who lead the drab life of the modern toiler, needs and craves an occasional 'good time.' Indeed, we all need to glow, tingle, and *feel life intensely* now and then."

The admen instinctively grasped this idea and offered up consumer culture as a therapeutic answer to the dual crisis of individual autonomy and experiential living. "Go to a motion picture . . . and let yourself go," began a typical ad in *The Saturday Evening Post.* "Before you know it you are *living* the story—laughing, loving, hating, struggling, winning! All the adventure, all the romance, all the excitement you lack in your daily life are in—Pictures! They take you completely out of yourself into a wonderful new world. . . . Out of the cage of everyday existence! If only for an afternoon or an evening—escape!"

Though working people might not have enjoyed several crucial benefits of meaningful citizenship—a responsive government, autonomy in the workplace, fair wages, and economic security—at least they could drown their troubles in a sea of consumer plenty. However more subtle today's advertisements seem by comparison, the same promise of a more authentic, fulfilling life surely permeates American media.

Not everyone shared Madison Avenue's enthusiasm for the new consumer culture. A few years after the Jazz Age had come and gone, the English critic Denys Thompson complained that "advertising tries to conceal the emptiness and make life feel good. It is as if the forces of advertising had decreed that the individual man or woman must not be allowed to develop his or her own potentialities." This could be all too true of working women, whose economic, social, and (until 1920) political rights were sharply curtailed but who faced a steady barrage of advertisements urging them to find self-definition and freedom in $1.95 "Joan Crawford Hats."

If advertisers only had to teach Americans to embrace a more self-indulgent ethos, their task would have been hard enough. But they also had to initiate citizens into an emerging national market in which brand names—a completely new invention—meant something. People who were used to buying soap and sugar out of large vats at the local dry goods store needed to be taught to prefer prepackaged cakes of Ivory and prewrapped packets of Domino sugar. Housewives accustomed to baking their own desserts and growing their own produce required instruction on the virtues of Uneeda biscuits (manufactured by the National Biscuit Company) and White Diamond corn.

In the first years of the twentieth century, brand names sprang by the thousands from the wild imaginations of enterprising businessmen and, with the help of Madison Avenue, the new home of national advertising, were seared into the minds of ordinary Americans. Crisco, Gillette, Coca-Cola, Colgate, Kodak, Sherwin-Williams, Waterman's, Jell-O, Kellogg's Toasted Corn Flakes, Wrigley's Doublemint chewing gum, Wrigley's Juicy Fruit chewing gum, Wrigley's Spearmint chewing gum . . . The competition for mind share was fierce.

Thanks to the highly successful efforts of advertising executives, by the eve of World War I, Americans were well on their way to becoming trained consumers, and consumer branding—a new form of intellectual property—was widely recognized as intrinsically valuable. When the U.S. Supreme Court broke up the American Tobacco Company in 1911, it appraised the total worth of its trademarks at $45 million—a sum equal to 20 percent of its total assets.

By 1920, grocers in Chicago had reported that more than three-quarters of their customers asked for baked beans by the brand name, while a national survey of three hundred men revealed that every last respondent could identify at least one brand name of a watch, soap, and fountain pen. Together, they pinpointed thirty-six different brand names of soft drinks.

In their effort to reshape attitudes about spending, advertisers profited from vast changes in the way Americans saw the world around them. Until late in the nineteenth century, representations of reality—photographs, mirrors, paintings, and the like—were primitive and hard to come by. Only wealthy Americans in the 1840s and 1850s could employ portrait artists, whose work usually captured a rough outline of their subject's appearance.

It wasn't until the invention of modern photography in 1839 and, even more so, the popular introduction of ferrotypes and tintypes sometime around the 1860s, that working men and women enjoyed affordable access to *cartes-de-visite*—small trading pictures that could be purchased for 10 cents on the dozen. At the same time, new technologies like halftone engraving, which came into wide use in the 1880s and 1890s, made it easier to reproduce photographs, oil paintings, and wash drawings in newspapers, broadsides, books, magazines, and advertisements.

Almost overnight, visual reproduction, once scarcely imaginable, became an everyday convenience for millions of Americans. The effects of this cornucopia of sight and sensation were dramatic.

In the 1880s and 1890s, around the same time that halftones became de rigueur, new printing techniques—particularly the chromolithograph (or chromo)—made it possible to introduce colors into trading cards, product wrappers, advertisements, mass-produced paintings, and even some photographs. And not just the primary colors. By the turn of the century, advances in coloration introduced as many as a thousand new tints into the color spectrum. Americans growing up just before World War I learned to recognize heretofore unknown shades like mauve and chrome yellow.

Advertisers were quick to exploit these advances in printing and coloration. In the 1880s, young women became avid collectors of trade cards—a cross between magazine advertisements (which came into wider use after 1890) and baseball cards (which wouldn't become popular until the 1920s)—that announced the arrival of new household products and brands. In her autobiography, *Little Town on the Prairie,* Laura Ingalls Wilder wrote of the delight that she took as a child in these collectors items. "The cards were the palest green," she remarked, "and on each was a picture of a bobolink swaying and singing on a spray of goldenrod."

In the remote mountain towns of Kentucky, farm and mine families clipped ads from mail-order catalogs and magazines, mounted them to the wall with a mixture of red pepper, rat poison, and flour-and-water paste (to keep the mice from gnawing at the paper), and coated them with a combination of sweet anise roots and arrowroot to leave a friendlier aroma. Color pictures of new food brands adorned the walls of their country kitchens; ads featuring new toys formed a backdrop in children's bedrooms; images of premade furniture and glass and porcelain finery decorated living rooms.

In 1905, a social worker surveyed working-class tenement homes in downtown Manhattan and found that most contained cheap chromos—either reproductions of paintings or consumer ads—on the walls.

The hunger of ordinary people for new pictures and colors held out part of the answer to the plague of underconsumption. Color, wrote Artemas Ward, an advertising industry pioneer, is a "priceless ingredient. . . . It creates desire for the good displayed. . . . It imprints on the buying memory. [It] speaks the universal picture language" and touches "foreigners, children, people in every station of life who can see or read at all." A billboard promoter summed up the point best. "It is hard to get mental activity with cold type," he said, but "YOU FEEL A PICTURE."

And pictures were there for the gazing. Between 1918 and 1920, the volume of annual consumer advertising doubled to an astounding $2.9 billion (equal to nearly $20 billion in today's money).

Most of these new appeals were concentrated in magazines, which shifted in the 1880s and 1890s away from the old business model of high prices and low circulation toward a more profitable system of low newsstand and subscription rates and high circulation. Under the new arrangement, magazines turned most of their profits from advertising revenues rather than direct sales.

Aided by the nation's extensive railroad system, the introduction of cheaper, second-class postal rates in 1879 and rural free delivery in 1896, and new technological advances like the rotary press, magazine circulation in the United States jumped to a whopping two hundred million in 1929, or 1.6 magazines per person, per month. By the time Scott Fitzgerald was writing for *The Saturday Evening Post,* his stories were reaching over a quarter of all households in cities like

Seattle, Washington. Other titles like *Good Housekeeping* and *Collier's* enjoyed similar appeal in places as far-flung as Omaha, Nebraska, and Grand Rapids, Michigan.

Though magazines remained a distinct trapping of the middle classes, the expansion of the magazine market created the first truly national institution combining both news and entertainment. In turn, this vital institution created a market for national branding and advertising where none had existed before.

Among the highest-circulation magazines were several that catered specifically to women: *Good Housekeeping, Women's Home Companion,* and *Ladies' Home Journal,* which concentrated principally on homemaking topics, and *McCall's, Delineator,* and *Pictorial Review,* which dedicated themselves increasingly to fashion and criticism. Other important women's magazines like *Vogue* and *Harper's Bazaar* had smaller circulations but exerted a disproportionate influence by virtue of their elite readership.

All told, between 1890 and 1916 a handful of women's publications attracted more than one-third of all magazine ad revenues, reflecting the commonly held (but never substantiated) belief that women accounted for the lion's share of all consumer purchases. This meant that advertisers tailored many of their appeals to women, who were thought to be responsible for household purchases of soap, cleaners, canned foods, furniture, toiletries, and clothing.

To coax women into this new world of getting and spending—to convince them of the need to purchase more goods for themselves and their families—advertisers introduced startling new ideas about body image and fashion. In so doing, they created a visual ideal of the flapper that many women would find difficult to achieve.

Fashion artist Gordon Conway, 1921, introduced millions of magazine readers in Europe and America to the visual style of the New Woman.

10,000,000 FEMMEſ FATALEſ

"HAPPY DREAMS AND illusions"—that's what magazine advertisements and illustrations offered to American women, or so said Frank Crowninshield, the legendary editor of *Vanity Fair.*

"Such pages spell romance to them," he observed. "They are magic carpets on which they ride out to love, the secret gardens into which they wander in order to escape the workaday world and their well-meaning husbands . . . after a single hour's reading of the advertising pages, 10,000,000 housewives, salesgirls, telephone operators, typists, and factory workers see themselves daily as *femmes fatales,* as Cleopatra, as Helen of Troy."

In the pages of the slick new consumer magazines lay the images that American women increasingly aspired to imitate, and by the 1920s, arbiters of culture like Frank Crowninshield enjoyed considerable influence in crafting popular tastes and styles. Illustrated magazine covers depicting sleek, angular women with skirts flapping in the wind, legs bared to the elements, and elegant garments falling naturally along their silhouettes dictated the image of the modern woman no less than the glossy advertisements nestled inside the front and back pages.

One of Crowninshield's star cover artists, Gordon Conway, wielded more influence than most. No fewer than 110 fashion houses—including all of the leading Parisian couture shops—invited her to sketch their work. Department stores commissioned her for print advertisements. Broadway directors hired her to design sets and costumes. Filmmakers in London and Paris turned to her expertise when they outfitted their silent screen actresses. Though few people outside the art and publishing worlds knew her name, anyone who subscribed to *Harper's Bazaar, Women's Home Companion, Vogue, Vanity Fair, Judge, Town & Country, Metropolitan, Country Life*—virtually every major fashion magazine of the era—knew her work. Anyone who saw a European film or took in a local production of a London or Broadway play saw her style.

Conway's flapper was slender, sleek, and brilliantly aloof. Her clothes were rendered with tremendous precision, yet her facial expressions and features were often distant and even obscure. For Conway, the New Woman's grace and being came from her willowy outline and modern attire.

Born in 1894 to John Conway, a prominent lumberyard owner, and Tommie Conway, his world-wise wife, Gordon spent the first years of an unusually privileged childhood roaming the grounds of her family's handsome Queen Victoria frame house in Cleburne, Texas. Marked out from all the other neighborhood homes by its distinctive, fish-scale shingle facade and the rows of books and paintings that adorned its interior, the Conway residence bespoke the family's unparalleled position in the community.

From an early age, Gordon was treated like a little lady—not a little girl. Her parents were local apostles of high culture and considered it de rigueur that their daughter attend the numerous dance and orchestra performances they sponsored in their home. Gordon grew up on chamber music, poetry recitals, and salons staged on the long porch that wrapped around the Cleburne house, bounded on one side by a hand-carved balustrade.

When Gordon was nine years old, her family—enjoying still greater prosperity from John's lumber business—moved to a stately new mansion in Dallas, right on the corner of Ross and Harwood, a neighborhood known locally as "Silk Stocking Row" and the "Fifth Avenue of Dallas."

Dallas was a boomtown in those days, and Gordon was lucky to be among the "so-called 400," the leading families who mattered most in the insular but wealthy community of Texas oil barons and lumber tycoons. There, in the blazing southwestern heat, the four hundred raised faux Gothic mansions and French châteaus, they lined their newly paved streets with tall trees from exotic places and paid one another visits in custom-made, horse-drawn carriages, each driven by a uniformed coachman.

As the daughter of wealthy socialite parents, Gordon enjoyed a host of opportunities that equipped her with the sense of cosmopolitan style that would serve her well in her later career. Even after her father died young and unexpectedly in 1906, Gordon enjoyed a level of refinement and comfort unknown to most Americans of their era. Raised on a steady diet of opera, ballet, modern dance, classic and modern poetry, and symphony music, Gordon honed her already refined sensibilities as a student at the National Cathedral School in Washington, D.C., where she studied piano, elocution, and dance and learned to speak Italian, Spanish, and French with relative ease, if not fluency. Tall, dark haired, and remarkably poised, Gordon was, according to her childhood friend Margaret Page Elliott, "as graceful as a fawn. She was not a beauty like her mother in a classic way, but she could just toss an old shawl around her shoulders and look as glamorous as all get-out. If the rest of us tried that we'd look like rough-dried laundry hanging on a clothesline."

Gordon's rigorous training in the arts and languages paid handsome dividends when, in August 1912, she and her mother sailed for Europe to spend the better part of two years traveling, studying, and meeting the men and women who were ushering in a modernist revolution in Western art and literature. In Munich, she gained extensive exposure to the work of continental futurists and cubists. "Ridiculous!" she wrote in her diary in response to the various works by Pablo Picasso and other leading innovators, though she would later help popularize these artistic conventions by incorporating them in her advertising and cover art.

Gordon and Tommie spent their two-year sojourn deeply enmeshed in European culture—both high and popular. They became well-known American customers at the leading Parisian couture houses, roughly around the time Coco Chanel was launching her signature line, and they frequented tea parties, dances, and recitals with leading members of the American expatriate community.

But the fun couldn't last forever. As the clouds of war gathered in the summer of 1914, Tommie and Gordon found themselves on a mad dash from the Alps, where they had been hiking through the Maloja Pass. They somehow managed to talk themselves onto the last train bound for Zurich and then plodded their way onward to Lausanne, where Gordon sporadically attended school.

As German soldiers broke through Belgium and headed west toward France, Gordon, holed up in her bedroom suite at the Hotel Royal, recorded her thoughts amid the steady clatter of heavy rain. "I am very sad on account of the war," she began, "for Germany is fighting and Renee"—a friend, perhaps a suitor—"is there . . . there is a revolution in Paris and Anibal"—another beau?—"is there. Silvio"—yet another smitten friend—"is stuck in France." Gordon pondered the fate of all the smartly dressed men who had courted her in Rome just a few months before and worried that the war would consume all of her "bounty of beaus."

In the days before their departure for America, Gordon and Tommie watched with great emotion as ten thousand Swiss soldiers swore an allegiance to God and country and marched off into the great unknown. Mother and daughter then managed to catch the last, overcrowded train from Geneva to Paris. Packed like sardines into ordinary coach cars, they endured a nineteen-hour journey and had to negotiate their way around vast crowds at the Gare de l'Est. "Paris has changed!" Gordon wrote in her diary. "There's no one on the streets and lights are not burning."

Though the German army was fast moving west, Tommie and Gordon found time for one last whirlwind shopping expedition at the houses of Worth, Poiret, and Patou. They then caught a ferry to England, wound their way up by train to Liverpool, and boarded the RMS *Olympic* for a safe return to New York. For now, their European adventure had drawn to a close.

Though she claimed no formal training as an artist, back in the United States, Gordon's vast knowledge of continental painting, steady hand at the drawing board, and—perhaps most important—extensive network of well-placed friends and acquaintances soon drew her to the attention of Heyworth Campbell, art director for Condé Nast's various high-end publications, including *Vanity Fair* and *Vogue*.

Headquartered in a stylish office suite (Mrs. Nast herself chose the decor—an art deco interior very much in line with new trends in architecture and design), Campbell and his boss, Frank Crownin-shield, drew on the talents of a wide circle of friends, including Dorothy Rothschild (later, Dorothy Parker), who had not yet become a leading light of the Algonquin Round Table, and Ted Shawn and Ruth St. Denis, the celebrated husband-and-wife team whose company, Denishawn, pioneered modern dance in America.

Through associates in New York, Gordon managed to snare an appointment with Campbell in September 1915. Something about her style, which captured the vibrant colors, modernist flair, and energy of Parisian couture, meshed with the cultural project under way at Nast headquarters, and within a month, she was a regular free-lance contributor to their magazines. Over the next ten years, Con-way worked with ease to convey to millions of people on both sides of the Atlantic the outline of the New Woman: elegant and lean, tall and linear, alluring yet remote. It was a hard act to follow.

Strange, then, that neither Conway's name nor her work ever stuck in the public mind quite as tenaciously as that of her chief rival, John Held. Though their designs would go a long way in determining how Americans in the 1920s and long after would "see" the flapper, Gordon Conway and John Held couldn't have been more different. Graceful and chic, Conway was to the manor born—an urbanite and a sophisticate who drew the flapper with an air of profound elegance. Held, on the other hand, was a wrangler. Born and bred in Utah, he was a westerner and a maverick.

An early friend of Harold Ross's—the two men attended high school together; Ross edited the school newspaper, and Held was its staff cartoonist—Held learned the crude art of sketching and woodblock printing from his father, John Held Sr., an eclectic musician who imbued in his namesake a love of regional crafts and art.

In 1910, Held—all of twenty-one years old, with little more than a high school education and $4 to his name—struck out for New York City, where, like so many young artists and writers converging on Gotham, he paid his rent by working in the advertising business. Cranking out artwork for the Collier's Street Railway Advertising Company, Held labored away at night on his own humorous sketches and drawings. He soon earned enough money to send for Myrtle Jennings, the dashing former society editor of the *Salt Lake City Tribune,* whom Held had married shortly before his venture to New York.

It was a good move. Where Held was talented but quixotic, Myrtle was canny and ambitious. She hawked some of his drawings around town, selling a few here and there, until 1912, when Crowninshield began snapping them up for *Vanity Fair.* He particularly liked Held's humorous renderings of society women. Soon the renderings were bringing in solid money, and Held was able to leave his advertising job. The only problem was that Crowninshield thought Myrtle was the artist. When the famous editor held a party in 1916 to honor the talented women who contributed to Condé Nast's publications, Myrtle—who couldn't draw so much as a stick figure—went so far as to bandage her hand and feign a broken wrist, lest someone ask her to sketch a cartoon frame on the spot.

The ruse lasted only so long, and by the time World War I engulfed America, "Jack" Held was widely recognized as the genius behind the artwork that appeared widely in Condé Nast magazines, but also in *Judge, Puck,* and *Life.*

Even before the war, Held claimed a specialty in drawing bold young women who flouted prevailing standards of dress, style, and comportment. An early cartoon for *Judge* depicts a tall woman elegantly attired in riding gear. "Do you like motoring sports?" inquires a young man standing beside a topless car. "Yes," she replies, "—all that I've seen." It was typical Held—dry and understated, yet hinging on a corny double entendre that seemed more Salt Lake City than West Village.

By the early twenties, Held's renderings of American youth—flappers and sheiks, collegians and the younger married set—featured prominently on the covers of the leading humor and literary journals. His flapper drawings especially were all the rage. Whereas Gordon Conway offered up sleek, graceful silhouettes, Held brought his cartoonist's sensibility to bear. His flappers were all bare legs and bare arms, short dresses flailing in the wind, round heads with beady eyes. His characters were always suspended in a midair Charleston maneuver or caught in some unenviable—often embarrassing—situation.

His young sheiks were no less frivolous. Clad in white dinner jackets and bow ties, with round, anonymous faces, they seemed always intent on working their hands up the skirt of a credulous young flapper or looking for a quick way to dispose of yet another empty champagne bottle.

Conway was interested in the clothing and style of the twenties. Held was interested in the era's freedom and frivolity. He claimed to have "no method, no name, no laws, no philosophy, no purpose, no message, no nothing." "When I draw a caricature," he claimed, "it's like writing. I simply pick out the characteristics of a person. I try to make the picture look like them more than they are like themselves. It usually shows something the person does not want shown. The caricaturist, if he does anything, wars upon the individual for the benefit of society."

It was an approach to art that won Held more than a few laughs. When F. Scott Fitzgerald published *Flappers and Philosophers,* the top brass at Scribner's knew exactly where to look for the cover art: John Held. When the Hearst newspaper empire was looking for a new syndicated cartoonist, it knew exactly where to look: John Held. His weekly strip, *Oh! Margy!,* regaled millions of readers nationwide with the rollicking adventures of a charming young flapper with a penchant for trouble.

Not surprisingly, when Harold Ross wanted to lend illustration to Lois Long's columns, he turned to his old high school chum John Held. Held's contribution—a map of Manhattan nightclubs, as reported by Lipstick—was but another example of how small and interconnected, yet vast and eclectic, was the world of Harold Ross.

Drawing the New Woman and illustrating the Jazz Age proved a lucrative business. Held, a onetime westerner, took to wearing expensive English tweed suits and at one point owned no fewer than four houses, including an estate in Weston, Connecticut, at which he employed upward of twenty servants. For fun he ran for town warden, and won. For more fun he ran for Congress, and lost.

As the mid-1920s approached, Held's flappers grew a little less whimsical. Unlike his sheiks, who retained their comic-strip bubble heads, his flappers took on more human characteristics. They still embodied the spirit and restlessness of Jazz Age youth, but with time, their creator lent them more dignity and poise.

But no matter how her image evolved, and no matter whether it was Held's interpretation of her or Conway's, the flapper was always long, slender, graceful, and in constant motion. It was this image of the female body—omnipresent and entirely new—that young women now aspired to. The pressure to slenderize was on.

At Smith College, most students between 1875 and 1910 aspired to *gain* weight, not lose it. Their letters home brimmed with descriptions of college food, pleas for care packages, and tales of succulent "spreads" they shared with friends and roommates.

"We had two kinds of crackers, chocolate, pine-apple cake, candy and nuts," one young woman reported, "such fun as we had."

"It is my ambition to weigh 150 pounds," Charlotte Wilkinson wrote to her parents in 1892. "I have never had so much going on in my life as this last month," she informed them later in the year. "But don't be afraid that I shall get tired out for I am bouncingly well. I weighed 137 pounds the other day."

By the 1920s, all this had changed. "I had the worst scare the other day, when I came down," Lucy Kendrew informed her family. "I weighed 119 or 122, Wednesday I weighed myself on the gym scales, & weighed 136½! Friday I got weighed on them in the same clothes & had lost 2½ pounds."

Now, freshmen orientation booklets went out of their way to advise new students, "Don't consider it necessary to diet before your first vacation. Your family will be just as glad to see you if you look familiar."

Clearly, some of the women needed to be reminded. TO DIET OR NOT TO DIE YET? read the headline of a college newspaper op-ed. "If preventative measures against strenuous dieting are not taken soon," the authors warned, "Smith College will be notorious, not just for the sylph-like forms but for the haggard faces and dull, listless eyes of her students."

And there was more. Flappers weren't supposed to look only slim; they were supposed to look white. No less than anyone else, Lois Long was guilty of reinforcing this racial standard. Reporting on one of her nighttime excursions to Harlem, she made the preposterous observation that "most of the Negro girls entertaining along Lenox Avenue would do well, either to take Charleston lessons from one of the five thousand flowers of American womanhood adorning our [downtown] choruses, or to invent a new dance." Never mind that African Americans had pioneered the Charleston.

In order to appropriate black culture for the flapper, she worked overtime to denigrate African Americans. In some of her most vicious prose, Long described the scene at Club Cabaret on Lenox Avenue and 130th Street in Harlem. "The entertainer there," she wrote with loaded admiration, "a girl whose name turned out to be Retta [was] one of the most vigorous animals that I have ever seen turned loose in public. . . . Never could I have believed that coon shouting could be as noisy, or that dancing could so completely engross the anatomy as hers did. The lady has no inhibitions and is proud of it. She is simply swell, and like the tattooed lady, worth going miles to see."

Lipstick's argument was slick and invidious all at once. It was okay to slum it in Harlem, she told readers, as long as they understood that the Charleston was a white woman's dance. Black women, by definition, could never be "flowers of American womanhood." At best, they could aspire to being exhibits in a freak show. Long revisited this theme again and again, reserving her most cutting invective for black women. Black men, after all, posed no status threat to the flapper.

When an irate bandleader from Harlem took exception to Long's critique of black women—no white girl could dance "the REAL

Charleston," he announced—Lipstick conceded only that "negro men are supreme at this dance . . . but as for the girls—I will just have to be shown. The ones I have seen get a certain curious swing that the white ones don't, but they are very self-conscious as regards the feet. And just for that I promise never to mention the name of Charleston again."

Lois Long's concerted effort to write African Americans out of flapper culture placed her squarely within the mainstream in the 1920s. Throughout the first decades of the twentieth century, advertisers initiated millions of new city dwellers to the wonders of mass consumption, often calling upon docile, grinning black "spokeservants" like Aunt Jemima, the Gold Dust Twins, and the Cream of Wheat Uncle to get their message across.

The logic was impeccable. Flappers were consumers, and they were white. Black women were servants; thus, they couldn't possibly be flappers. And they couldn't possibly dance the Charleston.

The same message was rigidly reinforced in places of leisure. Other than in the "colored" balconies, the only black face one was likely to encounter at the movies was a white actor smeared from forehead to neck in burnt cork, crudely misrepresenting African American characters on the silver screen. Clara Bow, Louise Brooks, and Colleen Moore, the great flapper triumvirate of 1920s Hollywood, had no black counterpart, and certainly no one ever encountered a black John Held flapper or a black Gordon Conway flapper on the cover of *The New Yorker, Vanity Fair, Vogue,* or *McCall's*. At fun parks like Coney Island, the only place for blacks was behind popular concessions that offered visitors a chance to "hit the Nigger—Three Balls for Five."

The message behind these advertisements and concessions was unmistakable: White Americans were citizens. Black Americans weren't.

The long, lean, white flapper, perfect in every way, without so much as a blemish on her skin, equipped with a new outfit for every occasion, was an ideal that many women hoped to achieve, but it came at a price. After all, could a John Held flapper or a Gordon Conway girl possibly survive on so few calories? Could young women be expected to sculpt their bodies into this unnatural form? How could real women really banish every last imperfection from their faces? Could anyone actually afford to keep pace with the latest in couture and fashion?

Madison Avenue had an answer to all these questions. Emphatically, yes.

A cigarette advertisement in 1929 exploits the new national obsession with personal appearance.

19

APPEARANCE/ COUNT

PERSUADING THE AVERAGE woman to spend absurd sums of money and countless hours to achieve an impossible ideal was no small task. But American advertisers approached it with gusto. And they had both Sigmund Freud and Woodrow Wilson to thank (at least indirectly) for sophisticated new methods of influencing consumer behavior—methods that would go a long way toward making flapper fashion and flapper accessories *necessary* possessions for the discerning New American Woman.

Some of those methods had emerged in the wake of World War I. When President Woodrow Wilson resolved in 1917 that the United States should enter the great conflict then engulfing Europe in a hailstorm of bullets and blood, his closest advisers understood that it would be a tough sell to the American public. Only months before, Wilson had been reelected by the narrowest of margins on the simple platform: "He kept us out of war."

Shortly after calling the nation to arms, the president considered a proposal by Arthur Bullard, a prominent progressive who had been his student at Princeton, where Wilson taught history before making a second career out of elective politics. Bullard urged the president to "electrify public opinion" in favor of the war by forming an official publicity office. The idea was quickly seconded by Walter Lippmann, the erstwhile progressive writer and influential co-founder of *The New Republic*.

Lippmann was deeply interested in a growing field of social psychology that concerned itself with mass opinion and politics. His ideas owed a great deal to Gustave Le Bon's 1895 work, *The Crowd: A Study of the Popular Mind,* which characterized labor unions, mobs, crowds—pretty much any mass assembly of ordinary citizens—as easily subject to demagoguery and "little adapted to reasoning." As individuals, the idea was, people were still given to rational argument and discourse. But gather them together and they became illogical, responding only to force or manipulation.

With that idea in mind, Lippmann encouraged the president to appoint leading advertising men, publicists, newspaper editors, and film directors to a new propaganda agency that would convince the American public that the war was a necessary step "to make a world that is safe for democracy." The end result was Executive Order No. 2594, which established the Committee on Public Information (CPI)—the so-called House of Truth—under the direction of George Creel, a well-known progressive journalist.

Although the committee's original mandate was to provide the public with hard facts and information, allowing citizens to reach their own conclusions about the war, it soon gave way to the manipulations of prominent advertising men on staff. Even Creel came gradually to admit that "people do not live by bread alone; they live mostly by slogans." Realizing that the CPI would have to appeal to raw emotions and sensations, Creel drew together a talented group of communications professionals and artists, including the painter Charles Dana Gibson, who headed the CPI's Division of Pictorial Publicity, and George Bowles, a Hollywood promoter who had largely masterminded the distribution of *The Birth of a Nation.*

The end result was a massive propaganda campaign that included the dissemination of two hundred thousand different slides, stereotypes, and photographs; the enlistment of several hundred thousand "Four Minute Men" who delivered stock pro-war speeches in movie theaters while the film reels were being changed; a massive censorship effort that struck at any visible form of printed or spoken dissent; and, most ominously, posters, broadsides, and flyers that appealed mawkishly to love of country and more darkly to ever present strains of fear and raw prejudice.

Not everyone involved with the project approved of its unanticipated trajectory, but as Gibson conceded, "One cannot create enthusiasm for the war on the basis of practical appeal. The spirit that will lead a man to put away the things of his accustomed life and go forth to all the hardships of war is not killed by showing him the facts." No—the only way to compel an unwilling nation to embrace war was to "appeal to the heart."

Typical CPI posters presented a beleaguered Statue of Liberty collapsing under the strain of German fire, set against a backdrop of a wasted, burning New York City; a giant poisonous spider wearing a German combat helmet, accompanied by a banner that read SPIES ARE LISTENING; and a map of the United States, renamed New Prussia, with familiar places bearing new names like Heineapolis, Denverburg, Cape U Boat, and the Gulf of Hate.

While many reformers watched with horror as a onetime progressive president turned the United States into a quasi police state, arrested thousands of political dissidents, and used crass propaganda methods to appeal to the public's basest sentiments, American businessmen basked in the glow of the CPI's success. Pressed to experiment with new forms of mind control, and endowed with enormous sums of the federal government's money, advertising and public relations professionals who worked for the CPI in 1917 and 1918 emerged from the war armed with new techniques that could be used to market consumer products.

"The war taught us the power of propaganda," Roger Babson, a leading business analyst, boasted in 1921. "Now when we have anything to sell the American people, we know how to sell it."

Even before the war, advertising agencies had been experimenting with new methods of scientific surveying and social psychology. In fact, Madison Avenue enlisted the talents of some of America's leading psychologists and psychiatrists. George Phelps, an ad executive who encouraged the marriage of social science and marketing, argued that the real challenge in advertising was "the process of getting people to do or think what you want them to do or think."

John B. Watson, a professor at the Johns Hopkins University and arguably the leading behavioral psychologist in America, led the way in 1922 when he resigned his university post and signed a lucrative contract with the J. Walter Thompson agency. Other prominent academics made the same leap soon after.

Ivy Lee, a preeminent New York adman, spoke for many in his profession when he admitted, "I have found the Freudian theories concerning the psychology of the subconscious mind of great interest." Lee, who once maintained that advertising was nothing more than disseminating facts, came around to the opinion that "publicity is essentially a matter of mass psychology. We must remember that people are guided more by sentiment than by mind."

Who better to consult on this subject than the master himself? If Madison Avenue didn't enjoy direct access to Sigmund Freud, it had the next best thing: his nephew Edward Bernays—father of the "torches of freedom" display at the 1929 New York Easter parade. Bernays, a Viennese émigré and Freud's nephew two times over—his mother was Sigmund's sister; his father's sister was Sigmund's wife—was a veteran of George Creel's CPI and America's leading "public relations counsel" in the 1920s. With a client roster that included some of the nation's most lucrative business concerns—the United Fruit Company, General Motors, Procter & Gamble, Philco, and Liggett & Myers, among them—Bernays aggressively championed the integration of marketing and psychology.

"Mass psychology is as yet far from being an exact science and the mysteries of human motivation are by no means all revealed," Bernays conceded. "But at least theory and practice have combined with sufficient success to permit us to know that in certain cases we can effect some change in public opinion . . . by operating a certain mechanism."

Though business practitioners of psychoanalytic theory badly mangled and conflated the work of Sigmund Freud, Gustave Le Bon, John Watson, and other important theorists, there emerged by the early 1920s a popular consensus among advertisers that humans were rarely, in writer Everett Dean Martin's words, "governed by reason or consideration." Rather, "instinctive impulses determine the ends of all activities and supply the driving-power by which all mental activities are maintained."

With this idea in mind, advertising professionals were particularly successful in changing expectations about personal appearance and thus creating a new set of assumptions about body image and fashion. The flapper was one of their finest creations.

Warnings, they found, were especially effective. "Critical eyes are sizing you up," asserted an ad for Aqua Velva aftershave. "Keep your face fresh, firm, fit."

"The Picture He Carries Away," another advertisement began. "Will it be an alluring image of charm and freshness, or the pitying recollection of a pretty girl made unattractive by a poor complexion?"

In an urban society that was less personal and more anonymous, where chance encounters were more frequent and where one's appearance spoke louder than his or her reputation, *first impressions mattered*. A lot. Indeed, everything was at stake.

"It ruins romance," warned an ad for Listerine. Beneath a picture of a young, well-groomed couple, each gazing suspiciously at the other, the text wondered: "Did you ever come face to face with a real cause of halitosis (unpleasant breath)? Can you imagine yourself married to a person offending this way?" Another ad delivered this lecture: "You will be amazed to find how many times in one day people glance at your nails. At each glance a judgment is made. . . . Indeed some people make a practice of basing their estimate of a new acquaintance largely upon this one detail."

If a mere warning didn't suffice, advertisers were happy to trot out a cautionary tale. "Always a bridesmaid, never a bride. . . . Edna's case was really a pathetic one. Like every woman her primary ambition was to marry. Most of the girls of her set were married—or about to be. . . . And as her birthdays crept gradually toward the tragic thirty-mark, marriage seemed farther from her life than ever. . . . Listerine."

Magazine readers could be forgiven for expressing shock and alarm. They didn't realize that maladies like halitosis were wholly made-up disorders. When Gerald Lambert, heir to the Lambert

Pharmaceutical fortune, found himself strapped for cash in the wake of the 1921 economic recession, he decided it was time to put the firm's household and topical antiseptic, Listerine, to better use.

Gerald, whose formative years were marked by unusual privilege—he rode in a chauffeured limousine between classroom buildings at Princeton University—later admitted that he was "quite used to having any material thing I wanted." He certainly wasn't about to let a little national recession plunge him into the depths of the upper middle class.

Up until then, Listerine had been used to clean cuts and scrapes. When a member of the Lambert research team happened across the word *halitosis* in a British newspaper, and when the company's staff scientists confirmed that there was no real health risk in swirling around a small dose of Listerine in one's mouth, young Gerald—seeing a clear way out of his economic straits—immediately instructed his advertisers to market Listerine as the only proven cure for a serious medical and social disease: bad breath.

"A few years ago," read a typical Lambert ad, "bad breath was condoned as an unavoidable misfortune. Today it is judged one of the gravest social offenses." Appealing to the anxieties of urban Americans who lived in proximity to one another and experienced the daily angst of anonymity and public scrutiny, the company saw sales of Listerine skyrocket by 33 percent after just one month of the new ad campaign.

So it went with all sorts of new disorders—dandruff, athlete's foot, body odor, face wrinkles, dry or oily hair, acne, rough skin. Beneath every imperfection lurked a disastrous end—a lost job, a lost love, a missed opportunity. And for every danger, there was a cure—a new face cream, antiseptic, soap, shade of lipstick, or hair tonic to ward off the looming threat of social failure. By the end of the decade, annual sales of toiletries and beauty services had mushroomed, and the volume of advertising for toiletries ranked second only to food.

Magazine ads promised beauty, youth, and success with fetching titles like "I Cured My Pimples—and Became a Bride," "How a Wife Won Back Her Youth—A Surrender to Ugliness That Nearly Cost a

Husband's Love," and "Do you wonder, when you meet a casual friend, whether your nose is too shiny?"

The accompanying pictures—featuring intimate scenes of married life, young love, office politics, random everyday encounters, and job interviews—gave the subtle impression that everywhere one turned there was always a keen eye trained on the most infinitesimal aspects of one's appearance. For the would-be flapper, this was a powerful message. "Will his eyes confirm what his lips are saying?" wondered an advertisement for Palmolive. "The kindly candles of last night, the tell-tale revealments of noon! Do you fear the contrast they may offer?"

On some level, the modern world did, in fact, lend itself to a more rigorous standard of examination. As recently as the mid–nineteenth century, most mirrors cast back cloudy representations of real life, leading one historian to speculate that "American women and men had only a hazy apprehension of their facial qualities." When Maria Lydig Daley gazed on her image in a hotel mirror, she was appalled at how "old and ugly" she appeared. Upon returning home, Daley was reassured by her own looking glass, which offered a more familiar image of youth and beauty. "How few of us have a perfect idea how we look," remarked an early photographer, "or who we resemble, or look like."

All of this had changed by the 1920s. People had better ways of examining themselves and those around them. The wall-to-wall mirrors in the department store (damning in their accuracy), the little girl on the street clutching a Kodak camera in her hand, the shiny, reflective storefront windows, the stranger on the commuter train with the suspicious gaze—each was quietly poised to sear an unflattering image into memory.

As advertisers encouraged the American consumer to take greater stock of his or her appearance—to ratchet up standards of cleanliness, grooming, and artificial enhancement, to abandon the Sunday bath for the daily shower, to sculpt one's features in the never-ending quest for eternal youth and perfection—old taboos against lipstick, mascara, rouge, and face powder gave way to a new imperative: self-improvement.

In the nineteenth century, the only women who dared wear makeup were stage actresses, whose morals were considered highly suspect, and prostitutes. Miners in western camps warned that

> Hangtown Gals are plump and rosy,
> Hair in ringlets mighty cosy.
> Painted cheeks and gassy bonnets;
> Touch them and they'll sting like hornets.

Popular convention held that makeup concealed one's inner spirit. And who but a guilty or scheming person would mask his or her true nature? In an era when cities were first starting to expand and where people were being thrown for the first time into a sea of anonymous faces, the dominant culture placed a high premium on "a perfectly transparent character." Moralists held that, for women especially, "the skin's power of expression" was a vital sign of one's innate spirit and integrity. Thus, women who "painted" their faces had something to hide, just as young ladies who "put on the tinsel"—fancy clothes, flashy adornments, nail polish—were playing a dangerous game, trying "to *seem* to be what they are not."

"The mask of fashion," as critics sometimes called it, was turning everyday life into a "masquerade, in which we dress ourselves in the finest fashions of society, use a language suited to the characters we assume;—with smiling faces, mask aching hearts; address accents of kindness to our enemies, and often those of coldness to our friends. The part once assumed must be acted out, no matter at what expense of truth and feeling."

By the 1920s, popular opinion had completed a 180-degree shift. Now accustomed to the anonymity of the modern world, public authorities—more likely to be advertisers than ministers—*encouraged* Americans to cultivate their exterior appearance and present as polished a facade as possible. Cosmetics companies like Armand even urged the New Woman to "Find Yourself" through the application of makeup. "The questions and answers will discover the real you—not as you think you are—but as others see you." What was once dismissed as "the mask of fashion" now held out the power to "make us look and feel more self-possessed, poised, and efficient." Self-invention was a right; self-reinvention was a necessity.

When a woman "begins to regard her appearance in her own mind as a fixed, unalterable quality," warned *Vogue's Book of Beauty,* "—that same moment, some vital, shining part of her is extinguished forever." Drawing on popular psychoanalytic argot, *Vogue's* editors found that an inattention to external appearance "destroys those potential personalities that psychologists tell us are lurking behind our ordinary selves."

Whereas Victorian moralists claimed that the use of makeup and a slavish attention to fashion somehow masked one's inner self, the new apostles of consumerism claimed that lipstick and nice clothes empowered the superwoman beneath the skin. When a distraught woman from Detroit wrote to "Frances Ingram"—the pen name for the advertising department at Ingram's Milkwood Cream—wondering if "maybe my appearance affected my chance at promotion," "Frances Ingram" replied that in the current "age of self-development" there was an intimate relationship between "internal cleanliness" and a "radiant, attractive, and likeable" exterior.

"When a woman has a bad complexion," advised "Frances Ingram," "people notice immediately, and they have to get past it before they really like a person. I believe that the dullness of your complexion may have reacted on your subconscious in such a way that your confidence in yourself has become impaired." The answer: Buy more Ingram's Milkwood Cream.

Change came swiftly: By the late 1920s, industry analysts claimed that 90 percent of adult women used face powder, 83 percent used talcum, 73 percent applied perfume, and 55 percent used rouge.

City women were more likely to use makeup than their small-town and country sisters, though even in the metropolis there was a wide gulf among women of different classes. An industry analyst noted that wealthy women in Chicago tended to use cosmetics "very carefully and sparingly," whereas working-class women "use it in astonishing quantities." Another commentator lamented that "the shop girl has lost all sense of perspective. Each of her cheeks is a blooming peony. Her eyes are two smudges of dusky, shadowy black. Her lips are cruel with scarlet."

Department store counter clerks learned to differentiate among customers—Arden for the smart set, Pond's for the working girl, Elcaya for everyone in between. And in cities like New York and Chicago, it was common knowledge that young "Jewish flappers" preferred Angelus lipstick in dark red or orange. "All Jewish girls use it," explained a counter clerk who, according to an interviewer, "never asks what brand they want but gets the Angelus drawer out when she sees them coming."

As for rural America, "Towns under 1,000 are hopeless," sighed a cosmetics account representative at the J. Walter Thompson agency. That wouldn't be the case for long. A study of two thousand rural women conducted by *Farm Journal* just before World War II found almost universal use of face powder and widespread use of lipstick.

Surveys of college women—the first generation raised on aggressive consumer advertising, movies, and radio—revealed that 85 percent used rouge, lipstick, face powder, and nail polish. At Vassar College, the J. Walter Thompson agency found that "again and again phrases that had been used in the Woodbury advertising were used by the girls, with apparent unconsciousness."

When prompted to describe the virtues of Woodbury cold cream, coeds at the University of Chicago repeated almost verbatim the product's advertising copy—"[it] actually draws the dust and dirt out of the pores," "one feels deliciously clean and fresh after using it." At Smith College, a student admitted without prompting that she used Woodbury cream because she "longed for romance and thought perhaps a beautiful complexion would make me more fascinating."

Even in small cities, by the 1920s well over half of local newspapers ran advertisements for beauty products.

Just as advertisers made makeup and toiletries compulsory in the 1920s, they constantly drove home the idea that "appearances count for a great deal in this critical world of ours." "The well-dressed man may be no better than his opposite," explained a clothing ad, "but he'll meet with more consideration every time. Therefore, if you're looking for success, dress well."

Advertisers encouraged women to "make up your LIPS for KISSES!" but also warned of the dire consequences that surely followed from inadequate attention to detail. A typical ad featured a woman who was "innocent yet men talked." She was wearing the wrong kind of lipstick—a brand that marked her as cheap. "You cannot afford to make yourself ridiculous," cautioned the new apostles of modernity, "if you have started for success, you want to attract a REAL man."

With trusted authorities like Dorothy Dix warning that "the world judges us by appearance," a local newspaper in Muncie detected a new everyday fastidiousness about style and dress. "People weren't as particular in former days about what they wore Monday through Saturday," but "the Sunday suit of clothes is one of the institutions that is vanishing in our generation. . . . Even the overall brigade is apt to wear the same suit week-day evenings as on Sunday."

"The dresses girls wear to school now used to be considered party dresses," marveled one mother. "My daughter would consider herself terribly abused if she had to wear the same dress to school two successive days."

When another Muncie homemaker sent her thirteen-year-old daughter to school clad in a pretty (and hardly inexpensive) gingham dress and lisle hose, she was shocked to find the girl on the verge of tears the next day. "Mother, I am just an object of mercy!" cried the daughter. Her parents reluctantly gave in and bought her a new wardrobe of silk dresses and silk stockings, in the popular flapper style.

High school sororities placed a high premium on attire. "We have to have boys for the Christmas dances," explained a popular Muncie High School student, "so we take in the girls who can bring the boys." A recent recruit explained her sudden, newfound popularity this way: "I've known these girls always, but I've never been asked to join before; it's just clothes and money that makes the difference. Mother has let me spend more money on clothes this last year."

It was harder for working families to keep their daughters suitably attired. A Muncie mother living on an annual household budget of $1,363 complained that her daughters, ages eleven and twelve, were "so stuck up I can't sew for them anymore."

Just making it to graduation day was an expensive affair. A

respectable girl "needs three or four new dresses for graduation," remarked another Muncie mom. And this wasn't counting the fifteen or so new dresses needed each year for Christmas dances, fraternity and sorority dances, school recitals . . .

If parents of would-be flappers were most concerned by the sky-rocketing costs of maintaining their daughters' popularity and self-esteem, newspaper editorials were more concerned by the political implications of flapper attire. As the Lynds recognized, the insistence on "more comfort, looser clothing, and greater freedom of limb" went hand in hand with the "newer freedom and aggressiveness of women." When a lawsuit erupted in a small town near Muncie over the right of schoolgirls to wear knickers instead of skirts, commentators could only ask, "Where will this freedom end?"

No doubt the young women who fought for the right to wear knickers saw it as a bid for personal freedom. But their audacious ideas about what to wear and how to behave were not entirely their own. Their imaginations were nurtured by Madison Avenue, of course, but it was the great Jazz Age movie moguls who really sealed the deal—who shaped popular notions about the female body and how it should be displayed that endure to this day.

Their story begins on a studio lot in Hollywood, California, where dry desert ground that was once surrounded by vast, rambling valleys lush with citrus groves was now cultivating a nation's dreams.

PART THREE

Screen actress Colleen Moore played the starring role in The Perfect Flapper, *1924.*

20

PAPA, WHAT IS BEER?

I N MID-1923, as millions of young women eagerly turned the pages of their glossy magazines in search of the latest flapper fashion tips, the national press was abuzz with news of a scandalous new film called *Flaming Youth*.

"Intriguingly risqué but not necessarily offensively so," one reviewer concluded. "The flapperism of today, with its jazz, neckerdances, its petting parties, and its utter disregard of the conventions, is daringly handled in this film. And it contains a bathing scene in silhouette that must have made the censors blink."

"This girl plays a flapper the way Scott Fitzgerald writes one," another critic wrote of Colleen Moore, the film's lead player. "She is an informer and a betrayer. And I think she is one of the most fascinating little devils on this or adjacent continents." To yet another observer, Moore embodied "the young flapper to the tip of her bobbed head. . . . Perhaps college professors will call it trashy. But the people who should be pleased, those who pack the movie houses every night. Those are going to crazy about it."

As far as story lines go, *Flaming Youth* left a lot to be desired. Colleen played the role of Pat Fentriss, the teenage daughter of well-to-do urban sophisticates. Pat's mother and father host wild parties in the family mansion, complete with jazz music, bootleg liquor, and skinny-dipping romps in the swimming pool. They don't set the best possible example for their daughter, and it shows.

Young Pat, still hemmed in by adolescence, is eager to emulate her parents' fast life. So she skips town with a seductive violinist a few years her senior and sets sail for Europe on a yacht. Trouble quickly ensues when the violinist tries to seduce Pat. Realizing that she is in way over her head, and desperate to escape her sexually aggressive escort, Pat jumps overboard into the deep blue sea, only to be rescued by a sailor who proves far better mannered and better intentioned than the rakish musician.

Lessons learned, Pat is bound back safely for shore and then back to her mother and father. She doesn't want to grow up too fast, after all.

The film told a new kind of story and provided a new kind of role for Colleen Moore.

Anyone who grew up with Moore, back when she was still Kathleen Morrison, must have known she was fated for the stage. When she was a girl of about nine or ten, someone in the neighborhood ordered a large upright piano for his family and disposed of the enormous wooden packaging crate outside his house. Before the garbage men could come to haul the box away, Kathleen—a short, precocious redhead with intense eyes—convinced her neighbor's yard man to drag the crate, which resembled a small stage, over to her backyard. "The American Stock Company was now in business," she remembered years later with a smile.

Kathleen wrote a series of short dramatic productions and recruited some of her friends to perform the supporting roles. The American Stock Company charged a penny per head for admission—a stiff price for ten-year-olds. "Business, unfortunately, was bad," she recalled. "We played to very small audiences, sometimes as small as one or two. But my vanity wasn't the only thing that suffered. I've always liked a paying business, and we sometimes couldn't even get the ones who did come to pay the penny we asked."

Sensing that her fledgling production company was about to hit the skids, Kathleen revamped her act. Hoping to capitalize on the success of Barnum & Bailey's Circus, which had recently played to sold-out audiences in town, she plastered the neighborhood with boldfaced signs—CIRCUS IN MORRISON'S BACK YARD—SATURDAY—

NO BOYS ALLOWED. It was a winning gambit. That weekend, her family's well-manicured lawn took a royal drubbing from dozens of girls and boys who were eager to watch Kathleen and her troupe perform a dazzling display of acrobatics.

"I was so carried away," she later wrote, ". . . that when I performed an acrobatic stunt with Cleve"—her younger brother—"hanging by my knees from a gym bar and holding him dangling, a leather book strap around his middle and the end of it clenched in my teeth, I twirled him around so fast I broke the edge off my new front tooth."

No matter. The show was a great success, and the end-of-the-day take—43 cents—was a vindication of Kathleen's dramatic aspirations.

Kathleen Morrison was born in 1900 to a middle-class, "lace Irish" Catholic family in Port Huron, Michigan, but she spent the better part of her youth in Atlanta, Georgia, and Tampa, Florida, where her father chased a variety of career opportunities and where she acquired a distinctive southern-midwestern accent.

Later in life, Kathleen would trace the spark of her lifelong love affair with the acting profession to a magic Saturday afternoon when she was five. That year, her mother took Kathleen to see a stage production of *Peter Pan*. When the title character ran down the center aisle in a blaze of footlights and invited "all children who believe in fairies to raise their hands" to save Tinker Bell, Kathleen did the audience one better. She leapt onto her seat, flailed her arms in the air, and cried, "I believe in fairies, I really do!"

"The audience burst into laughter," she remembered, "turning to look at me. I stared back at them, their laughter hitting me with a force I had never felt before. And when I realized that it was I—I—who was making them laugh, a curious feeling of power came over me—as if for those few brief moments I held that audience in my hand. That Saturday afternoon I knew—not hoped, knew—I would become an actress."

Like millions of other girls who came of age in the years just before and after World War I, Kathleen soon transferred her love of the stage to a near obsession with America's infant film industry.

As a junior high student in Tampa, each Friday afternoon she made a frantic dash for the Bijou Theater, where, amid the dazzling crystal chandeliers and beautifully upholstered, plush red seats, she and her friends swooned at the sight of Francis Ford and were awed by the polish and poise of Grace Cunard in *Lucille Love*. On Saturdays they flocked to the Strand Theater—equally grand, equally majestic— where they studied Mary Pickford's every move and gesture and mapped every line and curve on Marguerite Clark's petite, four-foot-ten-inch, ninety-pound frame.

The girls wrote fan letters to their favorite stars, clipped pictures and movie advertisements from magazines, and kept intricately detailed scrapbooks, with separate pages for each Hollywood luminary.

When she read in *Photoplay* magazine that Norma Talmadge, a leading lady of wide renown, believed all great actresses should be able to cry a river of tears on demand, Kathleen practiced for weeks until she was able to sob convincingly at a moment's notice. She cried on the way to school. She cried on the way back from school.

One day, when she was passing the time on a streetcar by practicing her mournful art, an old woman seated next to her asked, "What's the matter, little girl?"

"Oh, nothing, ma'am," Kathleen answered with a broad smile. Tears still streaming down her face, she explained, "I'm just practicing to be a movie actress."

It wasn't an uncommon story. Not by the dawn of World War I, anyway. Nevertheless, years later Kathleen would remember her Hollywood fixation as just a little exceptional. "The only difference between my movie scrapbook and those of my friends," she asserted, "was that I left a blank page in mine for my own picture after I became a movie star. Because I didn't just hope to go to Hollywood. I intended to."

Of course, Kathleen Morrison had something that a lot of other girls didn't: connections.

Walter Howey was the archetype of the hard-boiled newspaperman. He might have come straight from Central Casting, so convincingly did he play the part. A true son of the American heartland—born and bred in Fort Dodge, Iowa—as a young man,

Howey came to Chicago an ordinary hayseed without a clue about the big city and its alien ways. He spent the first two decades of the new century figuring it all out—scratching and clawing his way up the ranks of that city's famously competitive, no-holds-barred world of print journalism.

Howey was clearly in a line of work that suited him well. He had an uncanny knack for showing up everywhere and anywhere there was a story. Police roundups, murder scenes, catastrophic fires, smoky backroom political deals . . . if there was a story, Howey was there, and what's more, he was the first to get there. And when he committed his tale to paper, readers were enthralled.

His writing and editorial skills were so sharp that when he had a falling-out with the publisher of the *Chicago Tribune,* where he earned an annual salary of $8,000 as city editor, he stormed out of the office, slammed the door behind him, walked across the street to see William Randolph Hearst, and within half an hour scored a job as managing editor of Hearst's *Herald-Examiner*—the *Tribune*'s chief competitor for the morning news market. His new salary was $35,000 per year.

Howey's hard-driving style was media made, so much so that in 1928 Ben Hecht and Charles MacArthur wrote a satirical play about the newspaper business, *The Front Page.* Anyone who knew anything about Chicago journalism knew that the lead character, "Walter Burns," was patterned after Howey. *The Front Page* charmed audiences on and off Broadway for several years. In 1940, Hollywood asked Hecht and MacArthur to offer a new twist on their script for a second screen adaptation.

The result was *His Girl Friday,* featuring Cary Grant as a fast-talking, unrelenting big-city newspaperman. It immortalized Walter Howey for all time. Though they might not have known his name, millions of Americans came to know his type.

Lucky for Kathleen Morrison, the famous Walter Howey was also *Uncle* Walter. His wife, Lib, was the younger sister of Kathleen's mother. Lucky also for Kathleen that David Wark Griffith owed Uncle Walter a big favor.

Back in 1915, after he had sunk every penny of his savings into *The*

Birth of a Nation, Griffith faced the dreadful prospect that his three-hour masterpiece might never see the light of day. Under pressure from the National Association for the Advancement of Colored People, whose members objected to Griffith's crudely racist treatment of black characters, local censors threatened to ban the film. Griffith, in turn, agreed to remove a few of the most objectionable scenes.

Not that this helped a great deal; the final print was still patently offensive. It even rankled the good citizens of tiny Lancaster, Pennsylvania, who objected to Griffith's scathing treatment of Thaddeus Stevens, the antislavery politician who had represented the county in Congress during the Civil War and had championed the cause of emancipation and equal citizenship for black Americans. In Lancaster, as in many places, Griffith's picture was non grata.

Fearing that any controversy was bad for his picture, Griffith asked a few prominent members of the press to lend him aid and comfort in the pages of the newspapers and magazines. Uncle Walter was one such supporter. When *The Birth of a Nation* emerged as the industry's first real blockbuster, Griffith made it clear to Uncle Walter that he was eager to repay the favor. It wasn't long before the Howeys cashed in.

At a dinner party one night, they made their move.

Lib Howey began, "We have a niece——"

"Not a niece!" Griffith moaned.

Walter smiled back. "I'm afraid so."

Why not? Griffith thought. Such was the cost of doing business. His studio was already top-heavy with the daughters and nieces of big financial backers. What harm would one more "payoff" do? He'd put the Howeys' niece on a six-month contract for $50 per week, and if she was any good, he'd keep her; if she couldn't act—and they rarely could—then everyone would move on and there'd be no hard feelings. A handshake sealed the agreement.

Only one hitch remained: Kathleen's father. The year was 1916, and Mr. Morrison was decidedly cool to the notion that his sixteen-year-old daughter, an innocent, long-haired lass who had attended Catholic convent schools all her life, should venture off to the wilds of California, alone, to keep pace with the fast set in Hollywood.

Only the winning combination of Kathleen's tears—real ones—and Mrs. Morrison's determined support won over the deeply skeptical family patriarch.

That, plus a new stipulation: Kathleen's grandmother, a staid and proper Victorian, would accompany her out west and serve as her official chaperone. Sunset Boulevard was no place for unaccompanied young ladies.

A few weeks later, Kathleen and her grandmother packed their bags and set out by Pullman car for Chicago, where they would spend a few days with Walter and Lib Howey before boarding the *Santa Fe Chief* for Los Angeles. On their first night in Chicago, over a celebratory outing to the College Inn—"Aunt Lib told me it was a night-club," Kathleen later remembered. "When I asked her what that meant, Uncle Walter said, 'It's a place where they don't have lunch'"—Walter raised a champagne glass and offered a toast.

"Here's to Colleen Moore"—he beamed—"the newest Griffith discovery and a future movie star."

Kathleen raised her eyebrows.

"That's you, baby," Walter Howey informed his bewildered young niece. A new career demanded a new name, he explained. Something flashy, something dazzling—and something with fewer than twelve letters, which was the industry standard. "Kathleen Morrison" simply wouldn't fit on a movie billboard. "Colleen Moore" would. Also, Colleen Moore sounded Irish, and Uncle Walter "decided the time had come for introducing an Irish actress to the movies. There was a lot of good publicity in it."

Before Kathleen Morrison—now Colleen Moore—boarded the train for California, Uncle Walter scribbled a few words of parting advice. "Dear baby," he began, "Hollywood, where you will now be living, is inhabited by a race of people called Press Agents. The studios pay them a lot of money to think up stories about the players under contract and to persuade editors like me to print their stories. So the moral of this letter is, never believe one word you ever read about yourself."

It was good advice. By the time she became Hollywood's flapper queen, Colleen Moore would read a great many things about herself that didn't ring true. As far as the world knew, D. W. Griffith had "discovered" Colleen one night while dining at the Howey residence in Chicago. With the approval of her mischievous aunt and uncle, the spunky sixteen-year-old had donned a maid's outfit and tried to pass herself off as a house servant. By the time dessert rolled around, Griffith was so smitten by the Irish lass who had taken his coat and served up his potatoes that he grabbed his hostess by the arm and announced, "Mrs. Howey, you've just lost a maid, and I've gained a new movie star!" It was a good story, anyway.

According to a 1921 biographical index card she filed with Goldwyn Pictures Corporation, where she made several films after Griffith shut down his West Coast operations in 1919, Colleen arrived in Hollywood standing five feet three and three-quarter inches and weighing 110 pounds. She had long, reddish brown hair and dark brown eyes that didn't do much to set her apart from the dozens of other young leading ladies who were also trying desperately to emulate the wholesome girl-next-door look that was working such wonders for Mary Pickford's artistic career and bank account.

If Scott and Zelda Fitzgerald were setting the world on fire with their well-orchestrated apotheosis of the New Woman, Hollywood still seemed to prefer Plain Jane to Flapper Jane. What were Colleen Moore's pastimes, according to her file card at Goldwyn Pictures? Dancing and swimming. Her hobbies? "None—plain person." Reading interests? Blank. Ambition? "To become famous."

Colleen didn't become famous overnight, but between 1916 and 1923 she appeared in at least thirty-five feature-length films, almost always as a "leading lady" (playing a supporting role to the male star) or a "feature player" (appearing with a troupe of three or four prominent actors and actresses, all of whom shared equal billing). She was earning exceptionally good money—upward of $750 each week, or just shy of $40,000 per year (equivalent in today's money to an annual salary of $430,000).

At first, Colleen's appeal was her innocence and youth. Her long, curly hair—which photographed black, even though it was closer to auburn—and wide eyes lent her a look of incorruptibility, as did her well-practiced facial expressions. "There was a stage melodrama of many years before my time in Hollywood," she explained years later, "in which an innocent young thing turned to her father to ask in wonderment, 'Papa, what is beer?' That line carried over into vaudeville sketches and into the lingo of the silent film directors. The director would say to the girl playing the young, pure, innocent heroine, 'Get that "Papa, what is beer?" look on your face.' "

Colleen admitted that "this look was on my face through a great many movies—too many movies—too many made long after I knew full well what a beer was, and a number of other things as well."

Not that she had completely hit a rut. Colleen enjoyed opportunities to work with the motley assortment of characters who converged on Southern California just before and after World War I—men like Tom Mix, a marine veteran who was rumored to have fought in the Boxer Rebellion in China and the Boer War in South Africa, clocked time as a local sheriff in Oklahoma, and boldly escaped a firing squad in Mexico, where he fought with Francisco Madero's rebel forces, who were then in a pitched battle to overthrow President Porfirio Díaz.

Actually, none of this was true. Mix was a native Pennsylvanian who joined the army during the Spanish-American War and went AWOL in 1902 without seeing any action. He didn't escape a Mexican firing squad, but he did manage to elude both his first wife and the military police, who wanted him on charges of desertion.

Mix moved west to Oklahoma and reinvented himself as a sometime cowboy, cattle rancher, saloon keeper, and movie impresario. A veteran of the Miller Brothers 101 Real Wild West Ranch—a combination ranch and Wild West show—he proved such a skilled horseman, and so uncommonly nimble with a lasso, that he soon caught the attention of several filmmakers, who brought him to Hollywood to help invent the industry's stock country-western hero. Decked out in ten-gallon hats, expensive leather cowboy boots, and embroidered shirts, he circled around the set on his prized horse, Tony, to the delight of his adoring co-stars.

Colleen, who was still a teenager, appeared opposite the thirty-nine-year-old Tom Mix in several films and developed a hopeless crush on him.

Then there was Al Jennings, a rehabilitated train robber whom the big movie moguls recruited, predictably, to play the stock part of the villainous, horse-riding train robber in a series of boilerplate westerns. Jennings had done hard time in prison, but by the time Colleen had the chance to work with him in the feature production *Hands Up!,* his reputation for dastardly deeds far exceeded any crimes he might have committed in real life. Like many of the other leading ladies, Colleen was captivated by the onetime outlaw and trailed him around the set for weeks.

If life was good—and, to be sure, it was—Colleen nevertheless understood by 1923 that it was make or break time for her career. The "Papa, what is beer?" routine had brought her a long way from Tampa, but the headliner roles still eluded her.

"I just wasn't the accepted-and-acceptable model for a sweet young thing in the throes of her first love," she admitted. "The necessary curls I could manage, the same way Mary Pickford and the others did, with time and effort. But no amount of either could make my five-foot-five boyish figure into a curvy, petite five-foot-two or transform the sauciness of my freckled face with its turned-up nose into the demure perfection of a Mary Pickford."

Either Colleen would have to tap into a new aesthetic ideal or her days in pictures were numbered. "That was where my brother Cleve came in," she later wrote. "Cleve, and a man named Warner Fabian."

Cleve was now attending Santa Clara College in Northern California, and on the weekends he often came to visit Colleen—usually in the company of a different college girlfriend. Colleen had never met women like this before. "They were smart and sophisticated," she remarked, "with an air of independence about them, and so casual about their looks and clothes and manners as to be almost slapdash. I don't know if I realized as soon as I began seeing them that they represented the wave of the future, but I do know I was drawn to them. I shared their restlessness, understood their determination to free themselves of the Victorian shackles of the pre–World War I era and find out for themselves what life was all about."

Around the same time, someone loaned Colleen a copy of author Warner Fabian's best-selling novel *Flaming Youth,* a second-rate knock-off of an F. Scott Fitzgerald flapper tale. When First National—Colleen's new studio—bought the rights to *Flaming Youth,* she knew she wanted the lead role.

The question was, how? Flappers didn't ask, "Papa, what is beer?" They didn't dress like Victorian debutantes or spend hours combing their long, curly hair. They hardly *had* any hair.

Colleen's mother had the answer. Without any particular qualifications as a hairdresser, she picked up a pair of household scissors, walked over to her daughter, and, "whack, off came the long curls." Sculpting Colleen's hair into a Dutch bob, she instantly transformed her into the archetype of the collegiate flapper. Colleen breezed through her screen test and won the part. The movie, in turn, became a blockbuster hit. And Colleen Moore became one of the highest-grossing actresses in Hollywood, to the tune of $10,000 per week.

Hollywood had discovered the flapper.

"I was the spark that lit up Flaming Youth," Scott Fitzgerald wrote in the wake of the film's success. "Colleen Moore was the torch."

Famed director D.W. Griffith (seated) and screen legends Douglas Fairbanks and Charlie Chaplin (first and second from left) and Mary Pickford (far right).

21

OH, LITTLE GIRL, NEVER GROW UP

B Y THE TIME Kathleen Morrison—rechristened Colleen Moore—hopped the *Santa Fe Chief* for Los Angeles, the film industry had traveled a long road from guardian of Victorian morality to purveyor of youth culture.

In its first two decades, the motion picture industry left a lot to be desired. For one, the technology was bad. Rudimentary film projectors caused moving images to flicker and pulse. The film often came apart and crumbled after only a few screenings. Because projectionists still rotated the reels by hand, screen images often moved at erratic speeds.

But the problem wasn't just with the machinery. The plotlines were weak. Short clips featured everyday people engaged in mundane or humorous activities. Juggling. Running. Swimming. Sleeping. It didn't take long for people to realize that they could watch their husbands and wives do the very same things—but in real life, and for free. Somewhat more engaging, though salacious, were short takes like *What Happened on 23rd St., NYC* (the answer: The wind blew a woman's skirt over her head); *What Demoralized the Barber Shop* (the answer: A woman's skirt got snared on a foreign object and revealed some skin); and *The Pouting Water Model,* featuring a nude young woman with her back to the camera.

Around 1895, Alfred Clark, an early director, thought it might be a good idea to stage dramatic productions for film. His early short, *The Execution of Mary, Queen of Scots,* starred a male actor playing the lead role; just as the executioner's ax was set to fall on Mary's neck, Clark stopped the reel, substituted a dummy for his feature player, and resumed filming. The movie proved a sensational hit with audiences and inspired other attempts at plot-driven movies. The most ambitious of these projects was *The Passion Play,* a fifty-five-minute feature filmed in 1897 on a New York City rooftop. It was popular in theaters, but costly and difficult to produce. Another fifteen years would go by before motion picture directors revisited the idea of feature-length films.

Instead, early directors spent the next decade perfecting short, ten- or fifteen-minute movies. Edwin Porter, one of the industry's pioneers, raised the bar high with *The Great Train Robbery,* a pathbreaking production that used twenty separate shots, including close-ups, and several different indoor and outdoor sets. Audiences had never seen anything like it.

But nobody—not even Edwin Porter—appreciated the industry's potential for artistic growth more than David Wark Griffith. Born just ten years after Lee's surrender at Appomattox, Griffith— the son of a Kentucky planter who fought for the Confederacy— grew up as a displaced member of the old southern aristocracy. The emancipation of their slaves and the death of his father when David was just a boy left the family in a precarious financial situation. When David was fourteen years old, his mother was forced to sell the plantation and move to Louisville, where she operated a boardinghouse. It was a long way from the idyllic land of magnolias and mint juleps that David would later mythologize in his screen work.

Griffith spent his teenage years knocking around. He worked for a dry goods store and then a bookstore. He tried his hand at writing fiction and joined a traveling theater troupe that performed throughout the lower Midwest and California. He was going nowhere fast.

The dawn of the new century found Griffith in New York City, where he scratched out a living by selling short-story treatments to the Biograph Company—America's leading producer of motion pictures—and appearing in occasional film and stage productions. In 1908, the principals at Biograph decided to give Griffith a shot at directing a short feature, *The Adventures of Dollie.* It wasn't his most memorable work, but it did the trick. Within a few months, they offered him a contract to serve as Biograph's lead director.

Five months into his tenure at Biograph, he wrote and produced an experimental feature, *After Many Years,* adapted from Tennyson's *Enoch Arden*—the tale of a shipwrecked man who finds his way back to civilization, only to discover that his wife has remarried and his children have grown up and forgotten him.

The bigwigs at Biograph didn't know what to make of the film. Whereas other directors kept the camera at a respectable distance from the players, thus creating a sensation akin to that of attending a stage performance, Griffith moved it nearer the set so that his actors filled the entire frame. In some shots, he inched the camera so close to the action that the players appeared larger than the frame and were visible only from the waist up. Moviegoers could now study the actors' facial expressions.

Griffith also shot the same scenes from multiple perspectives and skipped back and forth between two complementary plotlines—the husband's ordeal on a desert island and his wife's perseverance back in civilization.

Not everyone was enthusiastic about these bold departures in film-making. "How can you tell a story jumping around like that?" one of the Biograph bosses asked him. "The people won't know what it's about!"

"Well," Griffith replied, "doesn't Dickens write that way?"

Though he didn't necessarily pioneer every new technique in the business—Edwin Porter had experimented with close-ups and multiple perspectives in his early work—Griffith soon acquired a reputation as the industry's most daring and innovative practitioner of the new art of cinematography. He placed cameras on rolling dollies so that he could follow his actors as they moved, thereby eliminating the vast, black space between the lens and the stage that occupied the bottom third of frames in other early productions. He merged short cuts from different perspectives to achieve a sense of action, motion, and complexity. In 1908, he even went so far as to use forty different shots in a single ten-minute film.

Almost single-handedly, he made the movies modern. His 1915 masterpiece, *The Birth of a Nation,* cost a record-breaking $60,000 to produce and ran over three hours. Filmgoers were enraptured by its intertwining plotlines, its colorful and detailed set designs, its intricate character development, and its dramatic historical reenactments. The climactic scene depicted hundreds of white Klansmen on horseback, galloping off to save white womanhood from the black rapists whose primitive fury was unleashed by emancipation and radical Reconstruction. It was bad history and suffused with the sort of Jim Crow mentality that pervaded American culture in those days. But because—not in spite—of that, the audiences loved it.

If he was the industry's leading trailblazer in those days, Griffith remained stubbornly backward in his social outlook. His films exalted the bygone world of the nineteenth century and scored the new urban-industrial order in which men found themselves wage slaves and women found their virtue compromised by the vice and corruption of the metropolis.

Lillian Gish, a popular actress who starred in many of Griffith's early masterpieces, believed the great director was fundamentally a solitary and forlorn figure who glorified Victorian femininity on-screen but was terrified of women in real life. His heroines weren't the "buxom, voluptuous form popular with the Oriental's mind," she observed with a tactlessness common to the time, but delicate, ghostly images who were the "very essence of virginity."

Lillian and her sister, Dorothy Gish, were exactly the kind of leading ladies whom Griffith favored. Growing up in the Midwest, they had attended convent schools. Lillian had even thought of becoming a nun. On the set, they were closely chaperoned by their mother. There was little chance they would try to circumvent the director's famously severe strictures against vice and intemperance.

So as to avoid even the "taint of scandal," Griffith forbade his women players to entertain men in their dressing rooms. They faced dismissal if they developed blemishes on their skin, as such imperfections, Griffith claimed, were surely a mark of a debauched character. And they were subjected to endless sermons on the virtues of clean living, for "women aren't meant for promiscuity," he explained. "If you're going to be promiscuous, you will end up with some disease."

So insistent was he on maintaining stringent standards of feminine virtue that Griffith forbade his on-screen characters to kiss. They could only embrace.

Though he used African American actors to play the parts of slaves in *The Birth of a Nation,* when the script called for black characters to assault white women, the director used white actors in blackface. It simply wouldn't do to have black men touching white women. Not in a D. W. Griffith production, anyway.

Griffith placed his leading ladies in front of white sheets, which reflected back the powerful glow of strobe lights and created a kind of "hazy photography" that served, in his mind, as "a great beauty doctor." The frail, angelic women who received this treatment personified the director's larger moral scheme. The movies were America's new, national pulpit, and Griffith eagerly ascended that pulpit to preach the nineteenth-century virtues of self-ownership, independence, reticence, sacrifice, and asceticism.

"It was all nonsense about youth going away from the old morals," he maintained. "Never since the beginning of time have there been so many girls and boys who were clean, so young, their minds are beautiful, they are sweet. Why? To win the dearest thing in the world, love from mankind. That is the motive that separates out civilization from dirty savages."

Griffith was well within the currents of the early motion picture industry. Most first-generation filmmakers were Protestant moralists who used the new medium to drive home the importance of virtue in an unvirtuous world. And this went double for women, whose intrinsic goodness was surely subject to a grave challenge from the forces of modernity.

Early movies like *The Fate of the Artist's Model* (1903), in which an innocent young lass is seduced into a sexual affair by a lecherous artist who then leaves her high and dry, and *The Downward Path* (1900), the story of a young country girl who is tricked by a depraved theater agent into becoming a soubrette and commits suicide before her parents can come to her rescue, continued to inform Griffith's style well into the late 1910s.

Writing a few years later, in 1925, the actress Linda Arvidson Griffith, Griffith's wife, acknowledged that this plotline was growing increasingly irrelevant in the years leading up to World War I. "We were dealing in things vital in our American life," she observed, "and [were] not one bit interested in close-ups of empty-headed little ingénues with adenoids, bedroom windows, manhandling of young girls, fast sets, perfumed bathrooms or nude youths heaving their muscles."

The problem was, by 1920 or so these were precisely the things that a lot of American moviegoers wanted to see. "D. W. Griffith is an idealist," observed Irving Thalberg, the production chief of MGM Studios in 1927, "and his love scenes on the screen were idealistic things of beauty . . . but his pictures are not stressed today because modern ideas are changing. The idealistic love of a decade ago is not true today. We cannot sit in a theater and see a noble hero and actually picture ourselves as him."

Thalberg had a point. The same social forces that were producing a revolution in morals and manners were rendering obsolete the didactic themes that informed Griffith's work.

Films produced between 1908 and 1912—those directed not just by D. W. Griffith, but by all the major production outfits—tended to follow set plotlines. Leading men and women turned inward to find strength and thereby prevailed over insidious threats to Victorian virtue—over alcohol, material indulgence, sexual urges, crime, passion. By 1913 or 1914, those themes began to give way to a glorification of pleasure, excitement, physical comedy, athleticism, and luxury—that is, to the consumer ethos that was coming by and by to dominate American culture. Moviegoers now reveled in the antics of Charlie Chaplin, "the little tramp," and the Keystone Kops, whose bumbling incompetence appealed to the lowest common denominator of popular humor.

The most popular film personages of the new era were Mary Pickford and Douglas Fairbanks, whose off-screen love affair—and, later, marriage—seemed to mirror perfectly the on-screen magic they produced in dozens of films. Doug was a man's man for the new age—athletic, handsome, dazzling, perfectly attired, and suave to a fault. Mary, on the other hand—"our Mary," "Little Mary"—was demure and childlike, yet carefree and full of life. She represented the altar of youth before which so many Americans were dropping to their knees. "We are our own sculptors," she advised her devotees. "Who can deny that passion and unkind thoughts show on the lines and expressions of our faces . . . young people seldom have these vices until they start getting old, so I love to be with them."

So compelling was her cinematic exaltation of youth and vivacity that the poet Vachel Lindsay composed an ode to Little Mary for *McClure's* magazine:

> *Oh Mary Pickford, Doll Divine,*
> *Like that special thing Botticelli*
> *Painted in the faces of his heavenly*
> *creatures. How you made our reverent*
> *passion rise, our fine desire you won.*
> *Oh, little girl, never grow up.*

In fact, Little Mary did grow up. When the big distributors began clamping down on talent—insisting on lower salaries and more artistic oversight—she and Fairbanks combined forces with D. W. Griffith and Charlie Chaplin to form a new company, United Artists, which arranged its own production deals and distributed its own films. Mary was a driving force behind the idea, and it made her one of the wealthiest women in America.

On-screen, though, she was still "Our Mary." And by the 1920s, the public craved something more. It would take a new breed of movie men to grasp that business was business.

"If the audience don't like a picture," Samuel Goldwyn insisted, "they have a good reason. The public is never wrong. I don't go for all this thing that when I have a failure, it is because the audience doesn't have the taste or education, or isn't sensitive enough. The public pays the money. It wants to be entertained. That's all I know."

If he wasn't the most articulate of wordsmiths, few could deny that Goldwyn had his finger on the pulse of the national film audience. He was a leading member of a small group of studio pioneers who were making the "movies"—a term that didn't come into popular use until the early twenties—a top-dollar entertainment industry. Over were the days of Victorian moralizing. In were the currents of change.

Clara Bow bids farewell to 1927.

22

THE KIND OF GIRL THE FELLOWS WANT

ECHNICALLY SPEAKING, Colleen Moore wasn't the first actress to portray the flapper on-screen. In 1920, a small production company released an unmemorable film entitled, simply, *The Flapper.* "In some sections you may have to define the title," one trade journal advised potential distributors, "though its meaning is pretty generally known by now."

The writer got it half-right and half-wrong. Even as D. W. Griffith was fighting a losing battle to wield film as a blunt cudgel in the fight against modern corruption, movie audiences in the decade before America's Jazz Age were growing accustomed to a new sort of female character—far more sexual, more wanton, and more dangerous than charming Mary Pickford or dear, sweet Lillian Gish.

There were several early varieties on the femme fatale, none of which could be properly termed "flapper." The "vamp," commonly associated with the actress Theda Bara, was an exotic, sexually charged creature who left behind a trail of ruined lives and craven men. By one expert assessment, Bara had "the wickedest face in the world, dark brooding, beautiful and heartless." Bara and others played this role expertly, and to wide acclaim, between 1914 and 1920.

In a world where female sexuality was increasingly discussed—but still feared and misapprehended—the vamp was a tantalizing yet sufficiently dark and distant figure for public consumption. There were fast women in the world, but they were still foreign and unusual creatures.

The vamp's days were numbered from the start. As moviegoers became more comfortable with overtly sexual women, they turned to a less menacing model—that of Cecil B. DeMille's crazy, debauched wife. In films like *Old Wives for New* (1918), *Don't Change Your Husband* (1919), *Male and Female* (1919), and *The Affairs of Anatol* (1921), De Mille fashioned a stock story line: Bored—and boring—housewife faces stiff competition from a faster, looser, younger woman (often her husband's secretary); husband leaves housewife (or considers leaving her); housewife dons makeup, hikes up skirt, and begins frequenting hot jazz clubs, often on the arm of a dark, mysterious sheik; husband falls in love with his wife again; marriage is saved.

Everyone—except perhaps the husband's secretary, who is left out in the cold—lives happily ever after. Little wonder that *Motion Picture* magazine hailed DeMille as "the apostle of domesticity." He was preaching a new gospel of personal freedom and sexual exploration, but within the bounds of matrimony.

In some respects, *The Flapper,* appearing in 1920, represented a bold new direction for the New Woman of the silver screen. The film was "no old, creaking vehicle for a star to ride in," announced *Moving Picture World,* and it turned its lead actress, Olive Thomas, into an overnight celebrity. Thomas played the part of Genevieve King, a typical middle-class girl who grows weary of life in tiny Orange Grove— a town that "didn't even have a saloon to close"—and persuades her parents to pack her off to boarding school in New York. Forsaking her wholesome boyfriend, Bill, Genevieve begins chasing after older men and falls in with a group of ne'er-do-well city slickers, including Richard Chenning, a handsome lech several years her senior, and a gang of jewel thieves who involve her in criminal mischief.

Genevieve, a good girl at heart, devises an elaborate plot to bring the crooks to justice. The film ends with the young protagonist safely back in Orange Grove, reunited with good old reliable Bill.

The film launched Olive Thomas's star, and it might easily have been Olive—and not Colleen Moore—who graced the cover of every fan magazine in the mid-1920s. But Olive was unlucky. On vacation with her husband in France, she mistook an unlabeled bottle of bichloride of mercury for common cold medicine. Maybe, as some of the papers suggested, she had trouble adjusting to fame and intended to kill herself. Either way, Olive Thomas was out of the picture. A few flapper films later, Colleen Moore was in.

With the release of *Flaming Youth* in 1923, the flapper became Hollywood's most lucrative character type, and Colleen Moore became the visual embodiment of the flapper.

Photoplay magazine offered a ringing endorsement of Colleen's flapper credentials, concluding that she "looks the part with her straight bobbed hair and her mischief-filled eyes. Once upon a time she wore curls—and a demure expression." But no longer. A writer in Muskegon, Michigan, went so far as to assert that Colleen was "the very apotheosis of the cult of unhampered youthful self-expression."

In her subsequent flapper movies—*Painted People* (1924), *The Perfect Flapper* (1924), *Flirting with Love* (1924), *We Moderns* (1925), *Ella Cinders* (1926), *Naughty but Nice* (1927)—Colleen played essentially the same role.

"Colleen Moore is a brilliant young flapper who contrives to disguise her flapperish appeal with the sweetness of the eternal maiden," a New Orleans newspaper observed. "If she is pert and naughty she makes you feel that your grandmother was, too. So all is forgiven. God forbid we hold anything against grandma! A very tricky young lady, Colleen, with a very wise bean, too."

Colleen's effectiveness as a flapper icon lay in her apparent willingness to bend the rules but never break them. She was the safe flapper—stylish, vivacious, full of verve and pluck, yet ultimately inclined to abandon life in the fast lane for more wholesome living. It was a winning combination: Young viewers loved Colleen for her modern sensibilities, and their parents loved Colleen for her fundamental decency. It was a balance she worked as hard to strike off-screen as on-screen.

"What kind of girl does a girl have to be," asked a Hollywood fan magazine, "—to be the kind of girl the fellows want? The girl of today has this problem to face, says Colleen Moore." Colleen explained that "a girl should not be too gaily dressed," but on the other hand, "she should not dress too plainly as a bit of tinsel is attractive; and she should remember that men want her to play but not to get soiled." Ultimately, Colleen maintained, "the golden glitter of tinsel is fine . . . but not acceptable in a wife."

If she was a conservative model for a flapper, Colleen was a talented performer nevertheless. She was an expert comedian, able to act with her whole body and to move her eyes and face in perfect synch with a part. In *Ella Cinders*—a clever nod to Cinderella—she played the part of a beleaguered modern-day stepdaughter who scrapes together money for professional photographs, wins a magazine contest, and travels to Hollywood to become a film star. Her comic timing and adorable antics struck a resonant chord among moviegoers—men and women alike.

Much of Colleen's commercial appeal clearly lay in the public's knowledge that she was happily married to John McCormick, a former publicist and now producer for First National, whom she wed shortly before filming *Flaming Youth*. If Colleen Moore, the archetype of flapperdom, could embrace the domestic ideal, then surely it was acceptable, if not wise, for American parents to allow their daughters a little harmless experimentation with bobbed hair and jazz. And maybe even liquor. Being a flapper didn't necessarily entail a blanket renunciation of marriage and motherhood. It was just a phase in every girl's life. A harmless, necessary, cathartic phase.

In press interviews, Colleen drove home precisely this point. "It's such fun asking my husband for money," she admitted with delight, "—not a bit like the funny papers say! And I just love it, too. And I'm just dying to bake a cake for John. John will eat it. He is brave and he loves me. I didn't know there was a domestic bone in my body, but all of a sudden I get such a thrill out of ordering milk and paying the butcher's bill! I always have breakfast with John—always fix his coffee for him. Do you think I'd let anybody else do that? I should say not. He takes one lump with cream. I'm trying to be a model housewife. . . ."

None of this was true. Colleen usually spent eighteen hours a day on the set and took most of her meals, including breakfast, at a bungalow on the studio lot. The mansion she shared with John McCormick was well staffed by an army of cooks and servants. She probably didn't even know where to find the coffee in her own kitchen.

No matter. For millions of young women torn between the romantic ideal of heterosexual love and marriage and Jazz Age glitz, Colleen held out hope that one could have her cake and eat it, too.

But hers wasn't the last word on the subject. By 1925, the other studios were eager to cash in on the flapper. They turned to Clara Bow, whose on-screen portrayal of the flapper was as different from Colleen Moore's as were her origins and upbringing. "Nobody wanted me t'be born in the first place," she once claimed. Sadly, it was probably an accurate assessment.

Clara entered the world in 1905 in a tenement slum on Sands Street in Brooklyn, a neighborhood strewn with garbage, rats, prostitutes, pawnshops, cheap saloons, and dangerous characters. Her parents, Robert and Sarah Bow, were a mismatch from the start. Robert was an alcoholic with an addiction to street prostitutes; Sarah was an emotionally unstable teenager who married to escape her even drearier childhood home. When their first child died two days after birth, Sarah threw her body into a trash bin outside the family's cheap railroad flat. A second baby also died in infancy. Sarah handed her over to the public health authorities for an anonymous burial.

Later in life, Clara was tight-lipped about her childhood in Brooklyn. "I have known hunger, believe me," she once admitted. "We just lived, and that's about all."

Life would have been hard enough if young Clara had only had to contend with her profoundly dysfunctional parents. But nothing else seemed to go right. For one thing, she stuttered. "H-h-h-ello, Clara," the other kids at P.S. 111 would greet her in scornful imitation. They mocked her ragged clothing and ridiculed her family. "I was the worst-lookin' kid on the street," she once acknowledged. Virtually alone in life, Clara learned how to protect herself against the roving street gangs that did unspeakable violence to neighborhood residents. "My right was famous," she boasted years later. "I could lick any boy my size."

She did have one friend—a local boy named Johnny who lived in the downstairs apartment. But even that friendship was too good to be true. One day, Clara heard a hair-raising cry from Johnny's flat. She ran downstairs to find the young boy engulfed in flames. There had been a kitchen fire. Clara smothered Johnny in a blanket and cradled him as he wailed out her name. He died in her arms.

School didn't offer much in the way of solace. Clara's education ended in seventh grade, and even that was a stretch. "I never opened a book and the teachers were always down on me," she confessed with typical self-doubt and deprecation. "I don't blame 'em."

Just getting up in the morning caused her heartache. Going to school was misery. The other kids were merciless. "They was always hurtin' my feelings, and I thought they was silly anyway. I never had no use for girls and their games." The only consolation she had in life came at the price of a nickel admission. "In this lonely time, when I wasn't much of nothin' and I didn't have nobody," she explained, there was "one place I could go and forget the misery of home and the heartache of school.

"That was the motion pictures."

Every spare nickel Clara could get her hands on, she fed right into the local movie theaters. "We'd go to the Carlton or the Bunny Theater," remembered John Bennett, one of her few friends from the neighborhood, "and see whatever was showing. I was the only one who would listen to her little tales of fantasy, her dreams." One day, as they sat out on the front stoop of her building, Clara "told me that she was going to be a great movie star. Of course, I didn't believe it."

Bennett would live to eat his words. In a sequence of events that could easily have been ripped from a Hollywood script (say, for instance, *Ella Cinders*), in 1921, at age sixteen, Clara entered a Fame and Fortune contest sponsored by *Motion Picture* magazine. Dressed in the only outfit she owned—"a little plaid dress, a sweater, and a red tam"—she dragged her father to a local photography studio at Coney Island and somehow persuaded him to pay a dollar for two cheaply produced snapshots. Clara thought the results were "terrible," but she hopped the subway to the offices of Brewster Publications, which owned *Motion Picture,* and submitted her application personally.

"Called in person—" the contest manager scrawled beneath her paperwork. "Very pretty."

Much to Clara's surprise, she made the final cut and was invited for a mock screen test. The other girls laughed at her worn clothes. How could someone win a Fame and Fortune contest with holes in her shoes? "I hadn't thoughta that angle," she acknowledged later. "I'd only looked at my face, and that was disappointin' enough."

The girls lined up for the screen test. They were to walk before the camera, pick up a telephone, fake a casual conversation, and then suddenly appear deeply concerned by the voice on the other line. While the other finalists scratched and clawed at one another for the privilege of performing first, Clara stood back.

"I sat through every one of those tests," she remembered, "watchin' everythin' that was done, everythin' they was told, every mistake they made. The trouble was, I thought, that they was all tryin' t'do it like somebody they'd seen on screen, not the way they'd do it themselves. When it came my turn, I did it the way I'd do it myself." Three days later, Clara received a call from Brewster Publications. She had won.

It was tough going at first. The contest carried a small role in a feature-length film, *Beyond the Rainbow*. Humiliatingly, it was only after she dragged several neighborhood girls to the local theater to see the film that she learned her part had been cut. But she was tenacious.

"I wore myself out goin' from studio t'studio, from agency t'agency," she told an interviewer years later. "But there was always somethin'. I was too young, too little, or too fat. Usually I was too fat."

Luck was bound to strike sooner or later, and it did. Though she had been cut from the final print, Clara's role in *Beyond the Rainbow* caught the attention of another director, who cast her in a film called *Down to the Sea in Ships*. That role, in turn, won her a part in *Grit*, a low-budget film produced by a motley group of Ivy League alumni and written by their friend F. Scott Fitzgerald. Both of these movies brought her to the attention of a producer named Jack Bachman, who persuaded his West Coast partner, B. P. (Ben) Schulberg, a former producer at Paramount who had formed his own outfit, Preferred

Pictures, to pay Clara's way out to California. She would start with a three-month trial contract at $50 per week. The year was 1923.

It didn't take long for Clara's career to take off. Her first several films caught the eye of executives at other studios, who began paying Schulberg for Bow's services. Under a system then common in Hollywood, she continued to earn $50 per week—soon raised to $200—while Preferred Pictures, her contractual employer, raked in several times that amount for loaning her out. This was the case in 1924, when First National retained Bow for a new flapper feature, *Painted People,* starring Colleen Moore.

Three weeks into production, Colleen and Clara began shooting a scene together. When the director, Clarence Badger, ordered some close-up shots of Clara, Moore objected sharply. "You don't need that close-up," she told him. Badger acquiesced. What else could he do? Colleen Moore was the star of the film and the toast of Hollywood. Her husband, John McCormick, was the film's producer and, by extension, Badger's boss.

Clara might not have been articulate, but she was street smart. She understood the dynamics at play. "You're a big star," she pleaded with Colleen. "Ya don't need close-ups like I do. Every close-up I get helps me. Why d'ya haveta stop 'em?" The answer was self-evident.

Miscast in a Victorian role, contemptuous of Colleen Moore, and generally desperate to extricate herself from the picture, Clara went to a doctor and asked him to perform sinus surgery that she had been putting off since her arrival in California. *"Now.* I want the operation *right now,"* she demanded. When she showed up on the set the next week in bandages, it was clear she would have to be replaced and all the scenes involving her reshot with a new actress.

Painted People went over time and over budget. And the last laugh was on Colleen Moore. "She made that bitch pay," recalled Artie Jacobson, Clara's then boyfriend, with a smile. It was the only time that Moore and Bow would work together.

Years later, Colleen condescendingly sized up her rival as an unsophisticated dimwit. "The only time I ever met Clara socially was at a party given by Adela Rogers St. Johns in her English country house at Whittier, California," she wrote. "The conversation was a fairly intellectual one, and Clara finally became bored, I guess, and decided the time had come to liven up the party. She livened it up considerably. She stood up and, after getting everyone's attention, proceeded to tell the dirtiest story imaginable, with such perfect pantomime that nothing was left to the imagination. I was as shocked as everybody else, but I had to laugh inside, she did such a first-rate job."

In fairness to Moore, Clara was, in fact, known for her off-color stories and her off-color lifestyle. In just four years—from 1925 to 1929—she burned through five fiancés, including Victor Fleming, who later directed *The Wizard of Oz* and *Gone With the Wind;* had affairs with a number of other men, including stuntman-turned-leading man Gary Cooper; and frequently boasted to friends—in the most indelicate language she could muster—of Cooper's physical attributes and sexual prowess.

Where Colleen Moore bought a mansion, Clara purchased a modest seven-room Spanish bungalow made of stucco for $15,000. She filled one room with dirt, so her dog would have somewhere to play at night. Her accent was working-class Brooklyn, and she made no apologies for it. Her grammar was terrible, and she made no apologies for it. In effect, she made no apologies for who she was.

But in her own way, Clara was a class act. In an industry teeming with prima donnas, she showed up to the set on time, worked well with the directors, and never hogged the camera. "She could cry at the drop of a hat," remembered Billy Kaplan, a prop man on the Preferred Pictures set, "and you'd *believe* her. A beautiful actress, just beautiful. And I often wondered to myself, 'Where did this young girl get all this knowledge, this understanding, this *feeling*?' "

Kaplan remembered that the entire crew had a crush on Clara. "We *all* loved her," he said, smiling. "The electricians, the grips, the painters . . . everyone loved Clara." She was one of them—working-class, unpretentious, without airs. "Clara was always a good guy on the set," Kaplan concluded. "Very professional, always on time."

She was also kind—a rarity in Hollywood, even in those early days—and particularly with Budd Schulberg, Ben Schulberg's shy thirteen-year-old son.

"Golly, Mr. Schulberg," she asked with a smile, "is this your little junior? Gee, he's cute as a button." Clara ran her hands through Budd's hair and teased, "How wouldja like ta drive up to Arrowhead this weekend, Buddy? Just the two of us."

"Now, Clara," replied Ben, "he's just a little boy."

"Okay, maybe we'll hafta wait a couple of years," she answered.

When Ben ushered his son out of the office, Clara gave him a big wave. "See ya, Buddy boy. C'mon 'n' see me on the set. Sincerely I'm very glad to've meetin' yuz."

Buddy would have occasion to take her up on the offer. He was on location at Pomona College when Clara filmed *It,* the movie that would immortalize her. With the entire cast and crew watching, Clara ran over to young Buddy, gave him a kiss on the cheek, and informed everyone present that he was her "secret boyfriend," her "steady fella." In between takes, Buddy sat with Clara in her brand-new red Kissel roadster—one of Clara's rare indulgences—and discovered they had something in common: Buddy had a terrible stammer. Over the next few weeks, while the young boy idled the time away on the set, waiting for his famous father to wrap up each day's business, Clara made a point of sidling up to him in the roadster, shoulder to shoulder, asking him how he was enjoying school—which, of course, he wasn't; the other kids were teasing him mercilessly—and sharing stories about her own unhappy childhood. She fed him sticks of gum and assured him that his father was "awful proud of ya. He's even showed me some of ya poetry. . . .

"Someday you'll grow up and be a big producer becuz of all the things he's teaching ya," she promised. "I know yuh gonna make me awful proud of ya, too." This was pure Clara Bow—more content to idle the time away with an unhappy thirteen-year-old than to flaunt her own importance. On some level, it was a defense mechanism.

"She was peppy and vivacious in front of people," one of her colleagues remembered, "but when you talked to her one on one, she was serious and sad."

"I liked her," recalled another actress, "but I didn't get to know her well. Nobody did. She was away from the crowd, a loner. . . . Clara was an awfully sweet girl, but a very *lonesome* sweet girl."

Budd Schulberg, who went on to become a screenwriter, seems to have gotten over his acute sensitivity. Years later, he callously misinterpreted Clara's kindness as a sexual overture and summed up his "secret girlfriend" as "an easy winner of the Dumbbell Award. . . . She was simply an adorable, in fact irresistible, little know-nothing. It was as if Father had picked out a well-made collie puppy and trained her to become Lassie."

Budd was clearly a quick study in the family business. His father, Ben Schulberg, and his uncle, Sam Jaffe, treated actresses like sex toys and seem to have compelled Clara into relationships that she could scarcely afford to decline in those early days. "She was scared of all the people in the business," an unrepentant Jaffe maintained years later, "but she trusted me. She was in love with me and wanted to marry me, but I couldn't think of marrying her. She came from *Brooklyn*. She looked cheap. Men wanted to screw her."

It was easy to dismiss Clara as a déclassé kid from Brooklyn, but what Colleen Moore, Budd Schulberg, and Sam Jaffe didn't understand was that Clara was a pro. She fashioned a new flapper image that was more dangerous and overtly sexual than Moore's winsome Irish flapper, and in so doing, she became a viable alternative for many young girls searching out a slightly more risqué standard-bearer than Colleen Moore.

In *The Plastic Age* (1925) Clara played Cynthia Day, a fast-living coed who catches the eye of a clean-living scholar-athlete, Hugh Carver, and leads him down a dim path away from books and football practice and toward an alluring nightlife involving lots of cocktails and lots of heavy petting. Chastised by his parents, who expect more of their son, the young hero steels himself for a slow march back to gridiron glory. But not without help. In a selfless gesture that few viewers would expect from a femme fatale, Clara's character, billed as "the hottest jazz baby in film," withdraws herself from the equation. For Hugh's own good—realizing that he will never crack the books or commit himself to football as long as she's around—Cynthia breaks off the relationship.

In the final scene, Hugh achieves lasting glory at the "big game," and the two protagonists are reunited. It was the role that made Clara Bow famous. "She has eyes that would drag any youngster away from his books," crowed one reviewer.

While on the set in 1927, Clara astonished Clarence Badger, who was directing her in a new film, with her astute grasp of audience dynamics. "Following my directions," he later explained, "Clara gazed at [her male counterpart] with an expression of lingering, calflike longing in her pretty face: perfectly all right if she had stopped there. But she did not. Continuing on, the camera still grinding away, her doll-like tantalizing eyes suddenly became inflamed with unwholesome passion. Then the rascal suddenly changed her expression again, this time to one of virtuous, innocent appeal."

It had been a long day, and Badger was on edge. "Cut!" he cried out, and demanded to know why Clara had taken it upon herself to direct the scene. "Well, Santa," she replied with a smile, using her pet nickname for the normally even-keeled, cheerful director, "if ya knew your onions like ya was supposedta, you'd know the first look was for the lovesick dames in the audience, and the second look, that passionate stuff, was for the boys an' their poppas, and the *third* look . . . well, just about the time all them old ladies're shocked an' scandalized by the passionate part, they suddenly see that third look, change their minds 'bout me havin' naughty ideas, and go home thinkin' how pure an' innocent I was. An' havin' got me mixed up with this girl I'm playin', they'll come again when my next picture shows up."

Badger had to admit that the logic was impeccable. If he had any lingering doubts, the box office returns would have set his mind at ease. Clara's next film, *It,* based on a best-selling novel by Elinor Glyn, turned her into the uncontested flapper queen of Hollywood. Bigger than Colleen Moore. Bigger than Joan Crawford. Bigger than them all.

In *It,* Clara played Betty Lou Spence, a lovesick lingerie salesgirl who falls for the wealthy son of the department store owner. "Sweet Santa Claus," she declares, "give me *him!*" The complex plotline runs the same course as Bow's other films. Her character is naughty but nice—sexy but sweet—red hot but redeemable. In the end, Betty

Lou gets her man, and Clara Bow became the first "It Girl"—a sobriquet Glyn came up with to describe a woman with that elusive sex appeal all women (supposedly) want but few (supposedly) have.

"It, hell," quipped Dorothy Parker. "She had *Those*."

Though Clara Bow never raked in the kind of salary that Colleen Moore made—in part because she was indifferent to the sort of Hollywood politics that Moore and McCormick excelled at—in the aftermath of *It* she hired an attorney. Together, they went to the mat with Paramount—Clara's new studio, now that Ben Schulberg and Adolph Zukor, Paramount's founder, had made amends and merged their operations.

Her new contract called for a salary of $5,000 per week, a limit of four films per year, a no-loan-out clause to prevent Schulberg from exploiting her talent, a $25,000 cash advance, and a $10,000 bonus for each film she completed. Unlike most contracts, Clara's did not contain a decency clause. She could not be summarily fired for landing on the front pages in some sordid sex scandal. Bow's only concession was that her bonus money would be held in escrow until 1931. Payment would be contingent on her satisfying the general decency code.

At the time, it seemed like a good deal.

Louise Brooks, "the girl in the black helmet," as she appeared in the mid-1920s.

23

ANOTHER PETULANT WAY
TO PASS THE TIME

HOUGH LATER IN LIFE she would prove exasperatingly coy on the subject of sex, in her prime, Louise Brooks showed little compunction about telling it like it was. "I like to drink and fuck," she announced to friends and acquaintances on more than one occasion. In a rare, candid moment, Brooks estimated privately that "at a modest 10 a year from [age] 17 to [age] 60," the number of men she had "been to bed with" numbered somewhere around 430.

When in the late 1920s her younger brother mistook one of her dispatches from Berlin (where she was shooting a film) as an indictment of the loose principles that governed Weimar Germany, Louise chastised him sharply. "You are either a fool or a liar to say I would comment on the low state of anyone's morals," she shot back, "—mine being non-existent."

If Colleen Moore was Hollywood's archetype of the safe flapper— unthreatening, endearing, hapless, more bark than bite—and if Clara Bow represented the naughty flapper who flirted and smoked a lot but could always be counted on to see the error of her fast-living ways, Louise Brooks was the real deal.

Ironically, of the three great flapper actresses who graced the silver screen in the 1920s, Brooks arrived in Hollywood last and exited first. Long before Colleen Moore and Clara Bow adopted the flapper mystique as their own, and long after both women abandoned that image for different kinds of roles, Brooks—with her distinctive jet black bob, piercing gaze, and lithe dancer's body—lived the life of the New Woman in ways that made Zelda Fitzgerald seem like a conservative schoolmarm.

Brooks was born in the small town of Cherryvale, Kansas, in 1906. Her father, Leonard, was an attorney for a local oil and gas company, and her mother, Myra, was a vain but uncommonly bright autodidact whose dual regrets in life were that she lived in Kansas rather than Chicago or New York and that she bore her husband four children whose needs and wants distracted her from more rarefied pursuits.

To her parents' great credit, Louise grew up surrounded by books, music, art, and ideas. Years later, she remembered their house in Wichita, where her family moved in 1919, as a "fourteen-room gray frame structure [that was] literally falling down with books. The foundation on the right side had sunk eleven inches from the weight of the lawbooks in Father's third-floor retreat. There were new books in the bedrooms, old books in the basement, and unread books in the living room."

As a child, Louise reveled in exploring the overstuffed shelves in the family's library. She pulled down volumes at random—Dickens, Thackeray, Tennyson, Darwin, Emerson, Hawthorne, Twain. "All these books I read with delight, not caring in the least that I understood little of what I read," she admitted. When she was five years old, Louise began learning to sound out words by following along as her mother read to her from *A Child's Garden of Verses* and *Alice's Adventures in Wonderland*. She never stopped reading. In the mid-1920s, when she was a feature chorus girl in *Ziegfeld Follies,* Louise passed the time in the communal dressing room devouring works like Aldous Huxley's *Crome Yellow.* "The other girls were reading the *Police Gazette,*" she sneered. "They would look at me and say, 'Who is this Kansas bitch? How dare she?' "

It didn't make her any more popular on Hollywood movie sets in the late twenties when she passed the time between takes with a dog-eared volume of Schopenhauer.

Intellectual pursuits aside, Louise's childhood appeared conventional enough. Like so many other girls coming of age in the early twenties, she was boy crazy. Her diary for 1921, when she was just fourteen years old, chronicled in considerable detail one ill-fated romance after another.

> May 7: Marene and I have some affair. We were together all evening, and he brought me home in Dinman's car. We rode around for *quite* a while, and oh, boy! . . . Well, I'm crazy about Marene, and I surely have him going. I suppose I'll be lovesick for a few days.

> June 14: Meridith and I are still devoted. We went down to see the river several times.

> June 22: Sally Lahey is crazy about Meridith, and she said not a few catty things to me. There was a boy who was hanging about me incessantly. Mercy! Don't boys love con-man stuff. I have let M. knock me around enough to ruin anyone. They love to lord it over us, and I pretend to be so weak.

> June 23: Honestly—I must be boy struck, I mope around all day now and take no interest in the things that used to be so nice. . . . I have been swimming a great deal lately with Campbells and Meridith. We have lots of fun. Robert is awfully rough. He throws me around considerably, but you know what women love. . . .

> June 30: I have a new one on the string—Everett Fox. I know I have him jolly well.

> A week later: Charles Corbett . . . kissed me five times—the villain—and some of the other boys tried it.

What Louise didn't confide to her diary, her parents, or her friends was that when she was nine years old, a local handyman, Mr. Flowers, lured her into his house with the promise of freshly made popcorn and sexually assaulted her. When she was fourteen, her

Sunday school teacher, a prosperous businessman named Mr. Vincent, seduced her into posing for provocative photographs and, a short while later, a sexual affair.

Quite possibly, these early crimes had something to do with her propensity to detach sex from emotion. "Love is a publicity stunt," she later mused, "and making love—after the first curious raptures— is only another petulant way to pass the time waiting for the studios to call." One got the sense that Louise Brooks liked sex, but only when it was divorced from other ways of feeling.

If she wasn't necessarily paying close attention to her daughter's well-being—once, when young Louise plaintively admitted to breaking a piece of her mother's prized Haviland china, Myra replied dismissively, "Now, dear, don't bother me when I am memorizing Bach"—Myra Brooks compensated for her lack of warmth by introducing her daughter to a world that extended far beyond the limits of rural Kansas.

While most of her classmates didn't even know what or who Condé Nast was, Louise was a subscriber—courtesy of her parents— to *Vanity Fair* and *Harper's Bazaar*. She accompanied her mother to orchestral and dance recitals, took several years of intense ballet training, and knew more about important currents in the performing arts than most New Yorkers, let alone Kansans. In particular, Myra and Louise were both admirers of the new modern dance methods then being pioneered by the disciplines of Isadora Duncan.

A week before Thanksgiving in 1921—only three days after Louise's fifteenth birthday—Wichita's Crawford Theater hosted a rare heartland performance by Denishawn, a prominent modern dance company headquartered in New York and directed by the trail-blazing husband-and-wife team of Ted Shawn and Ruth St. Denis. Dancing with the troupe that evening were Martha Graham and Charles Weidman, two figures who would leave a permanent imprimatur on American choreography.

Myra and Louise were in the audience that night, and they were spellbound. They knew a little something about modern dance, but they had never seen the likes of Denishawn. Among the twenty-three arrangements the company performed were "Revolutionary Etude," an early nod to proletarian art featuring Martha Graham and set to a stirring piece by Chopin, and "Xochitl," based on Aztec themes and set against a rich backdrop of costumes and set designs by the Mexican artist Francisco Cornejo.

Because they were well-known in local cultural circles, mother and daughter were invited backstage after the performance to meet Ted Shawn. Louise must have struck Shawn as uncommonly enthusiastic, lithe, or seductive—or perhaps just persistent. By the evening's end, he had offered her a place at Denishawn's summer school in New York—a feeder to the company's professional ranks. Louise accepted on the spot, and though it took some convincing, Myra was able to talk her husband into covering the $300 tuition and letting his fifteen-year-old daughter venture on her own to the wilds of Manhattan.

Almost on her own, that is. Leonard Brooks stipulated that his daughter be chaperoned by Alice Mills, a middle-aged neighbor whom Louise described as "a stocky, bespectacled housewife." As luck would have it, Louise and Mrs. Mills got along just fine. Louise "tolerated Mrs. Mills' provincialism" because they shared a "love of the theatre. Together, we saw all of the Broadway shows, one of them being a favorite of mine—the *Ziegfeld Follies*. In the first act, Fanny Brice's burlesque of Pavlova's swan dance filled the New Amsterdam Theatre with laughter."

That summer, Louise and Mrs. Mills shared a small railroad flat on West Eighty-sixth Street near Riverside Drive, just thirty blocks south of Columbia University. For four hours each day, Louise and the other protégés sweated through grueling lessons in balance work and body control in a sweltering church basement at Broadway and Seventy-second Street. "Even in the ballet work, we danced barefoot," Louise remembered, "which was painful for unaccustomed feet on the splintering pine floor. Having gone barefoot through Kansas summers, I was spared the torn soles and blisters that tormented some of the pupils."

Of all the summer students, Louise stood out—so much so that in August, Ted Shawn invited her to join the company and tour full-time with the other dancers. It was an offer she couldn't refuse. Louise was smitten by New York, and it didn't take long before she realized that returning to Wichita was not an option. She never went back to school, and except for a few years in the early 1950s, she never again lived in Kansas.

So began Louise's stab at the great American art of self-reinvention. It was one thing to take the country girl out of the country. Could she also take the country out of the country girl? With Mrs. Mills back in Wichita, Louise had a chance to find out.

"In 1922," she later wrote, "if I was to create my dream women, I had to get rid of my Kansas accent, to learn the etiquette of the social elite, and to learn to dress beautifully. I could not correct my speech at a fashionable girls' school. I could not learn table manners from escorts embarrassed by my social inferiority. I could not afford Fifth Avenue couturiers. Therefore, I went for my education directly to the unknown people at the bottom who were experts in such matters—the people at the bottom whose services supported the people at the top of New York."

For elocution lessons, Louise turned to a working-class undergrad at Columbia University who was financing his college education by moonlighting as a soda jerk at a Broadway drugstore. Addicted to fudge sundaes, Louise was a regular at the counter and just barely tolerated the young man's uncanny aptitude for mimicking her flat midwestern accent.

"One day when the soda jerk was making the customers at the fountain laugh with a story about 'mulking a kee-yow,' I stopped him, saying, 'Instead of making fun of me, why don't you teach me how to say it?' While he was concocting a banana split, he began to smile at the fancy of becoming my Pygmalion."

What the soda jerk lacked in charm—"Not 'watter' as in 'hotter,'" he snapped, "but 'water' as in 'daughter.' And it's not 'hep,' you hayseed—it's 'help,' 'help,' 'help!'"—he made up for in precision. A few weeks and not a few fudge sundaes later, Louise graduated from the drugstore academy pronouncing her words like a real northeasterner.

The soda jerk on Broadway wasn't much help when it came to clothing and comportment, but Louise was a quick study. Through one of her friends, Barbara Bennett, the scion of a prominent stage family, Louise met a wide assortment of bankers and lawyers "who made it possible for me to buy expensive clothes. These most eligible bachelors in their thirties, finding debutantes a threat, turned to pretty girls in the theatre." She would later describe the delicate game of give-and-take by which "the extravagant sums given to the girls for clothes were part of the fun—part of competing to see whose girl would win the Best-Dressed title. Sexual submission was not a condition of this arrangement, although many affairs grew out of it."

When her wealthy escorts weren't looking, Louise consulted the waiters at Manhattan's best restaurants—the same watering holes that Lipstick gossiped about in the pages of *The New Yorker*—for tips on what to order and how to order it. Her syllabus at the Colony included "how-to-bone-a-brook-trout night, how-to-fork-snails night, how-to-dismember-artichokes night, and so on, until we came to the bottom of the menu, which included a dessert [requiring] the understanding and proper pronunciation of French words."

It was easy enough for Louise to keep her romantic and sexual exploits from the Denishawn dancers when the company was rehearsing in New York. But when they were on the road, her loose lifestyle led her to clash with Ruth St. Denis, the famously stern matron of the company, who closely guarded her dancers' morals.

Louise was a skilled performer and an important member of the troupe. She enjoyed billings with Martha Graham. But "she was very flirty in the hotels," another Denishawn dancer recalled, "and it was quite easy for men to have a conversation with her. . . . Somebody did say one time that she stayed with somebody one night. We were so excited about that we didn't know what to do!"

Matters came to a head late in the spring of 1924, two years after Louise joined Denishawn. Rumors of Louise's extracurricular activities—not to mention her strong resistance to authority, which manifested itself increasingly during rehearsals—were causing a disruption among the other dancers. With the full company assembled, St. Denis dealt her a crushing, public blow. "Louise," St. Denis began, as everyone else looked on, "to be brief and to the point—not to keep you from your more pressing concerns—I am dismissing you from the company because you want life handed to you on a silver salver."

Louise didn't even know what a salver was. She had to ask Barbara Bennett. "At 17," she wrote years later, "my first and blackest humiliation—and in public too."

Things got worse. Shortly after her unexpected departure from Denishawn, Louise moved into a suite at the Algonquin Hotel. How she paid for it, she never explained. From a corner perch in the Rose Room, she observed "Robert Sherwood and Dorothy Parker and a lot of other people jabbering away and waving their hands at the Round Table, wondering what made them so famous."

But Louise's reputation quickly caught up with her. Before long, Frank Case, the owner-manager, cornered her as she walked out of the elevator.

"How old are you, Miss Brooks?" he asked.

"Seventeen," Louise replied.

"Are you sure you aren't fourteen?"

"Yes."

"Does your family know you are here?"

"Yes."

"Well, George Cohan"—George M. Cohan, the Broadway musical composer—"just phoned me to tell me last night that he came down the elevator with a fourteen-year-old black-haired girl in a little pink dress. Where were you going at two-o'clock in the morning?"

It didn't help matters when Louise admitted she had been on her way to Texas Guinan's El Fay Club. Case didn't need any trouble in his hotel. He arranged for Louise to move into the Martha Washington, "a respectable women's hotel on East Twenty-ninth Street."

Louise rebounded. She was an exceptional dancer, and she knew a lot of famous and influential New Yorkers. Late fall found her appearing in *George White's Scandals,* the great rival act to the *Ziegfeld Follies* and the very same show that saw a hopelessly inebriated Scott Fitzgerald strip off his clothes along with the professional performers back in 1920 or 1921.

Less stuffy and a little more risqué than the *Follies*—in many numbers, the dancers appeared almost completely nude—the *Scandals* was quick to incorporate into its acts the latest dance crazes sweeping black Harlem and white collegiate America. And Louise excelled like no other dancer at the Charleston, a Harlem import that dominated the Broadway stage in 1923 and 1924.

Restless as always, Louise quit the *Scandals* in 1924, spent a few weeks in London, where she danced in local cabaret performances, and returned, dead broke, to New York, where Florenz Ziegfeld was happy to hire her for the 1925 run of his *Follies*.

Life was pretty good as a *Follies* girl. The pay wasn't bad—normally between $250 and $300 per week (Louise would have been on the higher end of the scale), equivalent to an annual salary of about $150,000 in today's money. There were also plenty of ways to line one's pockets with still more money. "There was a hand-picked group of beautiful girls who were invited to parties given for great men in finance and government," she later explained to a correspondent. "We had to be fairly well bred and of absolute integrity—never endangering the great men with threats of publicity or blackmail. At these parties we were not required, like common whores, to go to bed with any man who asked us, but if we did the profits were great. Money, jewels, mink coats, a film job—name it."

It was an extraordinary lifestyle, quite unlike that led by most American women. Or was it? Though Louise Brooks dined at the best restaurants, wore the best clothes, went to the best shows, and associated with the best people, the delicate art she practiced every day—the unspoken exchange of sex and romance for material satisfaction and financial security—was being lived out on a lesser scale by millions of underpaid shopgirls, garment workers, and office secretaries whose every date to Coney Island or to the movie theater was fraught with subtext and negotiation.

Yet unlike those other women, Louise Brooks was plunged deep into the excess and affluence of the fabled 1920s. By mid-1925, she was newly installed in a plush apartment-hotel at 270 Park Avenue and was a regular at Texas Guinan's nightclubs, where adoring fans beseeched her to take the stage and dance the Charleston.

That same year, she entered into a summer affair with Charlie

Chaplin—arguably the most famous Hollywood figure of his time and certainly one of the most famous personalities of the age—who was in town for the premiere of his new film, *The Gold Rush*. Louise was eighteen; Chaplin was thirty-six. They spent weeks together, trolling the nightclubs until daybreak, sleeping until noon, and taking long walks—sometimes for hours—through Central Park and in downtown Manhattan. They also indulged each other's boundless sexual appetites. Over one weekend, Brooks and Chaplin disappeared into a hotel suite with their friends A. C. Blumenthal, a film financier, and Peggy Fears, a close companion and fellow Ziegfeld girl. They didn't emerge until Monday. Years later, Louise admitted to a friend that the foursome spent most of the forty-eight hours in a state of undress and complex sexual entanglement.

If someone had bothered to call Louise Brooks a flapper, she would have shrugged off the charge (or compliment). "The flapper," she wrote years later to her brother, "did not exist at all except in Scott Fitzgerald's mind and the antics he planted in his mad wife Zelda's mind." As for Louise, she was just living her life the way she knew how. She wasn't trying to be a flapper. She had, in fact, been wearing her hair bobbed since the age of nine or ten. But Hollywood had a different idea.

One of Louise's occasional paramours in 1925 was Walter Wanger, a producer for Paramount Pictures who persuaded her to do some motion picture work. Famous Players-Lasky, the studio that formed Paramount's core, was still headquartered in Astoria, Queens, so Louise could easily shoot scenes during the day and make it back to Manhattan by dusk to perform in the *Follies*.

Her debut screen performance, *The Street of Forgotten Men,* was so strong that it soon earned her competing offers of a five-year contract from Warner Brothers and Paramount, both of which were in bad need of a flapper starlet to compete with the likes of First National's Colleen Moore. (Clara Bow hadn't yet moved over to Paramount.) Louise wasn't particularly interested in the movies, but she was restless, and the money was good ($250 per week to start, rising to $750 per week by the end of the decade), and she figured she could still do some stage work.

Wanger told her to sign with Warner Brothers; their relationship was an open secret, and he didn't want her career or reputation to suffer from the whisperings of jealous rivals and gossipmongers. Louise ignored the advice and went with Paramount. Over the next two years, she churned out a series of box office flapper hits like *Love 'Em and Leave 'Em,* a comic exposé of "modern youth's system of loving," as the studio ads billed it. Brook's character, a department store salesgirl named Janie Walsh ("like the crazy flapper you fell for last year," Paramount promised viewers), steals her sister's boyfriend, gets in way over her head at the racetrack, and, for good measure, tries to make off with the Employees' Welfare League fund to pay off her gambling debts. The opening scene finds her luxuriating in bed, her jet black bob mussed and her negligee revealing more than just a little skin. It was easy for Louise to play the role. She was the real thing.

When Louise wasn't on the set, she could sometimes be found at William Randolph Hearst's vast, rambling estate, San Simeon, where the famous newspaper magnate lived with his mistress, actress Marion Davies. There was nothing quite like it. Acres of well-manicured grounds surrounded an enormous main castle, three guest villas, swimming pools, tennis courts, a working cattle ranch, horse stables, and a variety of wonderland attractions. Though theoretically a guest of Marion Davies's, Louise was really a favorite of the self-styled Young Degenerates—a motley group of teenagers and twentysomethings anchored by Pepi Lederer, Davies's seventeen-year-old niece. Pepi lived off Hearst's generosity and dedicated most of her time to liquor, women (she was unapologetically gay in an era when it was all but impossible to be out of the closet), and cocaine.

Louise wisely stayed away from the cocaine, but she passed weeks on end at San Simeon, drinking from Hearst's stockpile of expensive champagne, partying with the Degenerates, and working to circumvent the old man's strictures against hard liquor.

"The most wondrously magnificent room in the castle was the dining hall," Louise remembered. "I never entered it without a little shiver of delight. High above our heads, just beneath the ceiling, floated rows of many-colored Sienese racing banners dating from the thirteenth century. In the huge Gothic fireplace between the two entrance doors, a black stone satyr grinned wickedly through the flames rising from logs propped up against his chest. The refractory table seated forty. Marion and Mr. Hearst sat facing each other in the mottle of the table, with their most important guests seated on either side." Louise was normally relegated to "the bottom of the table, where [Pepi] ruled. . . .

"At noon one day," Louise remembered, "before Marion and Mr. Hearst were onstage, we were swimming in the pool when Pepi learned that a group of Hearst editors solemnly outfitted in dark business suits, was sitting at the table, loaded with bottles of scotch and gin, in the dining room of the Casa del Mar—the second-largest of the three villas surrounding the castle. Pepi organized a chain dance. Ten beautiful girls in wet bathing suits danced round the editors' table, grabbed a bottle here and there and exited." One of the stunned newspapermen turned to another and asked, "Does Mr. Hearst know these people are here?"

Louise had slept with women before, but usually in the context of group sex. For good measure, she slept with Pepi. Later in life she'd claim to have had little interest in women, but she never held to a hard and fast rule. Rumor held that she had even had a one-night stand with Greta Garbo. Privately, Louise acknowledged it was true.

If a dangerous flapper was what Paramount wanted, a dangerous flapper was what it got. The studio was pushing the envelope, and it had found just the right woman to play the part.

24

The Dreamer's Dream Come True

WRITING SHORTLY AFTER the halcyon days of the 1920s, novelist Nathaniel West captured brilliantly the central place that Hollywood occupied in the American imagination. "All their lives they had slaved at some kind of dull, heavy labor," he observed of his nameless countrymen, "behind desks and counters, in the fields and at tedious machines of all sorts, saving their pennies and dreaming of the leisure that would be theirs when they had enough. Finally, the day came . . . where else should they go, but to California, land of sunshine and oranges."

People who came of age in the 1920s knew exactly what he meant. Hollywood—ostensibly just an incorporated district of Los Angeles—had come to represent the apotheosis of American plenty. "No romance has ever unfolded on the silver screen," boasted a Jazz Age author, "no fantastic tale from the pen of Jules Verne has ever depicted the glamorous drama of Hollywood, America's real, live Fairyland—the dreamer's dream come true. Brilliant as the eternal California sunshine, soft and languid as the California moon, the beauty of Hollywood is the glorious envy of the artist, the never-to-be-obtained goal of the poet."

Originally headquartered in cold, windy, snow-blown New York City, the movie barons flocked en masse to California just after World War I in pursuit of a virgin setting where labor was cheap, land abundant, and the vista unspoiled by industrial blight and decay. By the

Chinese American actress Anna May Wong challenged the popular belief that flappers need be white and native-born.

1920s, Hollywood—the Los Angeles neighborhood so many of them staked out as home—had "become the Enchanted City."

"Mohammadans have their Mecca," a writer observed, "Communists have their Moscow, and movie fans have their Hollywood."

Forget for a moment that the moguls chose Los Angeles mainly for pragmatic reasons—its extreme hostility to organized labor, its lower tax rates, the extra hours of sun for outdoor shooting, and its proximity to desert, ocean, and mountain panoramas. To millions of readers of fan magazines and faithful attendees of Saturday matinees, Hollywood represented the twin dreams of abundance realized and self-reinvention achieved.

"In the strange place which is Hollywood," observed a writer for *Motion Picture Classic* in 1927, ". . . when success does come, it comes swiftly and almost without effort. Youngsters, without any preparation, receive immense contracts for a trick of smiling, a tilt of nose, the curve of cheek."

Everyone was there, even Scott Fitzgerald, who took an unsuccessful stab at writing for the movies. In 1927, he contracted with United Artists to write a new flapper film. The end result was weak. Set, as always, in Princeton, *Lipstick* was the story of a young girl who is unjustly held captive but then discovers a magic tube of lipstick that makes every boy want to kiss her. The studio executives were unimpressed. Scott's film was never produced, and he had to settle for his $3,500 advance rather than the full $16,000 payment provided for in his contract. In Hollywood, either you had it or you didn't. Scott didn't.

The silent film stars built vast monuments to consumer plenty. Their rambling estates—Cecil B. DeMille's Paradise, Rudolph Valentino's Falcon's Lair, Mary Pickford and Douglas Fairbanks's Pickfair—represented all that was grand about the prosperous new era. Replete with sprawling master bathrooms, marble ballrooms, private theaters and projection rooms, sun decks, pipe organs, pagodas, and swimming pools—"They build the swimming pools first out here," observed a journalist, "and if there's still room on the lot, they build a home!"—the Hollywood mansions provided no end of entertainment to movie fans who faithfully soaked up every last bit of information about their favorite stars.

Colleen Moore later guessed that "we splurged on homes, partly because our intensive work schedules didn't permit such luxuries as travel, partly because what started out as necessities or conveniences became status symbols, and partly because most of us had more money than sense." The master suite in her own Bel Air home—with its wall-to-ceiling tiled mirrors, marble floors, expensive shag rugs, dark wood-paneled bedroom, and steamroom—was just the kind of shrine to excess that movie fans couldn't read enough about. It wasn't just *where* stars lived that interested the fans. It was *how* they lived. Whom they were dating. Whom they were marrying. Whom they were divorcing.

Since 1890, Americans had been led to believe that the frontier was closed. Hollywood suggested otherwise. The frontier was *here,* and the ordinary rules of life that bound shopgirls and factory workers to the clock and the whistle simply didn't apply.

To be sure, there was something special about Hollywood. It was young: Two-thirds of silent screen performers were under the age of thirty-five (and three-quarters of its female players were under twenty-five). It was exotic: All of the moguls were Jewish, and many of the crew were foreign-born. It was emancipated: Somewhere between one-third and one-half of the early screenwriters were women (the kind of women who didn't mind moving three thousand miles from home to start over). And it was urbane: The silent screen artists were usually city folks who had already cast off the shackles of small-town life. In an era when millions of young men and women were testing the boundaries of personal freedom, Hollywood seemed a haven for social and cultural experimentation—a "land of the future," as Charlie Chaplin put it, "a paradise of sunshine, orange groves, vineyards, and palm trees."

Little wonder that the stars received bottomless sacks of fan mail each day. "I am a girl twelve years of age," young Martha Meadows of Montgomery, Alabama, wrote to Clara Bow. "I am just wild about you. Your mouth, your eyes, and your hair. This craze for blondes never would last I knew."

"I bet you have many more admirers on the male side you naughty girl," one Connie Romero told Bow. "But don't worry we girls think a lot of you. . . . I like any girl who has personality. She's the one that stands above the crowd wherever she goes. . . . Goodness, I hope you don't get married and retire. If you marry please don't desert us, you will disappoint all your fans."

"I'm simply mad about your eyes," Audrey Ashuru of Brisbane, Australia, wrote to Clara. "They are the naughtiest, but most perfect, orbs I've yet seen. . . . I think you are the 'perfect flapper' of the screen."

The young movie fans weren't just watching; they were imitating. "I believe that watching the actions of people in the movies (the actors I mean) have led me to take up drinking and smoking," confessed a male undergraduate at the University of Chicago. "I sort of got the desire to smoke from watching some actor inhale a cigarette."

Another undergrad admitted that by watching romance films, he was able to give "considerable . . . attention" to the "technique of making love to a girl. . . . I learned to kiss a girl on her ears, neck and cheeks, as well as on the mouth, in a close huddle."

It wasn't just the young men who found their passions roused and techniques improved by the motion picture shows. Young women claimed to learn from their favorite on-screen flappers when to close their eyes during a kiss. "After I see a love picture," a sixteen-year-old high school junior confessed, "it just leaves me rather dopey. I always try to imagine myself in a like situation. Instead of making me feel like going out on a party with some men, I generally feel more ready to be loved. . . . The only benefit I ever got from the movies was in learning to love and the knowledge of sex." And a study of delinquent girls in the late 1920s revealed that three-quarters of them tried to boost their sex appeal by mimicking the way on-screen stars dressed, applied makeup, and fixed their hair.

"No wonder the girls of older days before the movies were so modest and bashful," concluded a young coed. "They never saw Clara Bow or William Haines. They didn't know anything else but being modest and sweet. I think the movies have a great deal to do with the present day so-called 'wildness.' If we didn't see such examples in the movies where would we get the idea of being 'hot?' We wouldn't."

She might have been selling her parents' generation a bit short. But the point was well-taken. The movies were having some effect. Young women reported developing intense crushes on leading men. "When I saw Rudolph Valentino in 'The Sheik,'" admitted one coed, "I could do nothing but think of him for days to follow. Several of my girl friends and I sent to Hollywood for the star's picture."

Many others were more closely fixated on the flappers themselves. When she watched "collegiate"—or flapper—films, reported a typical undergraduate, "I dreamed of being one of the most collegiate, the girl to be the football captain's friend."

"I often sat dreaming, planning what I would do when I got to go away to college," wrote another. "Oh, what a life! To be a popular co-ed, the member of a spiffy sorority! My first formal! What a hit I would be! When I saw these college romances develop before my eyes I wondered what my beau would be like. Of course, he would have to be a tall dark handsome boy; an athlete of repute. What would his first kiss be like? Would it send me to a world unknown, as some authors express it?"

The desire to imitate on-screen flapper heroines also helped enforce the same physical standards that young women encountered in magazine advertisements. For some women, the social pressure to lose weight—to resemble Colleen Moore and Clara Bow—created tremendous anxiety and internal conflict. "Resolved once more to cut down my diet," wrote Dorothy Dushkin of Smith College. "Betty and Fran's chief topic of conversation is dieting. It is extremely wearisome especially since they are both slender. I shall try once again to use my will power. I'm not going to say a word about it. I'm not going to foolishly cut meals and starve on certain days & relax on others as they do—but attend all meals & refrain from eating between meals."

Dorothy Dushkin wasn't writing in a vacuum. Immersed as they were in media images, young women couldn't help but notice that flappers were slim, angular, and sleek. John Held said so in his art. Gordon Conway said so in hers. Colleen Moore and Clara Bow, though not especially tall in real life, looked the part on-screen.

How many of the Smith girls knew that Colleen Moore's lucrative studio contract included a weight clause? Surely those who read the fan magazines knew that Clara Bow—who stood somewhere between five feet two and five feet four inches tall and whose weight in the 1920s fluctuated between a gaunt 100 pounds and a "plump" 132 pounds—suffered from chronic "curve trouble." In 1931, when Clara's new film, *No Limit,* premiered in Los Angeles, reviewers "thought Clara too plump" and speculated that her weight problem might cut short an otherwise brilliant career. Such musings couldn't have been lost on Clara's fans.

"Diet!" announced a writer for *Photoplay.* "It has put one world famous star in her grave [Barbara La Marr], has caused the illness of many others, has wrecked careers and has become, largely through its practice in Hollywood, the Great American Menace! For as Hollywood does so does the rest of the world. . . . The stars have set the styles in slim figures. The correct weight for a girl five feet two inches tall is 119 pounds. The average screen player of this height weighs only 108 pounds."

At Smith College and across the nation, young women subjected themselves to the "Hollywood Eighteen-Day Diet"—a strict regimen of five hundred calories per day in the form of toast, oranges, grapefruit, and eggs. It worked like a charm for Ethel Barrymore. Why not for everyone else? "Restaurants all over the country have bowed their heads before the Mayo-Hollywood 18-day diet," quipped *Photoplay.* ". . . It is running neck and neck with Lindbergh—and Lindbergh better look to his laurels."

"The slim figure is in the ascendant," observed a prewar writer. "Fat is now regarded as an indiscretion, and almost a crime. . . . Yet within living memory it was no disgrace to depress the scales to the extent of twenty stone [280 pounds] or more. . . . Fat . . . was indulgently tolerated, and even respected." In a world swollen with buying opportunities (home appliances, motorcars, clever copies of Parisian hats) and ways to indulge oneself (amusement parks, nightclubs, collegiate movies), it seemed that men and women were expected—or expected themselves—to show some restraint in how much they ate and how much they weighed. And in a world where individuals felt their vote counted little either in the political arena or the workplace, they could at least demonstrate authority over their own bodies.

On some level, the extra pressure that women faced to slim down might also have represented an attempt on the part of men to rein in a sex that was coming to enjoy more political, economic, and sexual autonomy. With the corset banished, women were free of the most crude, physical manifestation of social control. But they were still corseted—psychologically now—by the slender ideal.

Reinforced on the silver screen and in countless print advertisements, the expectation that they starve themselves in the interest of achieving flapperdom posed a real dilemma for many young women in the 1920s. " 'It's easy to be slender,' " announced the fan magazine *Picture Show* in 1924. "That's what Colleen Moore will tell you, anyway. When you see her on the screen she is generally moving too swiftly for you to do more than gather a general impression of youth and vivacity, but when you meet her you realize that the chief factor responsible for the impression is one of the most perfect figures ever seen. She has the lithe, youthful slenderness that all French designers seem to have in mind when they make their best models, slim, straight frocks that every woman wishes to wear and not one in a thousand can."

Readers learned that there was simply no "short cut to anything so desirable" as a Colleen Moore–like figure—that "no Turkish baths, medicines or reducing fluids will 'do the trick.' " Instead, would-be starlets were advised to follow Colleen's regimen—to avoid "too much white bread, potatoes, pastry, sweets, butter, oil, and fat" and to get "at least an hour's exercise, vigorous enough to stimulate the circulation, and to cause deep inhalations of air," each day.

For a nation still unaccustomed to the new worship of slenderness, this was a tough ideal to achieve. Still, most moviegoers were blind to the coercive potential of the flapper phenomenon. Young women still read the fan magazines religiously, taking note of informational articles, like "What It Costs to Be a Well-Dressed Flapper," which featured Clara Bow modeling a $25 silk blouse, doeskin gloves retailing at $8.50, rose beige chiffon stockings selling for $4.50, and a $30 lizard-skin pocketbook. They still lined up to buy Colleen Moore perfume, distributed by the Owl Drug Company. And they followed in great detail the subtle changes in Louise Brooks's bob.

By the late 1920s, the flapper craze had extended well past the white, middle-class neighborhoods where it began. Even if the media imagery was lily white, young black women, no less than their white peers, aspired to flapperdom. On campus at Spelman College, an all-black women's institution in Georgia, they donned imitation Chanel dresses, bobbed their hair, applied lipstick and eye shadow, and dangled strings of fake pearls from their necks.

The same was true of young Mexican women in Los Angeles, who frequented the movies, read the Hollywood fan magazines, and adopted the trappings of flapperdom as the most obvious means to acculturate to the Anglo world. "I was going to be Clara Bow," recalled Adele Hernández Milligan with a smile.

There were even Asian flappers like Anna May Wong, Hollywood's only Chinese flapper, and Flora Belle Jan, a young essayist and short-story writer for the *San Francisco Examiner* whose exploits and adventures, but for their ethnic twist, could have substituted any day of the week for Lois Long's.

For these young immigrant women, becoming a flapper was a way of accommodating the old world to the new. Every woman of that generation, it seemed, no matter her background or means, wanted to be a flapper. The social revolution that Scott Fitzgerald had announced—or stumbled upon—just a few years earlier had come full circle.

Zelda and Scott Fitzgerald, with daughter Scottie, on a Paris street in the mid-1920s.

25

ſUICIDE ON THE INſTALLMENT PLAN

ONE OF THE most vivid accounts of Scott Fitzgerald and his madcap—and increasingly mad—wife comes from Ernest Hemingway's memoir of expatriate Paris. Hemingway, a frustrated, undiscovered author, and Fitzgerald, the celebrated writer squandering his talents on booze, were bound to lock horns. And they did.

Written just a few years before Hemingway took his own life, *A Moveable Feast* was, by an ex-wife's admission, a scathing and at times scathingly unfair portrait of those sons and daughters of the American Midwest who took refuge in the cheap hotels and smoky cafés that lay set back along the windy, stone streets of the Sixth Arrondissement. There, by the tawny Parisian sunset and in the long shadow of the Eiffel Tower, these American moderns scratched out a body of art and literature that helped cast the United States as a creative force heretofore unappreciated and unknown. It was ironic that some of their best work was achieved more than three thousand miles from home.

In his assessment of Scott and Zelda Fitzgerald, who lent him countless hundreds of francs, promoted his novels when he was still an obscure and struggling writer, and helped him secure his first major publishing deal in the United States, Hemingway was particularly brutal. But, then, "Ernest could be brutal," Hadley Hemingway, his ex-wife, remarked.

Scott Fitzgerald and Ernest Hemingway first met in the late spring of 1925 at the Dingo Bar, a popular watering hole on rue Delambre where the local "sporting set" customarily retired each day after hours of boxing and vigorous calisthenics at the nearby Montparnasse Gymnasium.

Hemingway, who regarded himself as a man of action, was whiling away the time at the long, zinc bar with "some completely worthless characters" when America's flapper king strolled over and introduced himself. Scott had read some of Hemingway's short stories and had been talking him up with great enthusiasm among literary friends in both France and the United States. Each man had been eager for some time to make the other's acquaintance.

Even by his own account, Hemingway's career was stuck in low gear. Scratching out a meager existence as a freelance magazine correspondent, trying to make ends meet and support his small family, he was beginning to fear that whatever talent he had as a writer would forever remain a well-kept "secret between my wife and myself and only those people we knew well enough to speak to." That a celebrated author like Scott Fitzgerald took interest in his work came as a great shot of confidence, and at just the right time.

Smartly clad in a Brooks Brothers suit, starched white shirt, and black knit tie, Scott was already well on his way to inebriation when he arrived at the Dingo. Nevertheless, he ordered several bottles of champagne for the small party.

Hemingway later sized him up as "a man who looked like a boy with a face between handsome and pretty. He had very fair wavy hair, a high forehead, excited and friendly eyes and a delicate long-lipped Irish mouth that, on a girl, would have been the mouth of a beauty."

It was pretty well-known around town that Scott had a drinking problem. That is, he just couldn't handle his liquor. "He could take two or three drinks at most and be completely drunk," said his friend Carl Van Vechten. "It was incredible. He was nasty when he was drunk, but sober he was a charming man. . . ."

Hemingway didn't know this at the time. So he was in for a surprise.

"Ernest," Scott began, "you don't mind if I call you Ernest, do you?" Hemingway shrugged.

"Don't be silly," Scott reproached. He was slurring his words. "This is serious. Tell me, did you and your wife sleep together before you were married?"

"I don't know," Hemingway replied. (How does one answer a question like that? he thought.)

"How can you not remember something of such importance?"

"I don't know. It is odd, isn't it?"

"It's worse than odd. You must be able to remember."

"I'm sorry. It's a pity, isn't it?"

"Don't talk like some limey," Scott barked. "Try to be serious and remember."

"Nope," replied Hemingway. "It's hopeless."

"You could make an honest effort to remember."

And so their conversation went for what must have been the better part of a half hour, until Scott, with one arm poised against the bar and the other clutching a half-spent champagne bottle, turned as pale as "used candle wax" and started to buckle and cave. As the other patrons stared on, Hemingway helped his new acquaintance into a waiting taxi and watched in disbelief as Fitzgerald disappeared into the night. Or so Hemingway chose to remember the meeting.

Sara Mayfield, Zelda's girlhood friend from Montgomery, was working as a European correspondent for the *International Herald Tribune* in those days. She recalled Hemingway as "tall and well built but thin, almost gangling." Either by virtue of his grinding poverty or his patent disregard for high couture, he stood out like a sore thumb in fashionable Paris with his "dirty singlet," "old corduroy trousers," and "grimy sneakers."

The truth was that Hemingway was jealous of Scott's success. Hemingway was poor, and Scott, if not rich, was living as though he expected to be rich very soon. While Scott wore Brooks Brothers and Zelda draped herself in evening wear by Coco Chanel and Jean Patou, Hadley Hemingway shopped for cheap knockoffs at Au Bon Marché, a discount French department store. While Scott and Zelda moved between lavish apartments and expensive hotel suites in the fashionable Eighth Arrondissement, the Hemingways lived in a stark, unfurnished flat above an old sawmill in the Latin Quarter, a cut-rate neighborhood flooded with penniless bohemians and hungry students.

How could a man like Scott Fitzgerald enjoy such wide renown for publishing flapper stories in *The Saturday Evening Post*? It baffled the mind.

Shortly after that first meeting at the Dingo Bar, the Fitzgeralds invited Ernest and Hadley over to their apartment for a light lunch. Years later, all that Zelda remembered of the afternoon was that she had garnished the dining room table with a Lalique turtle and white violets. All that Hemingway could remember was that Scott got drunk and Zelda struck him as certifiably "crazy."

In fact, for all his jealousy, Hemingway had a point. The Fitzgeralds were at the peak of their fame and influence in the mid-1920s, but they were beginning to betray signs of the self-destructive tendencies that would ruin them by the decade's close.

Scott's new novel, *The Great Gatsby,* had just been published to almost universal acclaim. Though the sales were modest, Scribner's sold the film and stage rights for $25,000 and the magazine serial rights for another $1,000. Scott reaped the larger portion of this windfall. More important, *Gatsby* was hailed as a path-breaking literary achievement—akin to what Thackeray did "in *Pendennis* and *Vanity Fair* and this isn't a bad compliment," the famously plain-spoken Gertrude Stein told him.

On the strength of Scott's growing reputation as a serious and important novelist and not just a purveyor of flapper stories, the Fitzgeralds of St. Paul, Minnesota, and Montgomery, Alabama, found themselves cavorting with the likes of Pablo Picasso, James Joyce, Cole Porter, Archibald MacLeish, John Dos Passos, Isadora Duncan, and Edith Wharton. Magazines were lining up to pay Scott on the order of $2,500 for each short piece he banged out, a sum that would balloon to $4,000 by the close of the decade.

At first, all of Paris seemed captivated by their antics. Clad in expensive evening wear, they dove fully clothed into the pool at the Lido cabaret. Scott somehow managed to requisition a three-wheeled delivery cart and drove it in circles at the Place de la Concorde, leaving two frustrated gendarmes to pursue him on their bicycles. He showed up late one night, rip-roaring drunk, at the offices of the *Paris Tribune,* where he bellowed out random song fragments and started shredding pages of news copy when a nearby cluster of reporters refused to join in the chorus. In desperation, James Thurber and William Shirer pulled him outside for another crawl of the neighborhood bars. When Scott finally passed out for a few minutes, they drove him back to rue de Tilsitt and deposited him at his doorstep.

The stories were legion. At a formal dinner thrown by Sylvia Beach (of Shakespeare & Company fame), Scott knelt before James Joyce and offered to jump out the window as a sign of his undying veneration of the great Irish writer. Joyce later confided to the assembled guests, "That young man must surely be mad. If he's not watched, he will certainly do himself some injury."

Those who saw the Fitzgeralds only on social occasions could make light of their increasingly peculiar behavior. Scott was very clever, after all, and surely he couldn't have been too dysfunctional an alcoholic to churn out such a prolific body of work?

But those who were closest to the Fitzgeralds saw the destructive side of Scott's drinking and Zelda's increasingly fragile grip on reality.

Dos Passos once saw Scott stagger out of a bar in the light of day and kick a tray of cigarettes out of the hands of an old woman who sold tobacco on the street corner.

Vacationing in Cannes, Scott and his friend Charles MacArthur stepped into a trendy resort café, roughed up a group of waiters, dragged one of them to the foot of a towering cliff, and threatened to hurl him into the cold blue waters of the Mediterranean.

On another occasion, they overpowered the bartender at a near empty restaurant, spread him across two adjacent chairs, and threatened to saw him open to see what his insides were made of. The charade stopped only when Zelda intervened, cheerily reassuring Scott that he'd find nothing but broken porcelain, cardboard menu scraps, and pencil stubs in the belly of the terrified barkeep.

In a moment of candor, Zelda confided to a friend that two drinks were enough to put Scott in a "manic state. Absolutely manic—he wants to fight everybody, including me. He's drinking himself to death." Her confidante agreed. "He's committing suicide on the installment plan."

But Zelda was hardly a poster child for good behavior. Driving with friends near Monte Carlo, she grabbed the wheel of the car and veered toward the edge of the sea cliff. On another occasion, in the daybreak hours of a raucous, all-night party, fellow revelers watched her lie down in the driveway and dare Scott to run her over with their car.

Of all their acquaintances in France, Hadley and Ernest Hemingway may have suffered the most consistent exposure to the Fitzgeralds' bizarre conduct.

When clearheaded, the Fitzgeralds could be loyal friends. Scott proved a deft literary critic who could be counted on for insightful analysis and advice. He and Zelda lent the Hemingways money and gave them use of their rented château on the Riviera—a luxury Ernest and Hadley could not have afforded on their modest budget—and an opportunity to hobnob with the influential writers and artists who converged each summer on the shores of southern France. Scott even managed to talk Max Perkins into signing Hemingway for Scribner's and introduced him to important literary figures back in the States.

But Scott and Zelda were "inconvenient friends," Hadley tactfully remembered many years later. "They would call [on us] at four o'clock in the morning and we had a baby and didn't appreciate it very much. When Scott wrote I don't know."

In the aftermath of a typical drunken intrusion, Scott wrote a plaintive letter to Ernest, begging absolution for waking his family from its deep slumber. "I was quite ashamed of the other morning," he began. ". . . However it is only fair to say that the deplorable man who entered your apartment Sat. morning *was not* me but a man named Johnston who has been often mistaken for me." The Hemingways weren't amused.

The relationship between America's two greatest Lost Generation families was almost always strained. Zelda despised Ernest Hemingway's faux bravado and wrote him off as an intellectual fraud. He was as "phony as a rubber check," she told Scott. As for *The Sun Also Rises,*

Hemingway's first acclaimed novel, it was no more than "bullfighting, bullslinging, and bullshit." Zelda was particularly incensed when, in 1926, Ernest left Hadley and the baby for another woman.

Hemingway, in turn, thought Zelda was a terrible shrew. He also tired of Scott's relentless charm offensive and came to view the famous writer as little more than a tragically washed-up man who was drowning his residual talent in a sea of expensive red wine and champagne. He ridiculed Scott for dumbing down short stories to make them more marketable to *The Saturday Evening Post* and for turning regularly to Zelda for editorial advice.

Had they alienated only Ernest and Hadley Hemingway, the Fitzgeralds might have emerged from their time in Paris with their reputations intact. But they drove away other friends, too—among them Gerald and Sara Murphy, a dashing American couple just a few years older than the Fitzgeralds.

Gerald, the son of a wealthy leather goods dealer in New York, and Sara, an heiress from Ohio, had fled the demands of family and business in the United States for the deep blue waters of the Mediterranean and the enchanting, tree-lined boulevards of interwar Paris. Pale and lean but exceptionally debonair (Archibald MacLeish once described him as "well-laundered"), Gerald was a world-weary Skull and Bones man who thought there was something fundamentally "depressing . . . about a country that could pass the Eighteenth Amendment." With his long sideburns, white Panama hats, and ostentatious liking for walking canes, he cut an impressive figure even in the trendy circles of French bohemia.

In Paris, he pursued his dream of painting. He and Sara befriended Pablo Picasso, Joan Miró, and Juan Gris. They studied scene design with the Russian émigré Natalie Goncharova, and in time Gerald became an artist of some note.

With their chiseled good looks, impeccable sense of style, and seemingly bottomless bank account, the Murphys became the toast of France. Paris was "like a great fair," Sara said many years later, "and everybody was so young." Their fourteen-room Moorish villa in Antibes, with its beige stucco walls, yellow shutters, and flagstone terrace, set high on a long, shaded bluff that dropped directly into the sea, was the scene of some of the grandest dinner parties of the 1920s. It was through the Murphys' generosity that Scott and Zelda were introduced to the creative minds who converged on France in the mid-1920s. The Fitzgeralds were lucky to be in the Murphys' good graces, and they knew it.

At first, there was a genuine and deeply meaningful affection between the two couples. "Most people are dull," Gerald wrote to Scott, "without distinction and without value," but "we four communicate by our presence rather than any means. . . . Scott will uncover for me values in Sara, just as Sara has known them in Zelda through her affection for Scott. Suffice it to say that whenever we knew that we were to see you that evening or that you were coming to dinner in the garden we were happy, and it showed to each other."

But Scott and Zelda's gradual surrender to their personal demons strained the bonds of friendship, and the glorious summers of 1924 and 1925 gave way to darker times.

Scott and Zelda argued more—over his drinking, and now over her decision to train full-time with the renowned ballet instructor Lubov Egorova. Though Scott continued to churn out an impressive body of short fiction, his alcoholism was stunting the natural progress of his work. One friend remarked that "Scott could write and didn't; couldn't drink and did." The more that progress eluded him on his next novel, the more he resented Zelda's determination to revive the dance career she had always hoped to nurture. He failed to appreciate that she had real talent as a performer and that she needed to be more than just Mrs. F. Scott Fitzgerald.

Gradually, it became impossible to be their friends. While dining with the Murphys at a restaurant in St.-Paul-de-Vence, Scott—well past his two-drink threshold—walked over to Isadora Duncan's table and knelt before the famous choreographer, who playfully tussled his hair. Observing this scene from the corner of her eye, Zelda put down her drink, stood up, and threw herself headfirst down a flight of stone steps. Luckily, she only bruised her arms and legs.

Worse were their reckless high dives off the cliffs that overlooked the sea at Antibes. Each would dare the other to execute a more perilous version of the headlong plunge past jagged rocks and ledges, much to the horror of Sara and Gerald Murphy, who were never able to persuade Scott and Zelda to call off this nerve-shattering game of chicken. It was a miracle nobody was killed.

"It's no fun here anymore," Zelda confided to a friend. "If we go out at night Scott gets pie-eyed; and if we stay at home we have a row." Scott was even arrested several times for getting into bar fights. At parties, he introduced himself with the stock line "I'm an alcoholic."

When the Murphys threw a bash at the Juan-les-Pins casino, Scott hurled ashtrays at the other guests, prompting Gerald to walk out on his own party. At another affair, Scott threw a fig at the Princess de Poix, clocked Archibald MacLeish in the face, and tossed Gerald's expensive Venetian glassware over the garden wall.

In a rare moment of clearheaded reflection, or maybe just plain old self-pity, he confided to Hemingway that his "latest tendency [was] to collapse about 11.00 and with tears flowing from my eyes or the gin rising to their level and leaking over, + tell interested friends or acquaintances that I haven't a friend in the world and likewise care for nobody, generally including Zelda and often implying current company—after which current company tend to become less current and I wake up in strange rooms in strange places."

There was still a fire within him, and when sober he produced remarkable work. But "when drunk," he admitted, "I make them all pay and pay and pay."

While Scott drank himself into a stupor, Zelda suffered small nervous attacks that were precursors to her more dramatic breakdown several years later. She seemed tired and distracted; her friends noticed that "the sparkle had gone out of her as it does of champagne that has been swizzled too often." She lost weight. Her blond hair turned a darker brown.

"Zelda could be spooky," Sara Murphy remembered of those days. "She seemed sometimes to be lying in ambush waiting for you with those Indian eyes of hers." Like many of the others, the Murphys started to withdraw.

The rest of the world was oblivious. To the millions of magazine readers who enjoyed Scott's work, the gossip column devotees who followed tales of their more benign exploits, and the countless Americans who regarded the Fitzgeralds as poster children for a new generation, Scott and Zelda continued to represent all that was bold and experimental and grand about the new decade. Above all, Scott and Zelda were still called on to explain the flapper.

In the mid-1920s, *McCall's* magazine commissioned the Fitzgeralds to write companion articles under the headline "What Becomes of Our Flappers and Our Sheiks?" Readers would have easily understood the reference to the 1921 blockbuster *The Sheik,* in which Rudolph Valentino played a dark and mysterious man endowed with uncommon sex appeal.

In her contribution to the piece, Zelda struck contradictory chords of triumphalism and regret. "The flapper! She is growing old . . . ," Zelda opined. "She is married 'mid loud acclamation on the part of relatives and friends. She has come to none of the predicted 'bad ends,' but has gone at last, where all good flappers go—into the young married set, into boredom and gathering conventions and the pleasure of having children, having lent a while a splendor and courageousness to life, as all good flappers should."

Zelda seemed to view herself as an aging specimen, sounding deeply ambivalent about the path she was following in life and skeptical that the flapper had any real staying power. But if the magazines and couture shops and department stores and mail-order catalogs and silver screen were any indication, the character type known widely as the flapper was at the pinnacle of her influence. From her self-imposed exile in France, Zelda might not have appreciated this.

Yet if she was premature in her eulogy, Zelda might have grasped what few other cultural critics understood: The flapper was not long for this world. Like the Fitzgeralds, who began the decade in a burst of optimism and gusto, the Jazz Age was always too euphoric—and too manic—to sustain itself over the long run. It was fitting that Scott and Zelda, who were there from the start, began to unravel just as America began its steady descent into the Great Depression.

CONCLUSION

UNAFFORDABLE EXCESS

O N OCTOBER 29, 1929—Black Tuesday—the stock market collapsed and America's Jazz Age was officially over. So long to "I Love College Girls" and "The Sheik of Araby." Hello to "Buddy, Can You Spare a Dime?"

In fact, the stock market crash had little to do with the onset of the Great Depression. Very few Americans in the 1920s owned stocks or securities. Certainly the crash helped provoke the collapse of the nation's banking system a year or so later. And with bank failures came a rash of personal bankruptcies and evictions. But the banks were bound to fail anyway. They were a slapdash affair—poorly regulated, unevenly capitalized, overextended.

The simple truth was that America's most prosperous decade had been built on a deck of cards. There was a price to pay for so lopsided a concentration of the nation's riches. Good times relied on good sales, after all. The same farmers and workers who fueled economic growth early in the decade by purchasing shiny new cars and electric washing machines had reached their limit. By the late twenties, when advertisers told them that their cars and washing machines were outdated and needed to be replaced, the working class simply couldn't afford to buy new ones. Unbought goods languished on the shelves. Factories cut their production. Workers were laid off by the millions. With consumer demand hitting new lows, America's economy simply stopped functioning.

Young flappers in 1927. Three years later, in the wake of the Great Crash, the flapper slipped out of sight and into memory.

Still, Black Tuesday loomed large in the national imagination. A dramatic and singularly identifiable event, it struck many people as chiefly responsible for ushering out the abundance and frivolity of the 1920s and for ushering in a new era of scarcity.

With the passing of the Jazz Age came the passing of the flapper. The world of the 1930s—a world of breadlines, industrial strikes, Father Coughlin's radio rants, Huey Long's demagoguery, the mounting specter of European fascism, the serious work of those sober young New Dealers in Washington, D.C.—made the cocktail-drinking, cigarette-smoking, Charleston-dancing flapper an unaffordable excess. There were more important things to talk about. America moved on to other topics.

For the Hollywood flappers, the real crash had happened almost two years earlier. It was on October 6, 1927, during intermission at the New York City premiere of *The Jazz Singer,* that Walter Wanger—the Paramount executive who gave Louise Brooks her start in the motion pictures—raced to the lobby to make a long-distance call to his boss, Jesse Lasky, in California. "Jesse, this is a revolution!" he cried. Hundreds of moviegoers had just watched Al Jolson sing. Scratch that. *Heard* Al Jolson sing.

Others had tried and failed. Who would have thought it would be those Warner Brothers—Harry, Sam, Jack, and Albert—who would figure out how to synchronize sound and film? The Warner brothers were about as dysfunctional a family as ever existed. Harry had once chased Jack around the studio lot with a lead pipe, threatening to kill him. They were anything but professionals. But they'd just rendered every other studio obsolete. Overnight.

Thousands of nervous film stars lined up to take voice tests. Would they pass muster? Were they washed up, finished, kaput? Clara Bow and Colleen Moore soldiered on. They made a few talkies—and not bad ones at that. Clara even starred in a film with Kay Francis, Lois Long's former New York City roommate.

But their careers never survived into the new decade. It wasn't so much that the talkies killed them. More likely, the 1930s killed the public's taste for actresses typecast as flappers.

Facing more sober times, as well as mounting pressure from the decency lobby, the big film studios voluntarily cleaned up their act, adopted Will Hays's Motion Picture Production Code of 1930, and banished sexual themes and imagery from the silver screen. It would be another thirty years before Hollywood would so freely depict carnal desire.

CLARA'S GOOD LUCK ran out early on. Too trusting, too eager for affirmation, she lavished much of her income on hangers-on, including her father, who squandered more than his share on a string of bad business deals. Her affair with a married man ended in an embarrassing public scandal when his wife sued Clara for damages. Clara settled out of court, but Paramount seized her escrow account of $55,000 and counting, citing noncompliance with the morality clause in her contract.

Things got worse in 1931 when her former secretary, Daisy De Voe, went on trial for stealing large sums of Clara's jewelry and cash. As a parting shot, De Voe published a book chronicling Clara's alleged sexual exploits. All of Hollywood was agog. Rumor even had it that the flapper queen had entertained the entire University of Southern California football team in her bedroom. It wasn't true. But it didn't matter. B. P. Schulberg called her "crisis-a-day Clara" and fired her from Paramount.

Troubles at work meant troubles at home. A series of wellpublicized mental breakdowns ensued. With a mother and grandmother who had died in an insane asylum, Clara feared that she, too, would end her days in an institution.

Things improved in 1931 when she married Rex Bell, a cowboy film star who treated her well and fathered her two children. They lived in seclusion on a ranch in Nevada. Rex became the state's lieutenant governor. Though she tried several times to make a comeback on the silver screen, Clara Bow's career finally came to a halt in the mid-thirties. Throughout the 1930s and 1940s, Clara battled severe depression and began exhibiting signs of schizophrenia.

In the late 1940s, she began an intense course of psychotherapy at the Institute of Living in Hartford, Connecticut. There she unbottled a number of long-repressed childhood memories, including the knowledge that her father raped her repeatedly when she was a young girl. In the years that followed, Clara withdrew from therapy and moved to a small two-bedroom bungalow in Los Angeles. She rarely left the house.

Rex died on the ranch in Nevada, alone. A few years later, in 1965, Clara passed away at her small hideaway in Culver City.

"Miss Bow," someone once asked her, "when you add it all up, what is 'It'?"

Clara could only shrug. "I ain't real sure."

COLLEEN MOORE'S LIFE took a happier turn. Though she continued to make films until 1934—even playing opposite Spencer Tracy in *The Power and the Glory,* which she regarded as the best film she ever made—Colleen's public wanted her "to go on being a wide-eyed, innocent little girl."

"I was too old for that," she later wrote, "—and too tired of it in any case."

Colleen's marriage to John McCormick—unsteady from the start because of John's tendency to disappear on two-week benders—ended in divorce. A second marriage also fell apart.

The punishing routine she had kept for over ten years in the film industry—eighteen-hour workdays, constant travel, a fish-bowl existence—left her exhausted and yearning for a simpler life. In the late 1930s, Colleen married Homer Hargrave, a wealthy Chicago financier. She invested her film earnings in the market and made a killing. Then she wrote a book that instructed ordinary people on how to do the same. She rented out her Hollywood mansion and later sold it, preferring to reinvent herself as a devoted Chicago wife and stepmother to Hargrave's children.

Late in life, she wrote a lively account of her years in Hollywood.

If the crash ruined the fortunes of many a famous flapper, Colleen weathered the storm with anonymity and good cheer. "You just can't live comfortably on less than $2 million," she told an acquaintance.

She died in 1988, a wealthy and content woman.

UNLIKE COLLEEN MOORE, Louise Brooks despised Hollywood from the start. She had never intended to be an actress, much less a film star. "My [New York] friends were all literary people," she later remarked. "And in Hollywood there were no literary people. I went to Hollywood and no one read books. I went to the bookstore on Hollywood Boulevard—it's still there—and these Hollywood people would go in and say, 'I have a bookshelf, and I want to buy enough books to fill up the shelves.' And that was all the reading they did. Don't forget, most people in pictures, they were waitresses, they were very low-class people."

This wasn't the sort of attitude that was going to help Louise win friends and influence people in the rough-and-tumble world of studio politics. Still, when Paramount geared up in 1928 to make the transition to talkies and renegotiated the contracts of its major stars, Louise was one of the lucky ones. Ben Schulberg proposed to retain her at her current salary. No raise, but no pay cut, either. "You can stay on at $750 per week or leave," he told her.

Louise stunned Schulberg—and the entire film industry—by walking away. She was tired of Hollywood and of making less than Clara Bow and Colleen Moore.

Instead, she traveled to Berlin, where the German director G. W. Pabst recruited her to play the lead role in his pioneering work, *Pandora's Box*. It was arguably the last great film of the silent era, and it was her finest part ever. But the critics panned it. Louise stayed in Europe to shoot another film with Pabst and several more in England. Then she ran out of money. She crawled back to California on her knees.

But by the time she returned to Hollywood in 1930, Louise was persona non grata. Paramount blacklisted her on the grounds that she still owed the studio a film. For a time, there was talk of a contract with Columbia Pictures, but nothing ever came of it. Friends helped her secure a few minor parts here and there. By 1938, however, it was obvious that her film career was over. She moved back to Wichita and operated a dance studio for a few years. Then she returned to New York and worked behind the sales counter at Saks Fifth Avenue, picking up occasional voice-over work for radio soap operas.

Finally, she got desperate. For a time in the 1940s, she worked on and off for a high-priced escort service. For solace, she turned to liquor and pills.

Salvation came in the 1950s when film buffs, now inured to the talkies and in search of the industry's avant-garde past, rediscovered the silent era. In 1955, Cinémathèque Française featured Brooks in an exhibit entitled "Sixty Years of Cinema." The following year, with few other prospects, she accepted an invitation to move to Rochester, New York, where she began a new career as a film historian at the Eastman House. Her writing appeared in several important journals and earned acclaim for its brisk style and trenchant analysis of old Hollywood.

By 1979, when Kenneth Tynan revisited her early career in the pages of *The New Yorker*—his article was entitled, simply, "The Girl in the Black Helmet"—Louise had been canonized as one of the most brilliant and sexually alluring figures of the silent film era. Yet personal happiness eluded her. Louise's two marriages ended in divorce. A born loner, she retreated from old friends and family in later years as her health faded.

Louise Brooks died alone at her house in Rochester in 1985. She was seventy-eight years old.

LIFE TREATED LOIS Long somewhat more kindly. Harold Ross's bad-girl columnist carried on as the *New Yorker*'s in-house fashion columnist until 1970, when she retired to a farm in Pennsylvania.

Her work continued to set new standards for fashion commentary. William Shawn, who followed Harold Ross as editor of the magazine, believed that Long was "the first American fashion critic to approach fashion as an art and to criticize women's clothes with independence, intelligence, humor, and literary style." All of which was true. Yet after the 1920s, Long lost her place in the elite circle of *New Yorker* staff writers.

The magazine matured slowly from its origins as a lighthearted journal of urban "sophistication" and humor into a serious outlet for political discourse, biography, poetry, and cultural commentary. Lois Long never made the parallel journey. Her writing was still crisp and irreverent, but it was eclipsed by works of greater and more lasting import.

Lois Long and Peter Arno had a daughter together but divorced in 1931. Other staff members couldn't help but notice that Lois sometimes came to work with black-and-blue marks on her arms and bruises on her face. She never discussed the matter, but few of her colleagues were surprised. Arno's temper was as famous as his wit.

When she died in July 1974 at the age of seventy-three, *The New York Times* accidentally ran a picture of the wrong person next to her obituary. The last laugh was on Lois Long. She would have approved.

OVER THE COURSE of her long career as a fashion journalist, Long had plenty of occasion to cover the new spring lines at the House of Chanel. As she could have testified, Coco's reputation as a leading innovator of women's couture and accessories hardly diminished. In 1922, she launched Chanel No. 5—known as much for its distinctive bottle as for its scent. The thirties saw her refine the signature Chanel style: Hemlines dropped and waistlines crept up. But the fundamental idea behind Chanel's designs—comfort and elegance for the New Woman—remained the same.

In 1939, the House of Chanel turned out an evening dress in ivory cotton organdy, with red, white, and blue embroidery—part of her "tricolor" collection celebrating French nationalism. The piece was uncharacteristically mawkish, but with Western Europe besieged by the Axis threat, the times seemed to call for such a design.

Two years later, with Nazi Germany firmly in control of northern France and a puppet government installed in the south, Coco did as she always did—she cozied up to power. Indeed, shortly after the war, when a British MI6 agent interrogated Walter Schellenberg, an SS officer and top aide to Heinrich Himmler, the resulting interrogation report revealed that Coco, who was then in her late fifties, and Schellenberg, who was in his early thirties, spent the war years as lovers. Chanel used her connection to Schellenberg to keep her residence at the Ritz, which housed ranking Nazi officials stationed in Paris. Schellenberg, in turn, used Chanel in an ill-fated effort to reach a détente with the British government.

Because Coco enjoyed close ties to Winston Churchill and to the Duke and Duchess of Windsor, both of whom harbored pro-Nazi sympathies, Schellenberg hoped she might be useful in forcing a regime change in London and drawing Britain out of the war. At the behest of her Nazi patrons, Coco even embarked on a bizarre and unsuccessful peace mission to England.

In the days following the liberation of Paris, Coco was arrested and released by French gendarmes. She fled the country before she could be subjected to formal charges and trial—and before she could be rounded up with hundreds of other "horizontal collaborators," shaved bald, and paraded through the streets. Instead, she spent the better part of ten years in self-imposed exile in Switzerland.

Exile, however, did not suit Coco. In 1954, she staged a dramatic comeback, reclaiming her place as the world's leading designer of haute couture. Much as she had given the New Woman jersey and tweed, she now gave the New Woman's granddaughter pea jackets and bell-bottoms.

Coco was in her studio, hard at work, when she died in 1971. She never married.

Shortly after World War I, Boy Capel—the great love of Coco's life—wed another woman. Months later, he died in a car crash in southern France. Coco drove to the site of the accident and wept.

In 1926, she introduced the "little black dress." She told close friends that she had put the whole world in mourning for Boy.

THE OTHERS GOT on with their lives, too. John Held lost a fortune on the stock market and several wives to his own weird capriciousness.

Oh! Margy! didn't make much sense in the postflapper world, but still he managed to scratch out a respectable living as a gentleman farmer in New Jersey and an occasional contributor to magazines and newspapers.

He died in 1958 of throat cancer, just as he was on the verge of being rediscovered by a generation of art critics who had been too young to appreciate his work when it first appeared.

Gordon Conway married and divorced. Then, strangely, for reasons no one ever really understood, she withdrew in the 1930s from the world of commercial art. After a long but happy retirement, she died on her farm in Virginia in 1956, at the age of sixty-one.

In 1937, Bruce Barton, the adman who gave new meaning to the works of Jesus Christ, won a special election to Congress from New York's silk stocking district. He served three years in Washington before going down to defeat in an ill-fated U.S. Senate race in 1940. Along with his House colleagues Joseph Martin and Hamilton Fish, his outspoken opposition to American involvement in World War II earned him the opprobrium of Franklin Roosevelt, who delighted crowds with scathing references to the apocryphal firm of "Martin, Barton & Fish."

When he died a rich man in 1967, Madison Avenue hailed him as a founding father of modern advertising.

It was Scott and Zelda Fitzgerald, of course, who seemed in some uncanny way to embody perfectly the end of the Jazz Age, just as they had helped spark its beginning.

In 1930, while they were traveling in Europe, Zelda suffered the first in a series of debilitating mental breakdowns. She would spend most of the balance of her life in hospitals—sometimes teetering on the edge of sanity, other times lucid and upbeat.

Scott and Zelda kept up a furious correspondence throughout the thirties, but they rarely lived together. Their long, heartfelt letters revealed two people incapable of reconciling themselves to the passing of time. They lingered over distant memories of the early days in Montgomery, Manhattan, and Antibes—of "the strangeness and excitement of New York," Zelda wrote, "of reporters and furry smothered hotel lobbies, the brightness of the sun on the window panes and the prickly dust of late spring; the impressiveness of the Fowlers and much tea-dancing and my eccentric behavior at Princeton. There were Townsend's blue eyes and . . . a trunk that exuded sachet and the marshmallow odor of the Biltmore. . . . There were flowers and nightclubs. . . . At West Port, we quarreled over morals once, walking beside a colonial wall under the freshness of lilacs. . . ."

In their never-ending, frenetic attempt to recapture each sight, sound, scent, and sensation of the past, Scott and Zelda seemed to acknowledge that their best years were over. Where did it all go? they wondered. What became of this beautiful flapper and her handsome sheik?

Zelda may never have known the depth of Scott's despair. His next novel, *Tender Is the Night,* met with critical acclaim but lackluster sales. Deep in debt to Scribner's and to his literary agent, no longer able to trade on his reputation as the flapper king in an age that had little use for flappers, Scott struggled to keep pace with Zelda's mounting hospital bills. In that fight, he was his own worst enemy. The mid-1930s found him bloodshot and paunchy from sleepless nights and countless binges.

In 1937, desperate to pay off his debts, Scott moved to Hollywood and worked as a screenwriter for Metro-Goldwyn-Mayer. He considered it dreary and humiliating work, but the money—$1,000 per week, soon raised to $1,250—was excellent, and he couldn't afford to say no. He received only one screen credit, but MGM kept him on. Everyone knew that he was a vanity hire. Even he knew it.

In 1938, Scott tried his best to sum up his relationship with Zelda in a brutally honest letter to their daughter, Scottie, who was just about to start college at Vassar. "When I was your age," he wrote, "I lived with a great dream. The dream grew and I learned how to speak of it and make people listen. Then the dream divided one day when I decided to marry your mother after all, even though I knew she was spoiled and meant no good to me. I was sorry immediately I had married her but, being patient in those days, made the best of it and got to love her in another way. . . . She realized too late that work was dignity . . . but it was too late and she broke and is broken forever."

On his occasional trips back east, Scott visited with Zelda. They even took a few vacations together—to South Carolina in 1937, Virginia in 1938, and Florida in 1939. By then, Scott had found another life partner—a Hollywood gossip columnist named Sheila Graham, who remained his companion until the day he died. Graham never entirely displaced Zelda, whose bond with Scott—in life and in letters—endured even as the couple saw less and less of each other.

But Zelda was thousands of miles away in December 1940, when her husband died of a heart attack. He was forty-four years old.

Except for periodic stays with her mother in Montgomery, Zelda spent the remainder of her life at the Highland Hospital in Asheville, North Carolina. In 1948, a fire broke out on the top floor of the sanatorium. Zelda perished in the flames.

It took some time before her charred body could be positively identified. When it was, she was buried beside her husband in Rockville Union Cemetery. In 1975, they were reinterred at the Fitzgerald family plot at St. Mary's Church, also in Rockville.

"It is the custom now to look back on ourselves of the boom days with a disapproval that approaches horror," Scott wrote toward the end of his years. "But it had its virtues, that old boom: Life was a great deal larger and gayer for most people, and the stampede to the spartan virtues in times of war and famine shouldn't make us too dizzy to remember its hilarious glory. There were so many good things. These eyes have been hallowed by watching a man order champagne for his two thousand guests, by listening while a woman ordered a whole staircase from the greatest sculptor in the world, by seeing a man tear up a good check for eight hundred thousand dollars."

The days of "hilarious glory" were gone. All that was left were the words in Scott's books.

In early 1928, over a year before the stock market crash, the editorial page of *The New York Times* boldly declared that there were "No More Flappers." "Who has seen in recent days this creature," the editors wondered, "described by the [Junior League] as the typical postwar flapper? Her hair was furiously frizzled. Her smoking was overenthusiastic. Her chewing gum was too loud and too large. Her vocabulary was imported directly from the trenches. She was startlingly picturesque—and now she is no more."

The *Times* wasn't entirely wrong. For the better part of a decade, the flapper—part reality, part invention—had dominated the national imagination. But Americans living through depression, war, and the

Red scare could scarcely afford to indulge in the frivolities of the 1920s. So the flapper slipped out of sight and into memory.

Her influence, however, endures.

Though hemlines would continue to rise and fall over the century, the sexual and romantic revolutions in which the flapper was a star-ring player never really subsided. The sharp rise in sexual experimentation that had begun even before World War I continued over the course of the ensuing decades, aided by the social and demographic upheavals of World War II and by new forms of birth control like "the pill," which was licensed by the Food and Drug Administration in 1960 and became extremely popular among single women by the late 1960s. In the aftermath of World War II, when he scandalized the nation with his two-volume study, *Sexual Behavior in the Human Male* (1948) and *Sexual Behavior in the Human Female* (1953), research scientist Alfred Kinsey was only reminding Americans that the flapper and her boyfriend enjoyed sex even as they matured into middle age.

Moralists of the cold war era blamed the "sexual revolution" on a variety of social ills, among them technology (the pill), politics (feminism and communism), and culture (pornography). They even tried to shoot the messenger by blaming Kinsey. But the same trends that had converged earlier in the century to produce a vast change in morals and manners—the migration from country to cities, the mass entry of women into the workforce and classroom, the expansion of the middle class, the shift from an industrial and agricultural economy to a service economy, the emergence of a youth culture—continued in the cold war years to undermine the already shaky basis of Victorian-era morality.

Today, as Americans debate the question of same-sex marriage, they are in effect picking up where the flapper left off. In the 1920s, she attracted scorn for suggesting that romance was an individual prerogative and that there was an important place for sex outside of procreation. Eighty years later, gays and lesbians are extending the logic of this argument in asserting the legitimacy of their own bonds.

In the same way, today's debate over consumerism hearkens back to the flapper and her era. Mass production and mass purchasing power first came under serious public scrutiny in the 1920s. Arriving on the scene when she did, the flapper brought into sharp relief the new American propensity to speak of rights in material terms—as so many items bought and consumed—and to regard freedom as a function of marketplace choice. Even as most Americans grew more distant from political and economic elites, they came to regard access to fashionable dresses, lipstick, and jewelry as a "democratization" of everyday life.

As in the 1920s, Americans today are living amid rising economic inequality and a widespread feeling of alienation from the corridors of government. Even so, many people cling to the notion that consumption—purchasing a bigger house, a fancier car, a designer dress, or an expensive suit, even at the cost of deep household debt—is the great social leveler.

If the sexual and consumer revolutions of the 1920s continue to play themselves out today, so does the curious cycle of celebrity and style. It was never clear whether Scott Fitzgerald "invented" the flapper, "discovered" her, or exploited her. Can anyone today pinpoint the moment, or the reason, that Paris Hilton became famous? As in the twenties, a small but influential group of media and advertising professionals continues to wield a great deal of influence over the images we see, the celebrities we idolize, and the fashions we embrace.

Writing in the 1920s, Loren Knox, a culture critic for *The Atlantic Monthly,* lamented that "though we, the people of the United States, boast of our individuality, we are regarded to-day by those who cater to our wants as an absorbent mass, rather than as discriminating units. Great agencies of supply give us a range of selection, it is true. But each differentiation is the standard choice of so large a number that it becomes a class itself. . . .

"In foods, we are shipped train loads of ready-to-eat, sometimes predigested, breakfast foods, biscuits, meats, soups and desserts," he continued. "In clothes, all of us who are not museum freaks are offered ready-to-wear, uniformly designed suits, shirts, underwear, collars, hosiery, and shoes. . . . In music, the ready-to-grind phonographs and pianolas have given the art of the few to the mob. . . . All, all, is ready prepared."

Knox's eulogy for the American individual, though surely an overstatement, is as important today as in the 1920s. Then, as now, ordinary people struggled to carve out their own identities in an increasingly impersonal, prefabricated world. Millions of flappers embraced a controversial lifestyle in a spirited attempt at self-definition. But they did so in concert, buying the same brands of clothing, makeup, and cigarettes, emulating Clara Bow and Colleen Moore, and adopting the same jargon ripped from the pages of Scott Fitzgerald's latest short story. Eighty years later, their great-granddaughters struggle with the same dilemma.

The flapper was, in effect, the first thoroughly modern American.

Noteſ

Introduction: Tango Pirateſ and Abſinthe

1   *On May 22, 1915:* For a review of the Eugenia Kelly affair, see *New York Times,* May 23, 1915, C5; May 25, 1915, 8; May 26, 1915, 8; May 30, 1915, SM16; August 8, 1915, 7; October 1, 1915, 5; November 18, 1915; and Lewis A. Erenberg, *Steppin' Out: New York Nightlife and the Transformation of American Culture, 1890–1930* (Westport, CT: Greenwood Press, 1981), 77–85.

2   *$10 million:* Eugenia Kelly was due to inherit $600,000 on her twenty-first birthday. According to the Federal Reserve Bank of Minneapolis's consumer price index calculator, in 2003 dollars that sum equals just over $10 million.

5   *1920s fashion writer:* Kenneth A. Yellis, "Prosperity's Child: Some Thoughts on the Flapper," *American Quarterly* 21, no. 2 (Spring 1969): 49.

5   Webster's: Gerald E. Critoph, "The Flapper and Her Critics," in Carol V. R. George, ed., *"Remember the Ladies": New Perspectives on Women in American History* (Syracuse, N.Y.: Syracuse University Press, 1975), 145.

5   *"flappers don't like":* Critoph, "The Flapper and Her Critics," 145.

6   *"Concern—and consternation":* New York Times, April 16, 1922, 49.

6   *"flippancy of the . . . flapper":* New York Times, October 1, 1922, 20.

6   *"lowest degree of intelligence":* New York Times, July 6, 1922, 8.

6   *Florida State Legislature:* New York Times, April 4, 1929, 22.

6   *It wasn't until 1929:* William E. Leuchtenberg, *The Perils of Prosperity: 1914–1932,* rev. ed. 1993 (Chicago: University of Chicago Press, 1958), 158.

6   *fourteen-year-old:* New York Times, June 4, 1923, 7.

7   *"Flapper Jane":* Bruce Bliven, "Flapper Jane," *New Republic,* September 9, 1925, 65–67.

Chapter 1: The Most Popular Girl

13 *"brown-shingled building"*: Sara Mayfield, *Exiles from Paradise: Zelda and Scott Fitzgerald* (New York: Delacorte Press, 1971), 1.

13 *"sophisticated for her age"*: Mayfield, *Exiles,* 1–2.

14 *climbed to the roof:* James R. Mellow, *Invented Lives: F. Scott & Zelda Fitzgerald* (Boston: Houghton Mifflin, 1984), 5.

14 *Stutz Bearcat:* Mayfield, *Exiles,* 24.

14 *"most popular girl"*: Mayfield, *Exiles,* 24.

14 *pear trees:* Nancy Milford, *Zelda: A Biography* (New York: Harper & Row, 1970), 9.

15 *cut school:* Milford, *Zelda,* 22.

15 *"I do love my Charlie so"*: Milford, *Zelda,* 12.

15 *"the last to deny"*: Mayfield, Exiles, 22–23.

16 *During the summer:* Milford, *Zelda,* 16.

16 *legendary Christmas bop:* Matthew J. Bruccoli, *Some Sort of Epic Grandeur: The Life of F. Scott Fitzgerald,* rev. ed, 1993 (New York: Harcourt Brace Jovanovich, 1981), 104.

16 *"I never let them down"*: Zelda Fitzgerald, *Save Me the Last Waltz,* in Matthew J. Bruccoli and Mary Gordon, eds., *Zelda Fitzgerald: The Collected Writings* (New York: Charles Scribner's Sons, 1991), 32.

16 *"the agreeable countenance"*: Thomas Alexander Boyd, "Scott Fitzgerald Here on Vacation: 'Rests' by Outlining New Novels," *St. Paul Daily News,* August 28, 1921, E6; also reprinted in Matthew J. Bruccoli and Judith S. Baugham, eds., *Conversations with F. Scott Fitzgerald* (Jackson, Miss.: University Press of Mississippi, 2004), 3.

17 *leave from the army:* Bruccoli, *Some Sort of Epic Grandeur,* 96–97.

17 *most eligible debutantes:* Mayfield, *Exiles,* 1.

17 *"great animal magnetism"*: Mellow, *Invented Lives,* 7.

17–18 *"two kinds of girls"*: Milford, *Zelda,* 17.

18 *"late dates with fast workers"*: Mayfield, *Exiles,* 2–3.

18 *"the handsomest boy"*: Mayfield, *Exiles,* 3.

18 *"like new goods"*: Zelda Fitzgerald, *Save Me the Last Waltz,* in Bruccoli and Gordon, eds., *Zelda Fitzgerald: The Collected Writings,* 39.

19 *"break up the stag lines"*: Mayfield, *Exiles,* 45.

19 *Zelda's attention:* Milford, *Zelda,* 22.

19 *passed their days:* Milford, *Zelda,* 33–34.

19 *"this dusty time"*: ZSF to FSF, undated [summer 1935], in Jackson R. Bryer and Cathy W. Barks, eds., *Dear Scott, Dearest Zelda: The Love Letters of F. Scott and Zelda Fitzgerald* (New York: St. Martin's Griffin, 2002), 214–15.

20 *An entry from 1935:* Bruccoli, *Some Sort of Epic Grandeur,* 106.

CHAPTER 2: *f*EX O'CLOCK IN AMERICA

21   *"'no ladies'"*: Sara Mayfield, *Exiles from Paradise: Zelda and Scott Fitzgerald*
     (New York: Delacorte Press, 1971), 11–12.
21   *sexual habits*: Alfred Kinsey, *Sexual Behavior in the Human Female* (Philadel-
     phia: W. B. Saunders, 1953), 298, 339. In his study of one hundred married
     men and one hundred married women who were born before 1900, G. V.
     Hamilton found that 67 percent of women born between 1886 and 1890
     but only 30 percent of women born between 1891 and 1900 were virgins
     at marriage. Hamilton's study is probably skewed by its small sample size
     and by the unusually active sex lives of its participants. See G. V. Hamilton,
     A Research in Marriage (New York: A. & C. Boni, Inc., 1929), 43–44.
23   *"Sex o'clock"*: "Sex o'Clock in America," *Current Opinion* 55 (August 1913):
     113–14; Agnes Repplier, "The Repeal of Reticence," *Atlantic Monthly* 113
     (March 1914): 297–304.
23   *noted with disapproval*: James R. McGovern, "The American Woman's
     Pre–World War I Freedom in Manners and Morals," *Journal of American
     History* 55, no. 2 (September 1968): 326.
23   *"Where Is Your Daughter"*: McGovern, "The American Woman's Pre–World
     War I Freedom," 324.
23   *magazine exposé*: Page Smith, *Redeeming the Time: A People's History of the
     1920s and the New Deal* (New York: McGraw-Hill, 1987), 9, 49.
23   *"You dare me"*: McGovern, "The American Woman's Pre–World War I
     Freedom," 323.
24   *"Take It from Me!"*: McGovern, "The American Woman's Pre–World War I
     Freedom," 323.
24   "I DO NOT DOUBT YOU": FSF to ZSF, February 21, 1919, in Jackson R.
     Bryer and Cathy W. Barks, eds., *Dear Scott, Dearest Zelda: The Love Letters of
     F. Scott and Zelda Fitzgerald* (New York: St. Martin's Griffin, 2002), 11.
24   "DARLING HEART": FSF to ZSF, February 22, 1919, in Bryer and Barks,
     eds., *Dear Scott, Dearest Zelda*, 12.
24   *dust from the Auburn incident*: Mayfield, *Exiles*, 46–47.
24   *"soft, warm nights"*: ZSF to FSF, undated [March 1919], in Bryer and Barks,
     eds., *Dear Scott, Dearest Zelda*, 13.
25   *"don't be so depressed"*: ZSF to FSF, undated [March 1919], in Bryer and
     Barks, eds., *Dear Scott, Dearest Zelda*, 15.
25   *122 rejection letters*: Matthew J. Bruccoli, *Some Sort of Epic Grandeur: The
     Life of F. Scott Fitzgerald*, rev. ed. 1993 (New York: Harcourt Brace
     Jovanovich, 1981), 111.
25   *"about as much control"*: F. Scott Fitzgerald, *The Crackup* (New York: New
     Directions, 1945), 25.
25   *"I must leave now"*: ZSF to FSF, undated [March 1919], Bryer and Barks,
     eds., *Dear Scott, Dearest Zelda*, 21.
25   *"Bill LeGrand and I"*: ZSF to FSF, undated [April 1919], in Bryer and Barks,
     eds., *Dear Scott, Dearest Zelda*, 24.

25   "'Red' said": ZSF to FSF, undated [May 1919], in Bryer and Barks, eds., *Dear Scott, Dearest Zelda,* 31–32.

26   "awfully silly": ZSF to FSF, undated [April 1919], in Bryer and Barks, eds., *Dear Scott, Dearest Zelda,* 24.

26   "Please please": ZSF to FSF, undated [late May 1919], in Bryer and Barks, eds., *Dear Scott, Dearest Zelda,* 32–33.

26   "Is that all . . . ?": Mayfield, *Exiles,* 75.

26   "added whiskey": Minnie Sayre to ZSF, enclosed in ZSF to FSF, undated [April 1919], in Bryer and Barks, eds., *Dear Scott, Dearest Zelda,* 28.

27   "asked me not to write": ZSF to FSF, undated [June 1919], in Bryer and Barks, eds., *Dear Scott, Dearest Zelda,* 37.

27   *Victrola records:* Nancy Milford, *Zelda: A Biography* (New York: Harper & Row, 1970), 51.

27   "While my friends": Fitzgerald, *The Crackup,* 25–26.

CHAPTER 3: WILL ∫HE THROW HER ARM∫ AROUND YOUR NECK AND YELL?

29   *economic and demographic forces:* Lynn Dumenil, *Modern Temper: American Culture and Society in the 1920s* (New York: Hill and Wang, 1995), 112–18; Joanne J. Meyerowitz, *Women Adrift: Independent Wage-Earners in Chicago, 1880–1930* (Chicago: University of Chicago Press, 1988), 4–5.

29   *real money . . . real freedom:* Paula S. Fass, *The Damned and the Beautiful: American Youth in the 1920s* (New York: Oxford University Press, 1977), 24.

29   *industrialization and urbanization:* Howard P. Chudacoff and Judith E. Smith, *The Evolution of American Urban Society* (Englewood Cliffs, N.J.: Prentice-Hall, 1995), 69–70, 111–12; William E. Leuchtenberg, *The Perils of Prosperity: 1914–1932,* rev. ed. (New York: University of Chicago Press, 1958), 225; James T. Patterson, *America in the Twentieth Century: A History* (New York: Harcourt College Publishers, 2000), 146.

30   "the farmer's daughter": Meyerowitz, *Women Adrift,* 9, 19.

30   "money for clothes": Meyerowitz, *Women Adrift,* 18–19.

30   "up to that time": Meyerowitz, *Women Adrift,* 18–19. Italics added for emphasis.

30   "mysteries of darkness": David Nasaw, *Going Out: The Rise and Fall of Public Amusements* (Cambridge, Mass.: Harvard University Press, 1993), 6.

31   *Across America:* Nasaw, *Going Out,* 1–9.

31   *more money and more time:* Roy Rosenzweig, *Eight Hours for What We Will: Workers & Leisure in an Industrial City, 1870–1920* (New York: Cambridge University Press, 1983), 179–180. Thanks to mechanization, the work week of the average urban blue-collar worker plummeted from 55.9 hours in 1900 to 44.2 in 1929; at the same time, real wages adjusted for inflation rose 25 percent in the first two decades of the new century.

31 *"throw her arms"*: Kathy Peiss, *Cheap Amusements: Working Women and Leisure in Turn-of-the-Century New York* (Philadelphia: Temple University Press, 1986), 134–35.

32 *Louisa*: Peiss, *Cheap Amusements*, 70.

32 *"one of the women"*: Peiss, *Cheap Amusements*, 70–1, 99, 108–09.

32 *Ina Smith . . . and John Marean*: Ellen K. Rothman, *Hands and Hearts: A History of Courtship in America* (Cambridge, Mass.: Harvard University Press, 1987), 204–05.

33 *"walking under the trees"*: Rothman, *Hands and Hearts*, 207.

33 *Otto Follin and Laura Grant*: Rothman, *Hands and Hearts*, 206.

33 *Marian Curtis and Lawrence Gerritson*: Rothman, *Hands and Hearts*, 223–35.

34 *"going out motoring"*: Robert S. Lynd and Helen Merrell Lynd, *Middletown: A Study in Modern American Culture* (New York: Harcourt, Brace and Co., 1929), 257, 524.

34 *Muncie's high school students*: Lynd and Lynd, *Middletown*, 257, 524.

35 *"off and away"*: Rothman, *Hands and Hearts*, 294–95.

35 *By 1925 . . . in Muncie*: Lynd and Lynd, *Middletown*, 258.

35 *the old order*: Beth L. Bailey, *From Front Porch to Back Seat: Courtship in Twentieth-Century America* (Baltimore: Johns Hopkins University Press, 1980), 16–17.

36 *"I'll be patient"*: Rothman, *Hands and Hearts*, 230.

36 *"If I get much hungrier"*: Rothman, *Hands and Hearts*, 230.

36 *This new system*: Meyerowitz, *Women Adrift*, 35–36, 69.

36 *crude double standard*: Peiss, *Cheap Amusements*, 68.

37 *"If they didn't take me"*: Peiss, *Cheap Amusements*, 54.

37 *"If I did not have a man"*: Meyerowitz, *Women Adrift*, 102.

37 *Consumer's League report*: Peiss, *Cheap Amusements*, 55.

37 MAN GETTING $18: Meyerowitz, *Women Adrift*, 102–03.

38 *Clara Laughlin*: Peiss, *Cheap Amusements*, 112.

38 *coed at Ohio State*: Paula S. Fass, *The Damned and the Beautiful: American Youth in the 1920s* (New York: Oxford University Press, 1977), 307.

CHAPTER 4: FLAPPER KING

39 *"recognized spokesman"*: Frederick James Smith, "Fitzgerald, Flappers and Fame," *Shadowland* 3 (January 1921): 39, 75, reprinted in Matthew J. Bruccoli and Judith S. Baughman, eds., *Conversations with F. Scott Fitzgerald* (Jackson, Miss.: University Press of Mississippi, 2004), 6.

39 *"originated the flapper"*: "Novelist Loved Atlanta Girl's Picture," undated news clip, source unknown, F. Scott Fitzgerald Papers, Firestone Library, Princeton University [hereafter FSF MS], Scrapbook III.

39 *"Flapperdom's Fiction Ace"*: Bart Fulton, "Flapperdom's Fiction Ace," undated clip [ca. 1922], FSF MS, Scrapbook III.

39   *"'eternal feminine'"*: "The Expert on Flappers," undated news clip [ca. 1921–1922], *Minneapolis Tribune*, FSF MS, Scrapbook III.

41   *"To Scott Fitzgerald"*: Undated, untitled clip, source unknown, FSF MS, Scrapbook II.

41   *"Transformation of a Rose"*: "The Parliament of Fools," The Wellesley [?] undated clip, FSF MS, Scrapbook II.

42   *"popular daughter"*: F. Scott Fitzgerald, *This Side of Paradise* (New York: Charles Scribner's Sons, 1920), 58.

42   *"saw girls doing things"*: Fitzgerald, *This Side of Paradise*, 59.

42   *"Mother, it's done"*: Fitzgerald, *This Side of Paradise*, 59–60, 178.

42   *forty thousand copies:* "The Bookman's Monthly Score," undated clip [ca. 1920], FSF MS, Scrapbook II.

42   *"Before he started"*: Untitled, undated clipping [ca. 1921–1922], FSF MS, Scrapbook III.

43   *2.75 million:* Matthew J. Bruccoli, *Some Sort of Epic Grandeur: The Life of F. Scott Fitzgerald*, rev. ed. 1993 (New York: Harcourt Brace Jovanovich, 1981), 125.

43   Main Street: Bruccoli, *Some Sort of Epic Grandeur*, 158.

43   *Ardita:* F. Scott Fitzgerald, "The Offshore Pirate," *Saturday Evening Post*, May 29, 1920.

44   *Myra admits:* F. Scott Fitzgerald, "Myra Meets His Family," *Saturday Evening Post*, March 20, 1920.

44   *one in every five households:* Robert S. Lynd and Helen Merrell Lynd, *Middletown: A Study in Modern American Culture* (New York: Harcourt, Brace and Co., 1929), 239.

44   *more popular interest:* Paula S. Fass, *The Damned and the Beautiful: American Youth in the 1920s* (New York: Oxford University Press, 1977), 29.

44   *number of children borne:* Steven Mintz and Susan Kellogg, *Domestic Revolutions: A Social History of American Family Life* (New York: Free Press, 1988), 51; Linda Gordon, *Woman's Body, Woman's Right: A Social History of Birth Control in America*, rev. ed. 1977 (New York: Grossman, 1976), 48. The average birthrate fell from 7.04 children in 1800 to 3.17 children in 1920.

45   *birthrates fell across the board:* Fass, *The Damned and the Beautiful*, 61.

45   *Smaller families:* Fass, *The Damned and the Beautiful*, 58–59; Howard P. Chudacoff, *How Old Are You?: Age Consciousness in American Culture* (Princeton: Princeton University Press, 1989), 92–116. The average household size fell from 4.7 persons in 1900 to 4.3 in 1920.

46   *college enrollments . . . high school attendance:* Fass, *The Damned and the Beautiful*, 124; John D'Emilio and Estelle B. Freedman, *Intimate Matters: A History of Sexuality in America* (Chicago: University of Chicago Press, 1997), 257.

46   *the Lynds observed:* Lynd and Lynd, *Middletown*, 211.

46   *"that generation's sex life"*: Fass, *The Damned and the Beautiful*, 21.

46   *"rather a joke"*: Lynd and Lynd, *Middletown,* 138.

46   *"petting parties"*: Lynd and Lynd, *Middletown,* 138.

46   *177 college women:* Geraldine Frances Smith, "Certain Aspects of the Sex Life of the Adolescent Girl," *Journal of Abnormal Psychology* (September 1924): 348–49.

46   *"Girls aren't so modest"*: Lynd and Lynd, *Middletown,* 141.

47   *Mrs. George Rose:* Mary Murphy, " '. . . And All That Jazz': Changing Manners and Morals in Butte After World War I," *Montana* 46, no. 4 (Winter 1996): 55.

47   *"A Novel About Flappers"*: Promotional advertisement, FSF MS, Scrapbook II.

47   *"timelessness"*: FSF to Maxwell Perkins, May 11, 1922, in Andrew Turnbull, ed., *The Letters of F. Scott Fitzgerald* (New York: Scribner, 1963), 158.

47   *"Fitzgerald, Flappers and Fame"*: Smith, "Fitzgerald, Flappers and Fame," 39, 75; "This Is What Happens to Naughty Flappers," *Detroit Free Press,* undated clip [ca. 1922], FSF MS, Scrapbook III.

47   *"worth hearing"*: B. F. Wilson, "F. Scott Fitzgerald Says: 'All Women Over Thirty-Five Should Be Murdered,' " *Metropolitan Magazine* 58 (November 1923): 34, 75–76, reprinted in Matthew J. Bruccoli and Judith S. Baugham, eds., *Conversations with F. Scott Fitzgerald* (Jackson, Miss.: University Press of Mississippi, 2004).

47   *"I sometimes wonder"*: "Fitzgerald and Flappers," undated clipping [ca. 1922], unidentified Philadelphia newspaper, FSF MS, Scrapbook III.

47   *"a variety of subjects"*: F. Scott Fitzgerald, *The Crackup* (New York: New Directions, 1945), 25–27.

47   *"I wish to state"*: "Scott Fitzgerald Speaks at Home," undated clip [ca. 1922], source unknown, FSF MS, Scrapbook II.

48   *"flapper is growing stronger"*: B. F. Wilson, "F. Scott Fitzgerald Says: 'All Women over Thirty-Five Should Be Murdered,' " *Metropolitan Magazine* 58 (November 1923): 34, 75–76.

48   *"broad moral views"*: Smith, "Fitzgerald, Flappers and Fame," 39, 75.

48   *Parker's whimsical poem:* Dorothy Parker, "The Flapper," *Life,* undated clip [ca. 1922], FSF MS, Scrapbook III.

CHAPTER 5: DOING IT FOR EFFECT

51   *"toploftiness"*: F. Scott Fitzgerald, *The Crackup* (New York: New Directions, 1945), 86.

51   *"all for taking a chance"*: Matthew J. Bruccoli, *Some Sort of Epic Grandeur: The Life of F. Scott Fitzgerald,* rev. ed. 1993 (New York: Harcourt Brace Jovanovich, 1981), 119.

51   *"Terms, etc."*: FSF to Maxwell Perkins, September 18, 1919, in Andrew Turnbull, ed., *The Letters of F. Scott Fitzgerald* (New York: Scribner, 1963), 139.

51 *"summer of despair"*: Fitzgerald, *The Crackup,* 77.

52 *"mighty glad you're coming"*: ZSF to FSF, undated [October 1919], in Jackson R. Bryer and Cathy W. Barks, eds., *Dear Scott, Dearest Zelda: The Love Letters of F. Scott and Zelda Fitzgerald* (New York: St. Martin's Griffin, 2002), 32–33.

52 *"so be-au-ti-ful"*: ZSF to FSF, undated [February 1920] in Bryer and Barks, eds., *Dear Scott, Dearest Zelda,* 43–44.

52 *"wild, pleasure loving girl"*: FSF to Isabelle Amorous, February 26, 1920, in Matthew J. Bruccoli and Margaret M. Duggan, eds., *Correspondence of F. Scott Fitzgerald* (New York: Random House, 1980), 53.

52 *"Called on Scott Fitz"*: Nancy Milford, *Zelda: A Biography* (New York: Harper & Row, 1970), 67.

53 *"not above reproach"*: FSF to Isabelle Amorous, February 26, 1920, in *Correspondence of F. Scott Fitzgerald,* 53.

53 *"He's going to leave"*: Nathan Miller, *New World Coming: The 1920s and the Making of Modern America* (New York: Scribner, 2003), 211.

53 *"they were the twenties"*: Mayfield, *Exiles,* 84.

53 *Between 1921 and 1924*: Miller, *New World Coming,* 149–50. Between 1921 and 1924, America's gross national product rose from $69 billion to $93 billion; aggregate wages rose from roughly $36.4 billion to $51.5 billion.

53 *Philadelphia banking family*: Irving Bernstein, *The Lean Years: A History of the American Worker, 1920–1933,* rev. ed. 1966 (Boston: Houghton Mifflin, 1960), 47.

54 *Lynds visited Muncie*: Bernstein, *The Lean Years,* 54–59.

54 *Brookings Institution*: Bernstein, *The Lean Years,* 63.

55 *"spent your summer canning"*: Robert S. Lynd and Helen Merrell Lynd, *Middletown: A Study in Modern American Culture* (New York: Harcourt, Brace and Co., 1929), 156–57.

55 *smaller portion of their wages*: Andrew Heinze, *Adapting to Abundance: Jewish Immigrants, Mass Consumption and the Search for American Identity* (New York: Columbia University Press, 1990), 23; Daniel Horowitz, *The Morality of Spending: Attitudes Toward Consumer Society in America, 1875–1940* (Chicago: I. R. Dee, 1992), Appendix A.

55 *money left over for nonessentials*: Lizabeth Cohen, *Making a New Deal: Industrial Workers in Chicago, 1919–1939* (New York: Cambridge University Press, 1990), 103–04; Horowitz, *The Morality of Spending,* chap. 7–8, Appendix A.

55 *fifty million tickets*: Cohen, *Making a New Deal,* 125.

55 *tempted by credit*: Miller, *New World Coming,* 152.

55 *mah-jongg . . . flagpole sitting*: Miller, *New World Coming,* 127–29.

56 *cult of self-examination*: William E. Leuchtenberg, *The Perils of Prosperity: 1914–1932,* rev. ed. (Chicago: University of Chicago Press, 1958), 164–68.

56 *Emile Coué:* Lynn Dumenil, *Modern Temper: American Culture and Society in the 1920s* (New York: Hill and Wang, 1995), 87–88.

57 *Lawton Campbell strolled:* Milford, *Zelda,* 68.

57 *"not doing it for effect":* Mayfield, *Exiles,* 59–60.

57 *basked in publicity:* Mayfield, *Exiles,* 65.

57 *"The remarkable thing":* Bruccoli, *Some Sort of Epic Grandeur,* 156–59.

58 *Dorothy Parker:* Milford, *Zelda,* 67.

58 *Scott's old eating club:* Bruccoli, *Some Sort of Epic Grandeur,* 166–67.

59 *"Mama and Daddy":* Mayfield, *Exiles from Paradise,* 58.

59 *"Within a few months":* Milford, *Zelda,* 67.

CHAPTER 6: I PREFER THI∫ ∫ORT OF GIRL

61 *average number of profiles:* Leo Lowenthal, "The Triumph of Mass Idols," in *Literature, Popular Culture and Society* (Englewood Cliffs, N.J.: Prentice-Hall, 1961), 111.

62 *"To write it, three months":* Heywood Broun, "Books," *New-York Tribune,* May 7, 1920, 14, FSF MS, Scrapbook II.

62 *"prefer this sort of girl":* Smith, "Fitzgerald, Flappers and Fame," 39, 75, reprinted in Matthew J. Bruccoli and Judith S. Baughman, eds., *Conversations with F. Scott Fitzgerald* (Jackson, Miss.: University Press of Mississippi, 2004), 6.

62 *"I love Scott's books":* "What a 'Flapper Novelist' Thinks of His Wife," *Louisville Courier-Journal,* September 30, 1923, 112, reprinted in Bruccoli and Baughman, eds., *Conversations,* 47.

62 *syndicated review of the book:* "Mrs. F. Scott Fitzgerald Reviews 'The Beautiful and Damned,' Friend Husband's Latest," *New-York Tribune,* April 2, 1922.

62 *"I'm deadly curious":* FSF to Maxwell Perkins, undated [ca. January 10, 1920], in Andrew Turnbull, ed., *The Letters of F. Scott Fitzgerald* (New York: Scribner, 1963), 141–42.

62–63 *"The girl is excellent":* FSF to Maxwell Perkins, ca. January 31, 1922, in Turnbull, ed., *Letters,* 152–53; Andrew Turnball, *Scott Fitzgerald: A Biography* (New York: Scribner, 1962), 130.

63 *"She is quite unprincipled":* F. Scott Fitzgerald, *This Side of Paradise* (New York: Charles Scribner's Sons, 1920), 170–71, 175, 181.

63 *"the flapper has grown up":* "Fitzgerald's Flapper Grows Up," *Columbus Dispatch,* undated clip [ca. 1922], FSF MS, Scrapbook III.

63 *"started the flapper movement":* "Family of Noted Author," *Washington Herald,* undated clip [ca. 1922]; advertisement, Heart's International, May 1923, both in FSF MS, Scrapbook III.

63 Midnight Flappers: Matthew J. Bruccoli, *Some Sort of Epic Grandeur: The Life of F. Scott Fitzgerald,* rev. ed. 1993 (New York: Harcourt Brace Jovanovich, 1981), 187.

64   *"Eulogy on the Flapper"*: Zelda Sayre Fitzgerald, "Eulogy on the Flapper," *Metropolitan Magazine,* June 1922, in Matthew J. Bruccoli and Mary Gordon, eds., *Zelda Fitzgerald: The Collected Writings* (New York: Charles Scribner's Sons, 1991), 39.

65   *the good life:* Warren I. Susman, *Culture as History: The Transformation of American Society in the Twentieth Century* (New York: Pantheon Books, 1984), xx–xxvi; 271–77.

65   *nature of work had changed:* Steven J. Diner, *A Very Different Age: Americans of the Progressive Era* (New York: Hill and Wang, 1998), 50–59.

66   *adman coolly explained:* Roland Marchand, *Advertising the American Dream: Making Way for Modernity, 1920–1940* (Berkeley: University of California Press, 1985), 24.

66   *"Sell them their dreams":* William Leach, *Land of Desire: Merchants, Power and the Rise of a New American Culture* (New York: Pantheon Books, 1993), 298.

66   "Road of Happiness": Lynn Dumenil, *Modern Temper: American Culture and Society in the 1920s* (New York: Hill and Wang, 1995), 89–90.

66   *"same old story":* Dumenil, *Modern Temper,* 89–90.

67   *"Why should all life":* Nancy Milford, *Zelda: A Biography* (New York: Harper & Row, 1970), 27.

67   *Margaret Sanger:* David M. Kennedy, *Birth Control in America: The Career of Margaret Sanger* (New Haven: Yale University Press, 1970), 131.

67   *erstwhile socialist organizer:* Kennedy, *Birth Control in America,* 10–11.

67   *"birth strike":* Ellen Chesler, *Woman of Valor: Margaret Sanger and the Birth Control Movement in America* (New York: Simon & Schuster, 1992), 86–88.

68   *"for the enemy—Capitalism":* Kennedy, *Birth Control in America,* 110.

68   *"love demands":* Chesler, *Woman of Valor,* 196–97.

68   *"liberation and human development":* Chesler, *Woman of Valor,* 209.

68   *"flirted because it was fun":* Zelda Sayre Fitzgerald, "Eulogy on the Flapper."

68   *young woman in Columbus:* Paula S. Fass, *The Damned and the Beautiful: American Youth in the 1920s* (New York: Oxford University Press, 1977), 307.

68   *"little town of Somerset": New York Times,* August 25, 1923, 7.

69   *"Personal liberty":* Fass, *The Damned and the Beautiful,* 76.

69   Chicago Tribune's *remark:* Nancy F. Cott, *The Grounding of Modern Feminism* (New Haven: Yale University Press, 1970), 172.

69–70 "personal liberties and individual rights": Fass, *The Damned and the Beautiful,* 37. Italics added for emphasis.

CHAPTER 7: STRAIGHTEN OUT PEOPLE

71   *Founded in 1866:* Eric Foner, *Reconstruction: America's Unfinished Revolution* (New York: Harper & Row, 1988), chap. 9.

71   *written by the losers:* Joshua Michael Zeitz, "Rebel Redemption Redux," *Dissent* (Winter 2001): 70–77.

73 *group of Georgians:* On the Klan revival, see David M. Chalmers, *Hooded Americanism: The History of the Ku Klux Klan* (New York: 1965), chap. 3–4.

73 *five hundred thousand women:* Kathleen M. Blee, *Women of the Klan: Racism and Gender in the 1920s* (Berkeley, Calif.: University of California Press, 1991), 2.

74 *man from Timson:* Chalmers, *Hooded Americanism,* 39–48.

74 *"straighten out our people":* Blee, *Women of the Klan,* 83.

74 *"the revolting spectacle":* Blee, *Women of the Klan,* 87.

74 *William Wilson:* William E. Wilson, "That Long Hot Summer in Indiana," *American Heritage* 16, no. 5 (May 1965): 56–64.

74 *burned down dance halls:* Blee, *Women of the Klan,* 85–86.

74 *members from cities:* On the character and makeup of the Ku Klux Klan in the 1920s, see Kenneth T. Jackson, *The Ku Klux Klan in the City, 1915–1930* (New York: Oxford University Press, 1967), parts 1, 5.

75 *Lyman Abbott:* Edwin Gaustad and Leigh Schmidt, *The Religious History of America* (New York: Harper & Row, 2002), 304.

75 *five theological "fundamentals":* On the early history of fundamentalism, see George M. Marsden, *Fundamentalism and American Culture: The Shaping of Twentieth Century Evangelicalism, 1870–1925* (New York: Oxford University Press, 1980).

76 *"crude beliefs and the common intelligence":* On the exchange between Bryan and Darrow, see Edward J. Larson, *Summer for the Gods: The Scopes Trial and America's Continuing Debate over Science and Religion* (Cambridge, Mass.: Harvard University Press, 1997), 3–8, 187–93.

77 *"age of Amen":* Larson, *Summer for the Gods,* 229.

Chapter 8: New York ∫ophi∫tication

79 *towns outside of Chicago:* Gerald E. Critoph, "The Flapper and Her Critics," in Carol V. R. George, ed., *"Remember the Ladies": New Perspectives on Women in American History* (Syracuse, N.Y.: Syracuse University Press, 1975), 153.

79 *Kearney, New Jersey:* Critoph, "The Flapper and Her Critics," 154.

79 *"flapper slouch": New York Times,* July 6, 1922, 8.

79 *"declaration of independence":* Critoph, "The Flapper and Her Critics," 154.

81 *Mrs. Anna Mesime: New York Times,* November 16, 1922, 10.

81 *at least $117: New York Times,* March 5, 1922, 3.

81 *"Eulogy on the Flapper":* Zelda Sayre Fitzgerald, "Eulogy on the Flapper," *Metropolitan Magazine,* June 1922, in Matthew J. Bruccoli and Mary Gordon, eds., *Zelda Fitzgerald: The Collected Writings* (New York: Charles Scribner's Sons, 1991), 391.

81 *Butte, Montana:* Mary Murphy, " '. . . And All That Jazz': Changing Manners and Morals in Butte After World War I," *Montana* 46, no. 4 (Winter 1996): 54.

82   *"a big-boned westerner":* Ben Yagoda, *About Town: The New Yorker and the World It Made* (New York: Scribner, 2000), 25.

83   *Algonquin Hotel:* Margaret Chase Harriman, *The Vicious Circle: The Story of the Algonquin Round Table* (New York: Rinehart, 1951), 21–22; Rian James, *Dining in New York* (New York: The John Day Company, 1931), 21–22.

84   *highbrow discussions:* Yagoda, *About Town,* 32.

85   *Dorothy Parker:* Robert E. Drennan, ed., *The Algonquin Wits* (New York: Citadel Press, 1968), 112–13.

86   *old lady in Dubuque:* Background on *The New Yorker* is culled from Yagoda, *About Town,* chap. 1–2.

CHAPTER 9: MISS JAZZ AGE

87   *"most dashing figure":* Brendan Gill, *Here at The New Yorker* (New York: Random House, 1975), 203.

89   *stumbled her way:* Gill, *Here at The New Yorker,* 203; "Lois Long" in *American National Biography* (New York: Oxford University Press, 1999).

89   *"exceptionally well-constructed":* Dale Kramer, *Ross and The New Yorker* (Garden City: Doubleday, 1951), 82, 212.

89   *later raised to $75:* Harrison Kinney, *James Thurber: His Life and Times* (New York: Henry Holt and Co., 1995), 378.

90   *"Drinks were a dollar twenty-five":* Kinney, *James Thurber,* 378–79.

90   *specially fitted wire:* Michael and Ariane Batterberry, *On the Town in New York* (New York: Scribner, 1999), 205.

90   *stock exchange bell sounded:* Rian James, *Dining in New York* (New York: The John Day Company, 1931), 227.

91   *"threw up in his cab":* Kinney, *James Thurber,* 378–79.

91   *amused her colleagues:* Kramer, *Ross and The New Yorker,* 82–83.

91   *"Lilly Daché hats":* Kennedy Fraser, *Ornament and Silence: Essays on Women's Lives* (New York: Knopf, 1996), 234.

91   *"the real excitement":* New Yorker, April 3, 1926, 42.

92   *"HAS been a week!":* New Yorker, November 14, 1925, 25. For a description of the County Fair, see Charles G. Shaw, *Nightlife* (New York: The John Day Company, 1931), 84.

92   *Most working women:* Winifred D. Wandersee, *Women's Work and Family Values, 1920–1940* (Cambridge, Mass.: Harvard University Press, 1981), 85. Thirty percent of women in the 1920s worked as domestic servants, 19 percent as clerical workers, 18 percent as factory workers, 6 percent as store clerks, and 9 percent as farmers.

93   *earned lower wages:* Lynn Dumenil, *Modern Temper: American Culture and Society in the 1920s* (New York: Hill and Wang, 1995), 115–16. Saleswomen earned only 42 percent of what salesmen brought home.

CHAPTER 10: GIRLIſH DELIGHT IN BARROOMſ

95   *$28,754.78:* Matthew J. Bruccoli, *Some Sort of Epic Grandeur: The Life of F. Scott Fitzgerald,* rev. ed. 1993 (New York: Harcourt Brace Jovanovich, 1981), 224–25.

96   *"where the $36,960 had gone":* Bruccoli, *Some Sort of Epic Grandeur,* 225.

96   *first week in Paris:* Sara Mayfield, *Exiles from Paradise: Zelda and Scott Fitzgerald* (New York: Delacorte Press, 1971), 94.

96   *never bothered to learn anything:* Bruccoli, *Some Sort of Epic Grandeur,* 275.

97   *Upon arriving in Valescure:* Nancy Milford, *Zelda: A Biography* (New York: Harper & Row, 1970), 106.

97   *sometime after July 13:* Bruccoli, *Some Sort of Epic Grandeur,* 230–33.

98   *"terrible four-day rows":* Bruccoli, *Some Sort of Epic Grandeur,* 245.

98   *Colony, at Sixty-first Street:* Rian James, *Dining in New York* (New York: The John Day Company, 1931), 187–88.

98   *Pirate's Den:* Stephen Graham, *New York Nights* (New York: George H. Doran Company, 1927), 32–33.

99   *"the crowd there": New Yorker,* November 21, 1925.

99   *"short, squat maiden": New Yorker,* November 14, 1925, 26; and December 18, 1926, 79.

99   *"snappy little roadster": New Yorker,* November 21, 1925, 22.

100 *"threw up a few times": New Yorker,* February 12, 1927.

100 *"spectacular dry raids": New Yorker,* January 1, 1927, 56.

100 *"it was nothing":* Harrison Kinney, *James Thurber: His Life and Times* (New York: Henry Holt and Co., 1995), 379.

100 *"hoped we could drink":* Kinney, *James Thurber,* 378–79.

101 *"Youth of America": New Yorker,* July 17, 1926, 47–48.

101 *a new cocktail:* Dale Kramer, *Ross and* The New Yorker (Garden City, N.Y.: Doubleday, 1951), 124.

101 *"grown-up sport": New Yorker,* July 24, 1926, 38.

102 *"Remedy for a dented flask": New Yorker,* July 3, 1926, 48; July 10, 1926, 48.

102 *"without a corkscrew": New Yorker,* December 4, 1926, 91–92.

102 *"girlish delight in barrooms": New Yorker,* September 12, 1925.

CHAPTER 11: THEſE MODERN WOMEN

105 *Charlotte Perkins Gilman:* Nancy F. Cott, *The Grounding of Modern Feminism* (New Haven: Yale University Press, 1970), 150–52.

105 *Lillian Symes:* Lillian Symes, "Still a Man's Game: Reflections of a Slightly Tired Feminist," *Harper's Magazine* 158 (May 1929): 678–79.

106 *"sex rights":* Cott, *The Grounding of Modern Feminism,* 42–43.

106 *"These Modern Women":* Elaine Showalter, ed., *These Modern Women: Autobiographical Essays from the Twenties* (New York: Feminist Press at the City University of New York, 1979), 5.

106   *Heterodoxy:* See Judith Schwartz, *Radical Feminists of Heterodoxy: Greenwich Village, 1912–1940* (Norwich, Vt.: New Victoria Publishers, 1986).

107   *"inquisitive and skeptical eye":* Symes, "Still a Man's Game," 678–79.

107   *"Declaration of Sentiments":* Eleanor Flexner, *Century of Struggle: The Women's Rights Movement in the United States,* rev. ed. 1975 (Cambridge, Mass.: Belknap Press of Harvard University Press, 1959), 74–75.

108   *Charlotte Woodward:* Flexner, *Century of Struggle,* 74–75.

108   "rights *of every human":* Cott, *The Grounding of Modern Feminism,* 19. Italics added for emphasis.

108   *According to prevailing wisdom:* Elaine Tyler May, *Great Expectations: Marriage and Divorce in Post-Victorian America* (Chicago: University of Chicago Press, 1980), 17–22.

109 *To many second-generation suffragists:* Paula Baker, "The Domestication of Politics: Women and American Political Society, 1780–1920," *American Historical Review* 89, no. 3 (June 1984): 620–47.

109   *"Why Women Should Vote":* Aileen S. Kraditor, *The Ideas of the Woman Suffrage Movement, 1890–1920,* rev. ed. 1981 (New York: Columbia University Press, 1965), 68–69.

109   *"Women's place is Home":* William H. Chafe, *The Paradox of Change: American Women in the 20th Century* (New York: Oxford University Press, 1991), 15.

110   *Over the preceding decade:* Cott, *The Grounding of Modern Feminism,* 135. By 1925, sixteen states banned women from working at night; thirteen states established minimum wages for women.

110   *to justify these laws:* Alice Kessler-Harris, *Out to Work: A History of Wage-Earning Women in the United States* (New York: Oxford University Press, 1982), 186.

111   *Alice Paul:* Cott, *The Grounding of Modern Feminism,* 122.

111   *Another member of the NWP:* Cott, *The Grounding of Modern Feminism,* 124.

111   *"the most important function":* Cott, *The Grounding of Modern Feminism,* 129.

112   *"slaves to the machines of industry":* Cott, *The Grounding of Modern Feminism,* 134.

112   *"flapper attitude": New York Times,* April 12, 1922, 5.

112   *"feminists—New Style":* Dorothy Dunbar Bromley, "Feminist—New Style," *Harper's Monthly Magazine* 155 (October 1927): 552.

112   *Bromley concluded:* Bromley, "Feminist—New Style," 560. Italics added for emphasis.

CHAPTER 12: THE LINGERIE SHORTAGE IN THIS COUNTRY

115   *sex was on the brain:* Mary Murphy, " '. . . And All That Jazz': Changing Manners and Morals in Butte After World War I," *Montana,* 46, no. 4 (Winter 1996): 58.

115   *"tall, urbane": New York Times,* February 23, 1968, 1.

116   *"fifteen and seventy-five": New York Times,* February 23, 1968, 1.

117 *"Maybe we began drinking"*: Harrison Kinney, *James Thurber: His Life and Times* (New York: Henry Holt and Co., 1995), 380.

117 *"I just learned"*: Harold Ross to Lois Long, May 16, 1930, *The New Yorker* Records, New York Public Library, Box 6, Lois Long Folder.

117 *"Zelda Fitzgerald figure"*: Kennedy Fraser, *Ornament and Silence: Essays on Women's Lives* (New York: Knopf, 1996), 234.

117 *Their marriage announcement:* James Thurber, *The Years with Ross* (New York: Little Brown and Co., 1957), 26–27.

117 *a Packard: New York Times,* November 30, 1929, 20.

117 *"All we were saying"*: Kinney, *James Thurber,* 380.

117 *nationwide alcohol consumption:* David E. Kyvig, *Daily Life in the United States, 1920–1940* (Chicago: Ivan R. Dee, 2002), 24.

118 *three-quarters of all college-age men:* Paula S. Fass, *The Damned and the Beautiful: American Youth in the 1920s* (New York: Oxford University Press, 1977), 275–77.

118 *"Imagine yourself kissed"*: Caroline Smith-Rosenberg, "The Female World of Love and Ritual: Relations Between Women in Nineteenth-Century America," in *Disorderly Conduct: Visions of Gender in Victorian America* (New York: Knopf, 1985), 57.

118 *"my girl of all the girls"*: Smith-Rosenberg, "The Female World of Love and Ritual," 58.

119 *"When a Vassar girl"*: John D'Emilio and Estelle B. Freedman, *Intimate Matters: A History of Sexuality in America* (Chicago: University of Chicago Press, 1988), 126.

119 *1870s to the 1920s:* Caroline Smith-Rosenberg, "The New Woman as Androgynye: Social Disorder and Gender Crisis, 1870–1936," in *Disorderly Conduct,* 253.

119 *Boston marriages:* Smith-Rosenberg, "The New Woman as Androgynye," 254.

120 *Bryn Mawr College:* Smith-Rosenberg, "The New Woman as Androgynye," 281.

121 *women in 1890:* Fass, *The Damned and the Beautiful,* 66.

121 *gay subcultures:* John D'Emilio, "Capitalism and Gay Identity," in Ann Snitow, Christine Stansell, and Sharon Thompson, eds., *Powers of Desire: The Politics of Sexuality* (New York: Monthly Review Press, 1983), 100–13.

122 *"Protestant Westerners"*: Kinney, *James Thurber,* 379–80.

122 *"lingerie shortage in this country"*: *New Yorker,* November 14, 1925, 24.

122 *"Turn about"*: *New Yorker,* October 19, 1925, 28–29.

123 *"perennial Greenwich Village Inn"*: *New Yorker,* August 1, 1925, 20.

123 *"Without being flapper"*: *New Yorker,* November 21, 1925, 22.

CHAPTER 13: A MIND FULL OF FABULATION∫

127 *rambling town house:* Axel Masden, *Chanel: A Woman of Her Own* (New York: Henry Holt, 1990), 128.

128   *"at the farthest corner"*: Marcel Hadrich, *Coco Chanel: Her Life, Her Secrets* (Boston: Little, Brown, 1971), 25.

128   *"I told myself"*: Masden, *Chanel*, 8.

128   *"little prisoner"*: Hadrich, *Coco Chanel*, 28.

129   *"concerned with independence"*: Hadrich, *Coco Chanel*, 33.

129   *"I—who never told the truth"*: Masden, *Chanel*, 4.

130   *"mind was full of fabulations"*: Masden, *Chanel*, 19.

131   *"I invited the chambermaid"*: Hadrich, *Coco Chanel*, 65.

131   *"reading cheap novels"*: Masden, *Chanel*, 40.

132   *"didn't know anything"*: Masden, *Chanel*, 39.

133   *"Forgive me"*: Hadrich, *Coco Chanel*, 75–79.

134   *"I was just a kid"*: Hadrich, *Coco Chanel*, 78.

134   *"It was very complicated"*: Hadrich, *Coco Chanel*, 79–80.

134   *"Two gentlemen"*: "Fashioning the Modern Woman: The Art of Couturiere, 1919–1939," The Museum at FIT, exhibition pamphlet, February 10, 2004, to April 10, 2004.

CHAPTER 14: AN ATHLETIC KIND OF GIRL

135   *The feminine aesthetic:* Caroline Rennolds Milbank, *New York Fashion: The Evolution of American Style* (New York: Abrams, 1989), 35–45.

137   *the daily torment:* Kate Mulvey, *Decades of Beauty: The Changing Image of Women, 1890s–1990s* (New York: Checkmark Books, 1998), 41.

138   *English magazine correspondent:* Helene E. Roberts, "The Exquisite Slave: The Role of Clothes in the Making of the Victorian Woman," *Signs: Journal of Women in Culture and Society* 2, no. 3 (Spring 1977): 561. The case study is drawn from Victorian England but is representative of corseting in the United States.

138   *study of fifty women:* Roberts, "The Exquisite Slave," 561–62.

139   *"ever present monitor"*: Roberts, "The Exquisite Slave," 564–65.

139   *"No one but a woman"*: Roberts, "The Exquisite Slave," 557.

139   *"Take what precautions"*: Roberts, "The Exquisite Slave," 556.

140   *J. Marion Sims:* Charles Sellers, *Market Revolution: Jacksonian America, 1815–1846* (New York: Oxford University Press, 1991), 256–57.

141   *"The corset-curse"*: Jenna Weissman Joselit, *A Perfect Fit: Clothes, Character and the Promise of America* (New York: Metropolitan Books, 2001), 49–50.

141   *Stanton put the matter:* Paula Welch, "The Relationship of the Women's Rights Movement to Women's Sport and Physical Education in the United States, 1848–1920," *Proteus* 3, no. 1 (1986): 36.

141   *"We only wore it"*: Joselit, *A Perfect Fit*, 46.

141   *"ladies of irreproachable character"*: Welch, "The Relationship of the Women's Rights Movement to Women's Sport," 36.

142   *"popular rise of sports"*: John Higham, "The Reorientation of American Cul-

ture in the 1890s," in John Weiss, ed., *The Origins of Modern Consciousness* (Detroit: Wayne State University Press, 1965), 25–28.

143   *"athletic kind of girl!":* Higham, "The Reorientation of American Culture," 30–31.

143   *"To men, rich and poor":* Welch, "The Relationship of the Women's Rights Movement to Women's Sport," 37.

144   *Dr. Edward Clarke:* Margaret A. Lowe, *Looking Good: College Women and Body Image, 1875–1930* (Baltimore: Johns Hopkins University Press, 2003), 2.

144   *"day's tramp":* Lowe, *Looking Good,* 47–49.

144   *"the biggest day":* Lowe, *Looking Good,* 49.

144   *"no skirts at all":* Lowe, *Looking Good,* 48.

CHAPTER 15: LET GO OF THE WAI/TLINE

147   *"King of Fashion":* Paul Poiret, *My First Fifty Years* (London: V. Gollancz, 1931), 285.

147   *"Parisian of Paris":* Poiret, *My First Fifty Years,* 11–12.

148   *"Women and their toilettes":* Poiret, *My First Fifty Years,* 19.

148   *"smash my pride":* Poiret, *My First Fifty Years,* 25.

149   *Four hundred copies:* Poiret, *My First Fifty Years,* 27, 36.

149   *"The women wore them":* Poiret, *My First Fifty Years,* 43.

150   *"Young man, you know":* Poiret, *My First Fifty Years,* 61.

150   *"You call that a dress?":* Poiret, *My First Fifty Years,* 63.

150   *clothing for the New Woman:* Amy De La Haye and Shelley Tobin, *Chanel: The Couturiere at Work* (Woodstock, N.Y.: The Overlook Press, 1996), 13; Sandra Ley, *Fashion for Everyone: The Story of Ready-to-Wear* (New York: Scribner, 1975), 53–55.

150   *"I waged war upon it":* Poiret, *My First Fifty Years,* 73.

151   *"shackled the legs":* Poiret, *My First Fifty Years,* 73.

151   *"despotism of fashion":* Poiret, *My First Fifty Years,* 290.

152   *supreme derision:* Poiret, *My First Fifty Years,* 146–47.

152   *"made for each other":* Axel Masden, *Chanel: A Woman of Her Own* (New York: Henry Holt, 1990), 55.

153   *"Chanel frock was born":* Masden, *Chanel: A Woman of Her Own,* 69; Marcel Hadrich, *Coco Chanel: Her Life, Her Secrets* (Boston: Little, Brown, 1971), 90.

154   *"let go of the waistline":* Masden, *Chanel,* 78.

155   Harper's Bazaar: De La Haye and Tobin, *Chanel,* 20.

155   *"leading the way":* New York Times, April 23, 1916, X2.

155   *Marie Louise-Deray:* Masden, *Chanel,* 80.

155   *"Let them take lovers":* De La Haye and Tobin, *Chanel,* 19.

156   *"flapper uniform":* Bruce Bliven, "Flapper Jane," *New Republic,* September 9, 1925.

156   *"feminized tweeds":* New Yorker, November 7, 1925, 28.

157   *masculine influences:* De La Haye and Tobin, *Chanel,* 42.

157   "misérabilisme de luxe": Masden, *Chanel,* 116–17.

157   *Parisian law student:* Valerie Steele, *Paris Fashion: A Cultural History* (New York: Berg Publishers, 1998), 256.

157   *"Oriental" or "primitive" themes:* Elaine Porter, "Women's Fashions in 1920s America," unpublished BA dissertation, Cambridge University, Spring 2005, 9–16.

158   *"hemline moveth slowly":* Washington Post, July 12, 1925, SM4.

158   DISPLAY OF SPRING FASHIONS: *New York Times,* January 22, 1927, 15.

158   *A Baptist pastor:* Jenna Weissman Joselit, *A Perfect Fit: Clothes, Character and the Promise of America* (New York: Metropolitan Books, 2001), 66.

159   *"adjust length to becomingness":* Joselit, *A Perfect Fit,* 60.

159   *"yearly cry":* New Yorker, October 10, 1925, 32.

CHAPTER 16: INTO THE STREETS

161   *"The whole position":* Eleanor Goodman and Jean Nerenberg, "Everywoman's Jewelry: Early Plastics and Equality in Fashion," *Journal of Popular Culture* 13, no. 4 (Spring 1980): 632–33.

162   *Alexander Hamilton:* Stewart and Elizabeth Ewen, *Channels of Desire: Mass Images and the Shaping of American Consciousness* (New York: McGraw Hill Publishers, 1982), 160.

162   *status quo changed slowly:* Ewen and Ewen, *Channels of Desire,* 166–67.

163   *Ellen Curtis Demorest:* Milbank, *New York Fashion: The Evolution of American Style* (New York: Abrams, 1989), 18.

163   *"A sketch is given":* Rob Schorman, *Selling Style: Clothing and Social Change at the Turn of the Century* (Philadelphia: University of Pennsylvania Press, 2003), 53–54.

164   *over six yards of forty-eight-inch fabric:* Jane Farrell-Beck and Joyce Starr-Johnson, "Remodeling and Renovating Clothes, 1870–1933," *Dress* 19 (1992): 39.

164   *under three yards of fifty-four-inch wool:* Farrell-Beck and Starr-Johnson, "Remodeling and Renovating Clothes," 43. Between 1870 and 1929, annual sales of factory-made women's clothes jumped from $12.9 million to $1.6 billion—roughly equivalent to $17.5 billion in current-day money.

165   *"The winter openings":* New Yorker, August 28, 1926, 44–46.

166   *"Fashion does not exist":* Amy De La Haye and Shelley Tobin, *Chanel: The Couturiere at Work* (New York: Overlook Press, 1994), 54.

166   *Madame Doret:* De La Haye and Tobin, *Chanel,* 54–55.

167   *"'Chanel' Rhinestone Bags":* New York Times, December 23, 1927, 7.

167   *"copies of Patou":* New York Times, November 28, 1926, 15.

167   *"Paris hats . . . so exact":* New Yorker, March 12, 1927, 7.

167   *even farm girls:* Jenna Weissman Joselit, *A Perfect Fit: Clothes, Character and the Promise of America* (New York: Metropolitan Books, 2001), 22.

168 *Rural free delivery and parcel post:* Thomas Schlereth, "Country Stores, County Fairs and Mail-Order Catalogues: Consumption in Rural America," in Simon J. Bronner, ed., *Consuming Visions: Accumulation and Display of Goods in America, 1880–1920* (New York: Norton, 1989), 342–45, 349.

168 *"on time":* Ewen and Ewen, *Channels of Desire,* 65.

168 *as little as $8.98:* Stella Blum, ed., *Everyday Fashions of the Twenties: As Pictures in Sears and Other Catalogs* (New York: Dover Publications, 1981).

169 *cheap imitation jewelry:* Eleanor Gordon and Jean Nerenberg, "Everywoman's Jewelry: Early Plastics and Equality in Fashion," *Journal of Popular Culture* (Spring 1980): 629–44.

169 *"Heinz pickle jars":* New Yorker, March 6, 1926, 41.

169 *parlor maid and the debutante:* Goodman and Nerenberg, "Everywoman's Jewelry," 633.

169 *"one big shop exclusively":* New Yorker, September 18, 1926, 54.

169 *"It is most annoying":* New Yorker, April 3, 1926, 34.

170 *"a second clue":* Robert S. Lynd and Helen Merrell Lynd, *Middletown: A Study in Modern American Culture* (New York: Harcourt, Brace and Company, 1929), 161.

170 *"Only a connoisseur":* Ewen and Ewen, *Channels of Desire,* 177.

170 *"Riverside Drive or East 4th Street":* Ewen and Ewen, *Channels of Desire,* 181.

170 *Jane Addams:* Joselit, *A Perfect Fit,* 39.

170 *"Let them copy":* Joseph Barry, " 'I Am on the Side of Women,' Said My Friend Chanel," *Smithsonian* (1971) 2, no. 2: 30.

170 *"Thanks to me":* Marcel Hadrich, *Coco Chanel: Her Life, Her Secrets* (Boston: Little, Brown, 1971), 119.

171 *"socialized into an average":* Loren H. B. Knox, "Our Lost Individuality," *Atlantic Monthly* (Dec. 1909), 820.

172 *"torches of freedom":* Stewart Ewen, *Captains of Consciousness: Advertising and the Social Roots of the Consumer Culture,* rev. ed. 2001 (New York: 1976), 160–61.

172 *prominent advertising guru:* Ewen, *Captains of Consciousness,* 31.

CHAPTER 17: WITHOUT IMAGINATION, NO WANT/

173 *"Fisher Body Girl":* Roland Marchand, *Advertising the American Dream: Making Way for Modernity, 1920–1940* (Berkeley, Calif.: University of California Press, 1985), 180.

173 *curious publishing phenomena:* Richard M. Fried, "Introduction," in Bruce Barton, *The Man Nobody Knows,* rev. ed. (Chicago: I.R. Dee, 2000; Indianapolis: Bobbs-Merrill, 1925), vii–x.

175 *he urged readers:* T. J. Jackson Lears, "From Salvation to Self-Realization: Advertising and the Therapeutic Roots of the Consumer Culture, 1880–1930," in T. J. Jackson Lears and Richard Wightman Fox, *The Cul-*

ture of Consumption: Critical Essays in American History, 1880–1980 (New York: Pantheon Books, 1983), 32.

176 *"the great advertiser"*: Barton, *The Man Nobody Knows*, 60, 65–72.

176 *As recently as the 1890s:* Stephen Fox, *The Mirror Makers: A History of American Advertising and Its Creators* (New York: Morrow, 1984), chap. 1.

177 *"goods must be moved"*: Susan Strasser, *Satisfaction Guaranteed: The Making of the American Mass Market* (New York: Pantheon Books, 1989), 22–25.

177 *"Without imagination"*: William Leach, *Land of Desire: Merchants, Power and the Rise of a New American Culture* (New York: Pantheon Books, 1993), 36–37.

177 *Nashville Ad Club:* Strasser, *Satisfaction Guaranteed,* 27.

178 *typical advertising expert:* Rob Schorman, *Selling Style: Clothing and Social Change at the Turn of the Century* (Philadelphia: University of Pennsylvania Press, 2003), 144.

178 *Helen Woodward:* Stewart Ewen, *Captains of Consciousness: Advertising and the Social Roots of the Consumer Culture,* rev. ed. 2001 (New York: McGraw-Hill, 1976), 86.

179 *"feel life intensely"*: Lears, "From Salvation to Self-Realization," 15. Italics added for emphasis.

179 *"let yourself go"*: Robert S. Lynd and Helen Merrell Lynd, *Middletown: A Study in Modern American Culture* (New York: Harcourt, Brace and Company, 1929), 265.

179 *Denys Thompson:* Ewen, *Captains of Consciousness,* 87.

179 *"Joan Crawford Hats"*: Stella Blum, ed., *Everyday Fashions of the Twenties: As Pictures in Sears and Other Catalogs* (New York: Dover Publications, 1981), 95, 127.

180 *American Tobacco Company:* Strasser, *Satisfaction Guaranteed,* 47.

180 *grocers in Chicago:* L. R. Geissler, "Association-Reactions Applied to Ideas of Commercial Brands of Familiar Articles," *Journal of Applied Psychology* 1 (September 1917): 218.

181 *invention of modern photography:* Neil Harris, "Iconography and Intellectual History: The Halftone Effect," in Neil Harris, *Cultural Excursions: Marketing Appetites and Cultural Tastes in Modern America* (Chicago: University of Chicago Press, 1990), 304–17.

181 *new printing techniques:* Richard Ohmann, "Where Did Mass Culture Come From?: The Case for Magazines," *Berkshire Review* 16 (1981): 99–100.

181 *Laura Ingalls Wilder:* Ellen Gruber Garvey, *The Adman in the Parlor: Magazines and the Gendering of Consumer Culture, 1880s to 1910s* (New York: Oxford University Press, 1996), 21.

181 *remote mountain towns:* Edward L. Ayers, *The Promise of the New South: Life After Reconstruction* (New York: Oxford University Press, 1992), 99–100.

182 *Artemas Ward:* Leach, *Land of Desire,* 43–45.

182 *annual consumer advertising:* Vincent Vinikas, *Soft Soap, Hard Sell: American Hygiene in an Age of Advertisement* (Ames, Iowa: Iowa State University Press, 1992), 34.

182 *magazine circulation:* Vinikas, *Soft Soap, Hard Sell,* 9–13; Richard Ohmann, "Where Did Mass Culture Come From?" 85–90. The most popular magazines reached between 10 percent and 50 percent of middle-class homes, but only 5 percent of working-class homes.

183 *one-third of all magazine ad revenues:* Mary Ellen Waller-Zuckerman, "'Old Homes, in a City of Perpetual Change': Women's Magazines, 1890–1916," *Business History Review* 63, no. 4 (Winter 1989): 726–35; Vinikas, *Soft Soap, Hard Sell,* 98.

CHAPTER 18: 10,000,000 FEMMES FATALES

185 *"10,000,000 housewives":* Raye Virginia Allen, *Gordon Conway: Fashioning a New Woman* (Austin, Tex.: University of Texas Press, 1997), ix.

187 *"as graceful as a fawn":* Allen, *Gordon Conway,* 20.

188 *recorded her thoughts:* Allen, *Gordon Conway,* 23.

189 *John Held:* see Shelley Armitage, *John Held, Jr.: Illustrator of the Jazz Age* (Syracuse, N.Y.: Syracuse University Press, 1987).

191 *"no method":* Armitage, *John Held,* 19.

192 *"two kinds of crackers":* Margaret A. Lowe, "From Robust Appetites to Calorie Counting: The Emergence of Dieting Among Smith College Students in the 1920s," *Journal of Women's History* 7, no. 4 (Winter 1995): 39–40.

192 *"Don't consider it necessary":* Lowe, "From Robust Appetites to Calorie Counting," 40.

193 TO DIET OR NOT: Lowe, "From Robust Appetites to Calorie Counting," 36.

193 *"most of the Negro girls": New Yorker,* December 12, 1925, 51.

193 *"The entertainer there": New Yorker,* December 12, 1925, 52.

193–194 *"the REAL Charleston": New Yorker,* December 26, 1925, 32–33.

194 *The same message:* Grace Elizabeth Hale, "'For Colored' and 'For White': Segregating Consumption in the South," in Jane Dailey, Glenda Elizabeth Gilmore, and Bryant Simon, eds., *Jumpin' Jim Crow: Southern Politics from Civil War to Civil Rights* (Princeton: Princeton University Press, 2000), 162–82; David Nasaw, *Going Out: The Rise and Fall of Public Amusements* (New York: Basic Books, 1993), 93, 80–95.

CHAPTER 19: APPEARANCES COUNT

197 *seconded by Walter Lippmann:* Stuart Ewen, *PR!: A Social History of Spin* (New York: Basic Books, 1996), 65–75, 106–08.

198 *CPI:* Ewen, *PR!,* 106–08; David M. Kennedy, *Over Here: The First World War and American Society* (New York: Oxford University Press, 1980), 59–78.

199   *Typical CPI posters:* Ewen, *PR!*, 115–17.

199   *"power of propaganda":* Ewen, *PR!*, 131.

199   *George Phelps:* Stewart Ewen, *Captains of Consciousness: Advertising and the Social Roots of the Consumer Culture,* rev. ed. 2001 (New York: McGraw-Hill, 1976), 83.

200   *Ivy Lee:* Ewen, *PR!*, 132.

200   *"Mass psychology":* Ewen, *Captains of Consciousness,* 83–84.

200   *"governed by reason":* Ewen, *PR!*, 138.

201   *"Critical eyes":* Roland Marchand, *Advertising the American Dream: Making Way for Modernity, 1920–1940* (Berkeley, Calif.: University of California Press, 1985), 213.

201   *"It ruins romance":* Vincent Vinikas, *Soft Soap, Hard Sell: American Hygiene in an Age of Advertisement* (Ames, Iowa: Iowa State University Press, 1992), 32.

201   *"You will be amazed":* Ewen, *Captains of Consciousness,* 38.

201   *"Once a bridesmaid":* Ewen, *Captains of Consciousness,* 44.

202   *"A few years ago":* Vinikas, *Soft Soap, Hard Sell,* 28–30.

202   *annual sales of toiletries:* Vinikas, *Soft Soap, Hard Sell,* xii; Kathy Peiss, *Hope in a Jar: The Making of America's Beauty Culture* (New York: Metropolitan Books, 1998), 97.

202   *Magazine ads:* Peiss, *Hope in a Jar,* 142, 184.

203   *cloudy representations:* Peiss, *Hope in a Jar,* 45.

204   *Hangtown Gals:* Peiss, *Hope in a Jar,* 27.

204   *"a perfectly transparent character":* Karen Halttunen, *Confidence Men and Painted Women: A Study of Middle-Class Culture in America, 1836–1870* (New Haven: Yale University Press, 1982), 52.

204   *"the skin's power":* Halttunen, *Confidence Men and Painted Women,* 63, 88.

204   *"The mask of fashion":* Halttunen, *Confidence Men and Painted Women,* 66.

204   *"as others see you":* Peiss, *Hope in a Jar,* 144.

205   *Vogue's Book of Beauty:* Peiss, *Hope in a Jar,* 155–56.

205   *Ingram's Milkwood Cream:* Peiss, *Hope in a Jar,* 155–56.

205   *industry analysts claimed:* Peiss, *Hope in a Jar,* 123–24, 168–73, 186, 190; Vincent Vinikas, *Soft Soap, Hard Sell,* 59.

206   *"appearances count":* Rob Schorman, *Selling Style: Clothing and Social Change at the Turn of the Century* (Philadelphia: University of Pennsylvania Press, 2003), 137.

207   *"innocent yet men talked":* Peiss, *Hope in a Jar,* 155.

207   *Dorothy Dix warning:* Robert S. Lynd and Helen Merrell Lynd, *Middletown: A Study in Modern American Culture* (New York: Harcourt, Brace and Company, 1929), 162.

207   *"dresses girls wear":* Lynd and Lynd, *Middletown,* 162.

207   *budget of $1,363:* Lynd and Lynd, *Middletown,* 163.

208   *Lynds recognized:* Lynd and Lynd, *Middletown,* 164–65.

CHAPTER 20: PAPA, WHAT IS BEER?

211 *"Intriguingly risqué"*: Film Review of *Flaming Youth,* undated [ca. 1923], Margaret Herrick Library, Academy of Motion Picture Arts and Sciences, Los Angeles, Colleen Moore Scrapbook #2.

211 *"the way Scott Fitzgerald writes"*: New York Exhibitors' Trade Review, December 1, 1923, Colleen Moore Scrapbook #2.

213 *"so carried away"*: Colleen Moore, *Silent Star* (Garden City, New York: Doubleday, 1968), 16–18.

215 *Lucky for Kathleen Morrison:* Moore, *Silent Star,* 11–18.

217 *"Dear baby"*: Moore, *Silent Star,* 24–25.

218 *"gained a new movie star"*: Moore, *Silent Star,* 26; "'The Close-Up': Colleen Moore," undated clipping [ca. 1927], source unknown, Colleen Moore Clippings File, Margaret Herrick Library, Academy of Motion Picture Arts and Sciences, Beverly Hills [hereafter CM Clippings].

218 *standing five feet three and three-quarter inches:* Biographical information, Goldwyn Pictures Corporation of New York, August 11, 1921, CM Clippings.

219 *"Papa, what is beer?"*: Moore, *Silent Star,* 43.

219 *motley assortment of characters:* Moore, *Silent Star,* 50.

221 *"I was the spark"*: "Colleen Moore: The Original Flapper in Bel-Air," *Architectural Digest* (April 1996): 216–21, 294.

CHAPTER 21: OH, LITTLE GIRL, NEVER GROW UP

223 *first two decades:* On early film, see Robert Sklar, *Movie-Made America: A Cultural History of American Movies* (New York: Random House, 1975).

225 The Birth of a Nation: Larry May, *Screening Out the Past: The Birth of Mass Culture and the Motion Picture Industry* (Chicago: University of Chicago Press, 1980), 76.

226 *"taint of scandal"*: May, *Screening Out the Past,* 75–76.

227 *"a great beauty doctor"*: May, *Screening Out the Past,* 75.

227 *Early movies:* Leslie Fishbein, "The Demise of the Cult of True Womanhood in Early American Film, 1900–1930," *Journal of Popular Film and Television* 12, no. 2 (Summer 1984): 68.

227 *Linda Arvidson Griffith:* Mary P. Ryan, "The Projection of a New Womanhood: The Movie Moderns in the 1920s," in Jean E. Friedman and William G. Shade, eds., *Our American Sisters: Women in American Life and Thought* (Lexington, Mass.: D. C. Heath, 1976), 502.

228 *Irving Thalberg:* May, *Screening Out the Past,* 200.

228 *Mary Pickford:* May, *Screening Out the Past,* 125–26.

229 *Samuel Goldwyn:* May, *Screening Out the Past,* 171.

CHAPTER 22: THE KIND OF GIRL THE FELLOW/ WANT

231   *"define the title"*: Sara Ross, "Banking the Flames of Youth: The Hollywood Flapper, 1920–1930," unpublished PhD, dissertation, University of Wisconsin–Madison, 2000, 48.

231   *"wickedest face"*: Mary P. Ryan, "The Projection of a New Womanhood: The Movie Moderns in the 1920s," in Jean E. Friedman and William G. Shade, eds., *Our American Sisters: Women in American Life and Thought* (Lexington, Mass.: D. C. Heath, 1976), 502.

232   *"apostle of domesticity"*: Leslie Fishbein, "The Demise of the Cult of True Womanhood in Early American Film, 1900–1930," *Journal of Popular Film and Television* 12, no. 2 (Summer 1984): 67–68.

232   The Flapper: Ross, "Banking the Flames of Youth," 66.

233   *"looks the part"*: Untitled photo caption, *Photoplay Magazine* (Chicago), March 1924, Colleen Moore Scrapbook #2.

233   *"very apotheosis"*: "Daily Movie Review," *Muskegon* (Mich.) *Chronicle,* January 21, 1924, Colleen Moore Scrapbook #2.

233   *"brilliant young flapper"*: "Player with 'Sex Appeal' Is Like a Rocket," Unknown Source (New Orleans), June 15, 1924, Colleen Moore Scrapbook #11.

233   *"kind of girl the fellows want"*: "How Girls Should Act Told by Screen Star," *Screen News,* Sacramento, March 8, 1924, Colleen Moore Scrapbook #2.

234   *"It's such fun"*: " 'I Love to Ask My Husband for Money,' Says Colleen Moore," *Movie Weekly,* undated, Colleen Moore Scrapbook #11.

235   *"Nobody wanted me"*: David Stein, *Clara Bow: Runnin' Wild* (New York: Doubleday, 1988), 5.

235   *Sands Street in Brooklyn:* Stein, *Clara Bow: Runnin' Wild,* 8.

235   *"I have known hunger"*: Stein, *Clara Bow: Runnin' Wild,* 11.

235   *"worst-lookin' kid"*: Stein, *Clara Bow: Runnin' Wild,* 11–12.

236   *Bennett would live to eat his words:* On Clara Bow's early years in film, see Stein, *Clara Bow: Runnin' Wild.*

238   *"the only time"*: Colleen Moore, *Silent Star* (New York: Doubleday, 1968), 147–48.

239   *"We all loved her"*: Stein, *Clara Bow: Runnin' Wild,* 50.

239   *"Golly, Mr. Schulberg"*: Budd Schulberg, *Moving Pictures: Memories of a Hollywood Prince* (New York: Stein and Day, 1981), 157–66.

240   *"I liked her"*: Stein, *Clara Bow: Runnin' Wild,* 43.

241   *"an easy winner"*: Schulberg, *Moving Pictures,* 158.

241   *Sam Jaffe:* Stein, *Clara Bow: Runnin' Wild,* 51.

241   *easy to dismiss:* Jeanine Basinger, *Silent Stars* (New York: Knopf, 1999), 411–50.

242   *"She has eyes"*: Stein, *Clara Bow: Runnin' Wild,* 55.

242   *Clarence Badger:* Stein, *Clara Bow: Runnin' Wild,* 83.

243   *"It, hell"*: Stein, *Clara Bow: Runnin' Wild,* 81.

243   *$5,000 per week:* Stein, *Clara Bow: Runnin' Wild,* 71.

CHAPTER 23: ANOTHER PETULANT WAY TO PA** THE TIME

245 *"drink and fuck"*: Ann Douglas, *Terrible Honesty: Mongrel Manhattan in the 1920s* (New York: Farrar, Straus, and Giroux, 1995), 48.

245 *"modest 10 a year"*: Louise Brooks to Tom Dardis, October 26, 1977, Louise Brooks Vertical File, Margaret Herrick Library, Academy of Motion Picture Arts and Sciences, Beverly Hills [hereafter LB Vertical File].

245 *"either a fool"*: Barry Paris, *Louise Brooks: A Biography* (New York: Knopf, 1989), 5.

246 *"fourteen-room gray frame"*: Louise Brooks, *Lulu in Hollywood* (New York: Knopf, 1982), 9.

246 *"'How dare she?'"*: Paris, *Louise Brooks,* 89.

247 *Mr. Flowers*: Louise Brooks to Tom Dardis, November 14, 1977, LB Vertical File.

248 *"first curious raptures"*: Paris, *Louise Brooks,* 4.

248 *"Now, dear"*: Brooks, *Lulu in Hollywood,* 7.

249 *"bespectacled housewife"*: Paris, *Louise Brooks,* 28–31.

249 *"Even in the ballet"*: Brooks, *Lulu in Hollywood,* 9.

250 *"my Kansas accent"*: Brooks, *Lulu in Hollywood,* 10–14.

251 *"very flirty in the hotels"*: Paris, *Louise Brooks,* 53–54.

252 *Algonquin Hotel*: Paris, *Louise Brooks,* 70.

252 *"How old are you"*: Brooks, *Lulu in Hollywood,* 15.

253 *Follies girl*: Paris, *Louise Brooks,* 72.

254 *Over one weekend*: Paris, *Louise Brooks,* 108–09.

254 *"Scott Fitzgerald's mind"*: Paris, *Louise Brooks,* 136.

255 *San Simeon*: Brooks, *Lulu in Hollywood,* 39–41.

CHAPTER 24: THE DREAMER* DREAM COME TRUE

257 *"All their lives"*: Larry May, *Screening Out the Past: The Birth of Mass Culture and the Motion Picture Industry* (Chicago: University of Chicago Press, 1980), 166.

257 *"No romance"*: Heather Addison, "Hollywood and the Reducing Craze of the 1920s," unpublished PhD dissertation, University of Kansas, 2001, 67.

259 *"In the strange place"*: Addison, "Hollywood and the Reducing Craze," 75.

259 *"They build the swimming pools"*: Addison, "Hollywood and the Reducing Craze," 76.

260 *"splurged on homes"*: "Colleen Moore: The Original Flapper in Bel-Air," *Architectural Digest* (April 1996): 216–21, 294.

260 *It was exotic*: May, *Screening Out the Past,* 188–89.

260 *"a paradise"*: May, *Screening Out the Past,* 185.

260 *"just wild about you"*: Martha Meadows to Clara Bow, October 20, 1926, Clara Bow Letters, Margaret Herrick Library, Academy of Motion Picture Arts and Sciences, Beverly Hills [hereafter CB Letters].

260 *"you naughty girl"*: Connie Romero to Clara Bow, 1926, CB Letters.

261 *"mad about your eyes"*: Audrey Ashuru to Clara Bow, undated, CB Letters.

261 *"watching the actions"*: Garth S. Jowett, Ian C. Jarvie, and Kathryn H. Fuller, eds., *Children and the Movies: Media Influence and the Payne Fund Controversy* (New York: Cambridge University Press, 1996), 254.

261 *"considerable . . . attention"*: Jowett, Jarvie, and Fuller, eds., *Children and the Movies,* 279.

261 *high school junior confessed:* Jowett, Jarvie, and Fuller, eds., *Children and the Movies,* 288.

261 *study of delinquent girls:* Peiss, *Hope in a Jar: The Making of America's Beauty Culture* (New York: Metropolitan Books, 1998), 191.

261 *"No wonder"*: Jowett, Jarvie, and Fuller, eds., *Children and the Movies,* 276.

262 *"I saw Rudolph Valentino"*: Jowett, Jarvie, and Fuller, eds., *Children and the Movies,* 247.

262 *"Oh, what a life!"*: Jowett, Jarvie, and Fuller, eds., *Children and the Movies,* 274.

262 *Dorothy Dushkin:* Margaret A. Lowe, "From Robust Appetites to Calorie Counting: The Emergence of Dieting Among Smith College Students in the 1920s," *Journal of Women's History* 7, no. 4 (Winter 1995): 241.

263 *those who read the fan magazines:* Addison, "Hollywood and the Reducing Craze of the 1920s," 232–34.

263 *"thought Clara too plump"*: Untitled review, [*Chicago*] *American,* undated, Clara Bow Notebooks, Margaret Herrick Library, Academy of Motion Picture Arts and Sciences, Beverly Hills [hereafter CB Notebooks].

263 *"Diet!"*: Addison, "Hollywood and the Reducing Craze of the 1920s," 59.

263 *"Hollywood Eighteen-Day Diet"*: Addison, "Hollywood and the Reducing Craze of the 1920s," 78.

263 *"The slim figure"*: Addison, "Hollywood and the Reducing Craze of the 1920s," 26.

264 *"'easy to be slender'"*: "Fashions & Fancies in Filmland," *Picture Show,* April 19, 1924, Colleen Moore Scrapbook #11.

264 *"What It Costs"*: Scott Pierce, "What It Costs to Be a Well-Dressed Flapper," undated news clipping [ca. 1920s], Clara Bow Clippings File.

265 *Colleen Moore perfume:* "Colleen Moore to Distribute Perfume," Los Angeles *Express,* July 19, 1923, Colleen Moore Scrapbook #2.

265 *Adele Hernández Milligan:* Vicki L. Ruiz, "Star Struck: Acculturation, Adolescence, and Mexican American Women, 1920–1950," in Elliot West and Paula Petrik, eds., *Small Worlds: Children & Adolescents in America, 1850–1950* (Lawrence, Kans.: University Press of Kansas, 1992), 67.

265 *Chinese flapper:* Judy Yung, " 'It's Hard to Be Born a Woman but Hopeless to Be Born a Chinese': The Life and Times of Flora Belle Jan," *Frontiers* 18, no. 3 (1997): 66–91.

CHAPTER 25: /UICIDE ON THE IN/TALLMENT PLAN

267 *"Ernest could be brutal"*: Nancy Milford, *Zelda: A Biography* (New York: Harper and Row, 1970), 117.

268 *Dingo Bar*: Ernest Hemingway, *A Moveable Feast* (New York: Scribner, 1964), 150.

268 *Carl Van Vechten*: Milford, *Zelda*, 98.

268 *in for a surprise*: Hemingway, *A Moveable Feast*, 151.

269 *"dirty singlet"*: Sara Mayfield, *Exiles from Paradise: Zelda and Scott Fitzgerald* (New York: Delacorte Press, 1971), 91.

270 *Lalique turtle*: Mayfield, *Exiles*, 106.

270 *$25,000*: Matthew J. Bruccoli, *Some Sort of Epic Grandeur: The Life of F. Scott Fitzgerald*, rev. ed. 1993 (New York: Harcourt Brace & Jovanovich, 1981), 288.

270 *Gertrude Stein*: Gertrude Stein to FSF, May 22, 1925 in Matthew J. Bruccoli and Margaret M. Duggan, eds., *Correspondence of F. Scott Fitzgerald* (New York: Random House, 1980), 164.

270 *cavorting with the likes of*: FSF to Ernest Hemingway, November 30, 1925, in Matthew J. Bruccoli, ed., *F. Scott Fitzgerald: A Life in Letters* (New York: Scribner, 1994), 130.

271 *James Thurber and William Shirer*: Bruccoli, *Some Sort of Epic Grandeur*, 276–77.

271 *James Joyce*: Bruccoli, *Some Sort of Epic Grandeur*, 311; Mayfield, *Exiles*, 135.

271 *the destructive side*: Mayfield, *Exiles*, 115.

272 *grabbed the wheel*: Mayfield, *Exiles from Paradise*, 115–16.

272 *"inconvenient friends"*: Milford, *Zelda*, 115.

272 *"I was quite ashamed"*: FSF to EH, November 30, 1925, in Bruccoli, ed., *F. Scott Fitzgerald: A Life in Letters*, 130.

272 *"phony as a rubber check"*: James R. Mellow, *Invented Lives: F. Scott & Zelda Fitzgerald* (New York: Houghton Mifflin Company, 1984), 241.

273 *"bullfighting, bullslinging"*: Mayfield, *Exiles*, 112.

273 *"well-laundered"*: Mellow, *Invented Lives*, 202.

273 *"depressing . . . about a country"*: Milford, *Zelda*, 105.

273 *"everybody was so young"*: Milford, *Zelda*, 105.

273 *fourteen-room Moorish villa*: Mellow, *Invented Lives*, 253.

274 *"Most people are dull"*: Gerald Murphy to FSF and ZSF, September 19, 1925, in Bruccoli and Duggan, eds., *Correspondence of F. Scott Fitzgerald*, 178.

274 *"could write and didn't"*: Mayfield, *Exiles*, 113.

274 *reckless high dives*: Bruccoli, *Some Sort of Epic Grandeur*, 296.

275 *"no fun here anymore"*: Mayfield, *Exiles*, 132.

275 *Juan-les-Pins casino*: Bruccoli, *Some Sort of Epic Grandeur*, 295.

275 *"pay and pay and pay"*: FSF to Ernest Hemingway, September 9, 1929, in Bruccoli, ed., *F. Scott Fitzgerald: A Life in Letters*, 168–69.

275 *"sparkle had gone"*: Mayfield, *Exiles,* 131.
275 *"Zelda could be spooky"*: Milford, *Zelda,* 124.
276 *"What Becomes of Our Flappers"*: F. Scott and Zelda Fitzgerald, "What Becomes of Our Flappers and Our Sheiks?" *McCall's,* October 1925, reprinted in Matthew J. Bruccoli and Mary Gordon, eds., *Zelda Fitzgerald: The Collected Writings* (New York: Scribner, 1991), 397–99.

CONCLU/ION: UNAFFORDABLE EXCE//

280 *Clara's good luck ran out:* "Clara Bow," American National Biography.
282 *"My [New York] friends"*: Barry Paris, *Louise Brooks: A Biography* (New York: Knopf, 1989), 187.
286 *"the strangeness and excitement"*: Jackson R. Bryer and Cathy W. Barks, eds., *Dear Scott, Dearest Zelda: The Love Letters of F. Scott and Zelda Fitzgerald* (New York: St. Martin's Griffin, 2002), part three.
287 *"When I was your age"*: FSF to Scottie Fitzgerald, July 7, 1938, in Andrew Turnbull, ed., *Scott Fitzgerald: Letters to His Daughter* (New York: Scribner, 1965).
288 *"It is the custom"*: F. Scott Fitzgerald, "Echoes of the Jazz Age," in *The Crack-Up* (New York: New Directions, 1945).
288 *"No More Flappers"*: *New York Times,* February 16, 1928, 22.
290 *Loren Knox:* Knox, "Our Lost Individuality," *Atlantic Monthly* 8 (Dec. 1909), 20.

PHOTOGRAPHY CREDITS

The illustrations and photographs are reprinted by permission of:

Bettmann/CORBIS: pages 22, 196, 210, 222, 230, 258.

Chicago Daily News negatives collection; courtesy of the Chicago Historical Society: pages 60, 135, 160, 278.

CORBIS: page 28.

Department of Rare Books and Special Collections, Princeton University Library: pages 12, 50, 266.

The family of Lois Long: pages 80, 88.

Gordon Conway Collection, Harry Ransom Humanities Research Collection, The University of Texas at Austin: pages 146, 184.

Hulton-Deutsch Collection/CORBIS: page 126.

John Springer Collection/CORBIS: page 244.

Library of Congress: pages 72, 94, 104, 114, 174.

Underwood & Underwood/CORBIS: page xii.

ACKNOWLEDGMENT/

LIKE ALL AUTHORS, I owe a tremendous debt to the legions of friends, family, and colleagues who provided me with critical support along the way.

At Crown, I had the good fortune to be paired with Rachel Klayman, a veteran editor of uncommon talent and wisdom. Rachel devoted countless hours to this book, reworking the manuscript until it was leaner and stronger, always delivering her sharp—and critical—insights with humor and wit. Ultimately, Rachel's hard work made this a far better volume, and for that, as well as for her friendship, she has my sincere gratitude. Thanks are also due to assistant editor Lucinda Bartley, who provided much-needed support toward the end of the writing process; Laura Duffy, who designed a brilliant dust jacket; Lauren Dong, who designed the book's interior; Patty Bozza, who so meticulously oversaw the copyediting and production editing of the book; Leta Evanthes, production manager; Sona Vogel, whose extensive copyedits saved me from many an embarrassing error and poor turn of phrase; Jill Flaxman, director of marketing, and Christine Aronson, senior publicist, for their tremendous work in promoting the book; as well as Kristin Kiser, editorial director, and Steve Ross, publisher, both of whom lent this project early and steadfast support.

I would never have found my way to Crown were it not for Susan Ginsburg, my agent at Writers House, and her assistant, Emily Saladino. Susan read more drafts of this book than either she or I would care to remember, suffered through marathon brainstorm sessions (in person and by e-mail), and provided both expert skill in guiding this book to publication, and great friendship along the way.

Troy Rondinone, a close friend and fine historian, generously helped me cull through the archives at the Academy of Motion Picture Arts and Sciences in Beverly Hills. Kathleen Lawton, Andy Trask, Erik Gillespie, and Andrew Stengel gave the manuscript a skilled read and provided the kind of honest and critical feedback that only friends can really offer up. Thanks go also to Josh Baran for offering sage advice on any number of book-related questions.

Cindi Leive, the editor-in-chief of *Glamour,* generously took time out of her busy schedule to read my manuscript and to share insights about the inner workings of the contemporary fashion cycle. Our conversation greatly informed the introduction and conclusion of my book.

Patricia Arno and her daughter, Andrea Brown, kindly agreed to share family pictures of Lois Long. I also owe a debt of gratitude to the staffs of the Library of Congress, Princeton University Library, Harry Ransom Humanities Research Center at the University of Texas at Austin, and the Chicago Historical Society, as well as Matthew Bruccoli, a leading Fitzgerald scholar, for their kind help in locating and reproducing some of the pictures that appear in this volume.

Many of the ideas in this book came to me during extended conversations with students at Brown University and Cambridge University. It's a pleasure and a privilege to work with such bright minds.

I might never have gravitated toward the historical profession were it not for Connie and Peggy Mewborn, dear friends who, over the years, became family to me and to my brother, Nate. Connie and Peggy bought me my first subscription to *American Heritage* when I was ten years old—which they renewed faithfully each year on my birthday—and helped kindle my fascination with the past. At the time, neither they nor I could have anticipated that one day I'd be fortunate enough to write for the magazine.

For five years it has been my privilege to count Richard Snow and Fred Allen, editor and managing editor, respectively, at *American Heritage,* as good friends. They've been incredibly supportive of my work and have shown, by example, that good scholarship and good writing need not be mutually exclusive.

Above all, I am deeply fortunate to have grown up in a house filled with books and ideas, and with two parents—Carl and Elaine Zeitz—who supported their sons' every whim and dream. My only regret is that my mother didn't live long enough to see this book in print. She was a modern woman who juggled career and family while balancing strongly held political convictions with a sense of style and grace. She knew that this book was on its way to publication, and I like to think she would have enjoyed reading it. In her memory, I'm pleased to thank a group of extraordinary friends from Bordentown, New Jersey—Randye Bloom, Rhea Goldman, Marsha Dowshen, Phoebe Nissim, Barbara Blair, Jeanette Poole, Heather Vail, Joanne Lutz, and Marlene Thompson—whose kindness to my family has been so great that it defies any adequate expression of gratitude.

Finally, my deepest thanks go to Juli-anne Whitney, who is my best editor, best critic, and best friend, all rolled into one. For her love and support—and for all the laughs along the way—this book is dedicated to her.

INDEX

Abbott, Lyman, 75
Abercrombie and Fitch, 101–2
abolitionists, 107–8
Adair, Perry, 27
Adams, Franklin, 84, 85
Addams, Jane, 109, 119, 170
Ade, George, 35
advertising:
    of brand names, 180–81, *196*
    and consumerism, 66–67, 68,
        177–82, 186, 194, 197, 206
    for cosmetics, 205–7
    cultural impact of, 65, 66
    of fashion, 151, 201
    illustrations in, 178, 181–82, 185
    and impulse buying, 201
    Madison Avenue, 85, 173, 179,
        208
    and personal image, *196*, 197,
        201–8
    pioneers in new field of, 9–10
    and propaganda, 197–99
    and publicity, 200
    and public relations, 171–72
    selling dreams, 66, 179, 185
    sexual images in, 115, 173
    and social psychology, 197–99
    and standardization, 168, 170

African Americans, 193–94, 216,
    226, 227
After Many Years (film), 225
Algonquin Round Table, 83–85, 189,
    252
American Tobacco Company, 171–72,
    180
amusement parks, 31–32, *60*
Anthony, Susan B., 107, 108
Arbuckle, Fatty, 61
Arno, Peter, 115–17, 284
automobile, 33–34, 35

Babson, Roger, 199
Bachman, Jack, 237
Badger, Clarence, 238, 242
Baker, Phil, 122
Baker, Ray Stannard, 158
Balsan, Etienne, 130–34, 152, 154
Bara, Theda, 231
Barrymore, Ethyl, 263
Barton, Bruce, 9–10, 173, 175–76,
    286
Beach, Sylvia, 96, 271
Beautiful and Damned, The (Fitzgerald),
    62–63
Bell, Rex, 280–81

Bellamy, Edward, 177
Benchley, Robert, 84
Bennett, Barbara, 251, 252
Bennett, John, 236
Bernays, Edward, 9–10, 171–72, 200
Berns, Charlie, 90
Biograph Company, 224–25
Birth of a Nation, The (film), 73, 216, 225–26, 227
Bliven, Bruce, 6–8, 156
Bloomer, Amelia, 141
Blumenthal, A. C., 254
Boston marriages, 119
Bow, Clara, 5, 9, *230,* 235–43, 260–64
    film career of, 237–38, 240, 241–43, 245–46, 254, 279, 280
    later years of, 280–81
Bowles, George, 198
Brandeis, Louis, 110
Brewster Publications, 236–37
Brice, Fanny, 259
Brill, A. A., 172
Britten, Florence, 35
Bromley, Dorothy Dunbar, 35, 112
Brooks, Louise, 9, *244,* 245–56
    and Denishawn, 248–49, 251
    film career of, 254–55, 279, 281–82
    later years of, 281–83
    reinvention of, 250–51, 265
    and sex, 247–48, 253, 254, 256
Brooks, Van Wyck, 83
Brooks Brothers, 163
Bryan, William Jennings, 76–77
Bullard, Arthur, 197
Burt, Maxwell Struthers, 97

Camp, Walter, 142
Campbell, Heyworth, 189
Campbell, Lawton, 17, 18, 57
Capel, Arthur "Boy," 132–34, 152–53, 155, 285

Carr, Rev. Henry, 5
Case, Frank, 85, 252
celebrity, focus on, 9, 56, 61
Chanel, Coco, 9, *126,* 127–34, 147, 152–57, 284–85
    and Balsan, 130–34, 152, 154
    and Capel, 132–34, 152–53, 155, 285
    copies of, 166–67, 168, 170
    costume jewelry, 169, 170
    House of Chanel, 134, 135, 153, 154–57, 159, 284–85
    signature style of, 156–57, 161, 162, 188, 284
Chaplin, Charlie, *80, 222,* 228, 229, 253–54, 260
Charles Scribner's Sons, 17, 20, 27, 47–48, 191, 270, 272
Chase, Stuart, 170
chromolithographs (chromos), 181–82
Churchill, Winston, 285
Clansman, The (Dixon), 73
Clark, Alfred, 223
Clark, Marguerite, 214
Clarke, Edward, 144
Cody, Dan, 18
Coe, George, 44
Cohan, George M., 252
Collier's, 61, 183
Committee on Public Information (CPI), 198–200
Connor, Ralph, 143
consumerism:
    and advertising, 66–67, 68, 177–82, 186, 194, 197, 206
    and choice, 68–70, 290
    impulse buying, 201
    in magazines, 185
    and standardization, 290–91
    trend toward, 9, 55, 66–67, 171, 177, 289–91
    and women, 183, 185, 290

Converse, Florence, 119
Conway, Gordon, 9, 184, 185–89, 191, 192, 262, 285–86
Cooper, Gary, 239
Corbett, "Gentleman Jim," 142
Cornejo, Francisco, 249
Coué, Emile, 56
Cowboy and the Flapper, The (film), 115
Crawley, Ernest, 158
Creel, George, 198, 200
Crowd, The (Le Bon), 198
Crowninshield, Frank, 80, 185, 189, 190
Curtis, Marian, 33

D'Alençon, Emilienne, 131, 132
Daley, Maria Lydig, 203
D'Arrast, Harry, 80
Darrow, Clarence, 76–77
Davies, Marion, 255–56
Davis, Al, 2–5
Dearborn, John, 24
Decourcelle, Pierre, 128–30
DeKay, Helena, 118–19
DeMille, Cecil B., 232, 259
Demorest, Mme. Ellen Curtis, 163
Dempsey, Jack, 61
Denishawn, 189, 248–49, 251–52
Deray, Marie-Louise, 155
De Voe, Daisy, 280
Dickerman, Don, 98
dieting, 262–64
Dix, Dorothy, 207
Dixon, Thomas, 73
Doret, Madame, 166–67
Dorr, Rheta Childe, 109–10
Dos Passos, John, 83, 97, 270, 271
Doucet, Jacques, 149
Dummer, Katherine, 36, 37
Duncan, Isadora, 270, 274
Dunning, William, 71
Dushkin, Dorothy, 262

Easter parade, 172, 200
Egorova, Lubov, 274
Ella Cinders (film), 233, 234
Elliott, Margaret Page, 187
Ellis, Havelock, 120
Emerson, Ella, 144
"Eulogy on the Flapper" (Z. Fitzgerald), 64, 81

Fabian, Warner, 220
Fairbanks, Douglas, 222, 228–29, 259
family life:
    alien threats to, 73–74
    and birthrate, 44–45, 68
    double standard in, 36–37
    erosion of, 34–35
    and wealth gap, 54, 55
family planning, 68
Famous Players-Lasky studio, 254
fashion, 146, 160, 184
    advertising of, 151, 201
    androgyny in, 157–58, 159
    and Chanel, 9, 135, 152–57, 159, 161–62, 166, 284
    comfortable and practical, 154, 156
    competitive world of, 149
    and consumerism, 178–79
    copies of, 166–67, 168–70
    corsets, 137–39, 141–42, 150–51, 154
    costs of, 207–8
    costume jewelry, 168–69, 170
    crinolines, 139–40, 142
    cycles of, 81–82, 135, 137, 151–52
    democratizing, 170
    garçonne look in, 156
    hemlines in, 158–59, 164, 284, 289
    hobble skirts, 139, 151

fashion (*cont.*)
  homemade, 162, 163–64
  "little black dress," 285
  live models of, 152, 166
  in magazines, 183–86
  in mail-order catalogs, 161–62
  makeup as mask of, 204–8
  in nineteenth century, 135,
    137–40
  paper patterns, 163–64
  Paris fashion shows, 165–66
  and Poiret, 147–52, 153
  ready-to-wear, 161–64, 170
  shirtwaists, 142
  as social control, 137, 138, 140,
    207
  and sports, 143–45
Fears, Peggy, 254
feminists, 105–13
  and choice, 69
  independence sought by, 7–8
  Seneca Falls convention of, 107,
    108
  and "sex rights," 106–7, 118
  social activism of, *104,* 106–12
First National studios, 221, 238, 254
Fish, Hamilton, 286
Fisher, Walter, 36
"Fisher Body Girl," 173
Fitzgerald, Frances Scott "Scottie," 65,
    96, *266,* 287
Fitzgerald, F. Scott, *50, 266*
  ad agency job of, 20, 27
  death of, 288
  drinking, 56–57, 98, 268, 270–72,
    274–75, 287
  early years of, 16
  on flappers, 5, 24, 29, 39–44,
    47–49, 61–63, 211, 221, 254,
    265, 270, 276, 290
  and Hemingway, 267–70, 272–73
  income of, 43, 95, 269
  media stories about, 39, 48, 62

movie adaptations of work by, 44,
    52, 221, 237, 257, 287
  in New York, 20, 23, 25, 27, 83,
    252
  novels by, 17, 20, 27, 39, 41–43,
    47, 51, 53, 61–63, 97, 270,
    287, 288
  personal traits of, 16, 17, 18, 57,
    96, 268, 271
  reputation of, 42, 44, 47–48, 61,
    270, 275–76, 287
  scrapbooks of, 20, 62, 63
  short stories and articles by, 20,
    25, 42–44, 47, 52, 95–96, 182,
    191, 270, 273, 274
  and women, 17, 26
  and Zelda, 13, 16, 17–20, 286–88;
    see also Fitzgerald, Scott and
    Zelda; Fitzgerald, Zelda
Fitzgerald, Scott and Zelda, *50, 266*
  correspondence of, 24–27, 52, 286
  courtship, 18–20
  daughter of, 65, 96, *266,* 287
  engagement of, 52–53
  fame of, 56, 58
  in France, 96–98, 267–76
  lifestyle of, 56–59, 95–98,
    269–72, 274–76, 286–88
  marriage of, 53
  and publicity, 57, 58, 64
Fitzgerald, Zelda:
  death of, 288
  early years of, *see* Sayre, Zelda
  as flapper, 62, 64, 68, 81, 105,
    246, 276
  media stories about, 62, 63
  and men, 97
  as out of control, 57, 271–72,
    274–75, 286
  personal traits of, 57, 273
  as reviewer, 62, 276
  and Scott, *see* Fitzgerald, F. Scott;
    Fitzgerald, Scott and Zelda

as source for Scott's writing, 24,
    42, 61–63
as writer, 63–65, 67, 68, 81, 276
flagpole sitting, 56
Flaming Youth (film), 211–12, 220–21,
    233, 234
Flapper, The (film), 231, 232
"Flapper, The" (Parker), 48–49
"Flapper Jane" profile, 7
flappers:
    behavior of, 23
    conformity of, 9
    costs of maintaining, 81, 207–8
    critics of, 105–6, 107, 112–13
    end of era, 279, 288–89
    enlarging the definition of, 8, 65,
        265
    fashions of, *146*, 153, *160; see also*
        fashion
    in international scene, 123
    in magazine illustrations, 9, *184,*
        186, 189–95, *278*
    media stories about, 5–8, 9, 24,
        39, 47–49, 63–65, 68, 81, 123
    in movies, 44, 115, 221, 231,
        233–35, 241–43, 245–46,
        254–55, 262–65
    popular image of, 81, *146,*
        193–95, 262–63, 276, 289, 290
    self-indulgence of, 65, 105, 107,
        112, 175–76
    and sex, *see* sex
    and social class, 93, 123, 265
    social impact of, 9, 64, 289–91
    use of term, 5–6
Flappers and Philosophers (Fitzgerald),
    40, 47, 191
Fleischmann, Raoul, 91
Fleming, Victor, 239
Follin, Otto, 33
Foote, Mary Hallock "Molly," 118–19
Ford, Henry, 34, 175
Foster, George, 30–31

Francis, Kay, 89, 279
Freud, Sigmund, 48, 56, 157, 197,
    200

Gallant, Barney, 101
Garbo, Greta, 256
Garland, Madge, 161
Garrison, William Lloyd, 107
George White's Scandals (revue), 57,
    252–53
Gerritson, Lawrence, 33
Gershwin, George, 83
Gibbons, Floyd, 54
Gibson, Charles Dana, 198, 199
Gill, Brendan, 87
Gilman, Charlotte Perkins, 105
Gish, Dorothy, 57, 226
Gish, Lillian, 50, 53, 57, 226, 231
Glyn, Elinor, 242–43
Godey's Lady's Book, 163, 164
Goldman, Emma, 67–68
Goldwyn, Samuel, 229
Goldwyn Pictures Corporation, 218
Goncharova, Natalie, 273
Graham, Martha, 248, 249, 251
Graham, Sheila, 287
Grant, Cary, 215
Grant, Jane, 83–86
Grant, Laura, 33
Grant, Ulysses S., 71
Great Depression, 276, 277
Great Gatsby, The (Fitzgerald), 97, 270
Great Train Robbery, The (film), 224
Griffith, D. W., 73, 215–16, 218, *222,*
    224–29, 231
Griffith, Linda Arvidson, 227–28
Gris, Juan, 273
Guinan, Texas, 252, 253

Hale, Ruth, 172
Hall, G. Stanley, 179

Hamilton, Alexander, 162
Hargrave, Homer, 281
Harper's Bazaar, 35, 86, 155, 183, 248
Hawes, Elizabeth, 166–67
Hays, Will, 280
"Head and Shoulders" (Fitzgerald), 52
Hearst, William Randolph, 215, 255–56
Hecht, Ben, 215
Held, John, 9, 114, 174, 189–92, 262, 285
Hemingway, Ernest, 267–70, 272–73, 275
Hemingway, Hadley, 269–70, 272, 273
Hernández Milligan, Adele, 265
Heterodoxy, 106
Hill, George W., 171
Hill, W. E., 62
Himmler, Heinrich, 284
Hollywood:
    lifestyles in, 259–60
    see also movies
homosexuality, 118–23, 289
Hooper, Lloyd, 18
House of Chanel, 134, 135, 153, 154–57, 159, 284–85
House of Doucet, 149
House of Worth, 149–50
Howey, Lib, 215–16, 217
Howey, Walter, 214–17
Hyatt, John Wesley and Isaiah, 168

Industrialization:
    commercial refrigeration and packaging, 55
    and gender roles, 109–12
    manufacturing productivity, 53, 65, 162
    and scientific management, 65
    trend toward, 29–30, 45, 177
    and unemployment, 53–54

Ingersoll, Ralph, 116
Ingram's Milkwood Cream, 205
intellectual property, 180
It (film), 240, 242–43

Jaffe, Sam, 241
Jan, Flora Belle, 265
Jazz Age, *114*
    beginning of, 13
    cultural transmission, 81–82
    dating in, 35–36, 37
    end of, 276, 277, 279
    flappers in, 8; *see also* flappers
    information revolution in, 54
    leisure culture in, 31, 37, 55, 66
    media stories about, 9, 30–31, 43, 63, 92
    moral revolution in, 29, 81
    movies of, *see* movies
    nightlife in, 30–32, 89
    public amusements in, 31–32, *60*
    pursuit of pleasure in, 65, 67
    romance and sexuality in, *22, 28,* 37–38, 173
    U.S. economy in, 53–55, 167–68
    visual style of, 192
    youth culture in, 44–46
Jazz Singer, The (film), 279
Jennings, Al, 220
Jesus Christ, biography of, 173, 175–76
Jolson, Al, 83, 279
Joyce, James, 270, 271
Jozan, Edouard, 97
J. Walter Thompson agency, 200, 206

Kaplan, Billy, 239
Kelly, Alvin "Shipwreck," 56
Kelly, Eugenia, 1–5
Kelly, Helen, 1–4
Kendrew, Lucy, 192

Kennedy, Julia H., 79
Keystone Kops, 228
Kinsey, Alfred, 289
Kirchwey, Freda, 106
Knox, Loren, 290–91
Kriendler, Jack, 90
Ku Klux Klan, 71–75, *72, 78*

Ladies' Home Journal, 158–59, 163
La Marr, Barbara, 263
Lambert, Gerald, 201–2
Lambert Pharmaceuticals, 201–2
Lasky, Jesse, 279
Laughlin, Clara, 38
League of Women Voters, 111
Le Bon, Gustave, 198, 200
Lederer, Pepi, 255–56
LeGrand, Bill, 25
Leland, Henry, 34
Leopold, Nathan, 61
Lewis, Sinclair, 43, 83
Lincoln, Abraham, 175
Lindbergh, Charles, 263
Lindsay, Vachel, 229
Lindsey, Ben, 44
Lippmann, Walter, 197–98
"Lipstick" (cocktail), 101
Lipstick (film), 257
"Lipstick" (Long), 89–92, 98–103, 117, 123, 192–94
Listerine, 201–2
Loeb, Richard, 61
Long, Lois, *80, 87–93, 88*
    and Arno, 115–17, 284
    earnings of, 92–93
    as fashion writer, 156, 159, 165–66, 169, 283–84
    as girl about town, 89–90, 92, 98, 101–3, 105, 115, 117, 122–23, 191
    insights of, 9, 89, 101, 122
    in later years, 283–84

as "Lipstick," 89–92, 98–103, 117, 123, 192–94
    and *New Yorker,* 86, 87, 91–92, 100–102, 123, 191
    and race, 193
Lost Generation, 272
Lynd, Robert and Helen, 35, 46–47, 54, 208

MacArthur, Charles, 215, 271
McCall's, 183, 276
McCormick, John, 234, 238, 243, 281
McGrath, Mary Josephine, 82
McGuffey's Reader, 75
McKaig, Alexander, 52–53
MacLeish, Archibald, 270, 273, 275
magazines, 182–83, 186
    advertising in, *see* advertising
    fashions shown in *see* fashion
    see also specific magazines
mail-order catalogs, 167–68, 181
Main Street (Lewis), 43
makeup, 204–8
Malinowski, Bronislaw, 158
Man from Home, The (Tarkington and Wilson), 84
Mankiewicz, Herman, 82, 86
Man Nobody Knows, The (Barton), 173, 176
Marean, John, 32–33
Marks, Jeanette, 119
Martin, Everett Dean, 200–201
Martin, Joseph, 286
Mayfield, Sara, 15, 19, 269
medicine, gynecology, 140–41
men:
    and cigarettes, 172
    civilizing influence of, 108
    defined by work, 65–66
    homosexual, 121
    more money than women, 37

men (*cont.*):
    and movies, 261
    roles of, 118
    in sports, 142–43
    women controlled by, 37, 137–41
Mencken, H. L., 84
Mesime, Anna and Ida, 81
Metro-Goldwyn-Mayer, 287
Metro Pictures, 52
Metropolitan Magazine, 63–65
Midnight Flappers (Fitzgerald), 63
Millay, Edna St. Vincent, 83
Mills, Alice, 249, 250
Miró, Juan, 273
Mix, Tom, 219
Montgomery Ward, 168
Moore, Colleen, 9, *210,* 211–21
    birth and early years of, 212–14,
        216–17
    film career of, 217–21, 232–35,
        238, 242, 243, 245–46, 279,
        281
    in *Flaming Youth,* 211–12, 220–21,
        233, 234
    flapper image of, 194, 221, 231,
        233–35, 241, 245, 254, 262,
        264–65
    later years of, 281
    mansion of, 239, 260
    name change of, 217
Morrison, Cleve, 220
Morrison, Kathleen, *see* Moore,
    Colleen
Motion Picture magazine, 236–37
Motion Picture Production Code,
    280
Moveable Feast, A (Hemingway), 267
movies:
    evolution of, 223–26, 229
    flapper image in, 44, 115, 221,
        231, 233–35, 241–43, 245–46,
        254–55, 262–65
    influence of, 8, 257, 259–63

    KKK monitoring of, 74
    and morality, 226–29, 280
    silent films, 259–62, 282, 283
    talkies, 279–80, 282
    technology of, 223–24
    tickets sold, 55
    vamps in, 231–32
Muller v. Oregon, 110
Muncie, Indiana, Lynds' social study
    of, 35, 46–47, 54, 55
Murphy, Gerald and Sara, 273–75
"Myra Meets His Family" (Fitzgerald),
    43–44

Nast, Condé, 84, 189, 190, 248
Nation, The, 86, 106
National Consumer's League, 111
National Woman's Party (NWP), 111
National Women's Trade Union
    League, 111
Nazi Germany, 284–85
neurasthenia, 139–40
New American Woman, *see* New
    Woman
New Deal, 279
New Republic, The, 6–8, 156, 197
New Woman, 7–9
    and equal rights, *see* feminism
    fashions for, 150, 152, 154, 156,
        284
    Fitzgerald's stories about, 61–63
    flappers, *see* flappers
    Long as embodiment of, 89, 92,
        122
    makeup used by, 204–8
    and sex, 21–27, 64
    songs about, 23–24
    visual style of, *184,* 186, 192
    see also women
New York:
    Algonquin Hotel in, 83–85, 252
    cultural origins in, 81–82, 83

Madison Avenue in, 85
nightlife in, 30–32, 90, 92, 98–99,
    122, 193, 251
New Yorker, The:
  beginning of, 82, 86
  cartoons in, 115, 116, 189
  evolution of, 283–84
  "Lipstick" writing for, 89–92,
    98–103, 117, 123
  narrative style in, 99–103, 122
  sophistication of, 86
  speakeasy of, 100–101, 116
  "Tables for Two" in, 92, 166, 191
New York Times, The, 69, 288
New-York Tribune, 30–31, 62

"Offshore Pirate, The" (Fitzgerald),
    43
Oh! Margy! (comic strip), 191, 285
Olds, Ransom, 34

Pabst, G. W., 282
Painted People (film), 238
Pandora's Box (film), 282
Paramount Pictures, 243, 254, 255,
    256, 280, 282
Parker, Dorothy, 48, 58, 84, 85, 89,
    189, 243, 252
Patent Office, U.S., 55
Paul, Alice, 111
Pelam Institute of America, 56
Pemberton, Murdock, 84, 85
Perkins, Maxwell, 27, 47, 51, 62–63,
    272
Phelps, George, 199
photography, invention of, 181–82
Picasso, Pablo, 187, 270, 273
Pickford, Mary, 214, 218, 220, *222,*
    228–29, 231, 259
Plastic Age, The (film), 241–42
plastics industry, 168–69

Poiret, Paul, 147–52, 153, 157
Porter, Cole, 83, 270
Porter, Edwin, 224, 225
Preferred Pictures, 237–38, 239
Prohibition, *94,* 100–102, 117
propaganda, 197–99
Proust, Marcel, 96
psychology, 56, 157, 197–200

Racism, and KKK, 71–75
radio, 54, 85
Reconstruction, 71
relativism, 69, 75
religion:
  and creationism, 75
  fundamentalism, 75–78
  literalism, 76–77
  and "Monkey Trial," 75, 76–78
Revolt of Modern Youth, The (Lindsey),
    44
Rice, Grantland, 54
Romantic Egoist, The (Fitzgerald), 17,
    20
Roosevelt, Alice, 15
Roosevelt, Franklin D., 286
Roosevelt, Theodore, 143
Rose, Mrs. George, 47
"Rosie the Riveter," 154
Ross, Harold, 82–86, 121–22,
    189
  and *New Yorker,* 82, 84–86, 87, 91,
    100–101, 116, 117, 122, 191,
    283
Royallieu (castle), 130, 131
Ruth, Babe, 61

St. Denis, Ruth, 189, 248, 251–52
St. Johns, Adela Rogers, 238–39
Sanger, Margaret, 67–68
San Simeon, California, 255–56
Sardeau, Helen, *80*

Saturday Evening Post, The, 42–44, 52, 61, 95–96, 173, 179, 182, 270, 273

Sayre, Anthony, 13–14, 21, 58–59

Sayre, Minnie, 21, 26, 58

Sayre, Zelda, *12,* 13–20, 37, *50*
   autobiographical novel by, 16, 18, 19
   and Fitzgerald, 13, 16, 17–20, 286–88; *see also* Fitzgerald, Scott and Zelda; Fitzgerald, Zelda
   as flapper archetype, 24, 29, 42, 61–63
   and men, 18–19, 24–27, 52
   personal traits of, 13, 52–53
   reputation of, 14, 16, 17–18
   scandalous behavior of, 13–16, 24, 53, 57

Schellenberg, Walter, 284–85

Schulberg, B. P. "Ben," 237–38, 239, 241, 243, 280, 282

Schulberg, Budd, 239–40

Scopes "Monkey Trial," 75, 76–78

Scribner's, 17, 20, 27, 47–48, 191, 270, 272

Scudder, Vida, 119

Sears, Roebuck & Co., 161–62, 168

self-indulgence, ethic of, 65, 105, 107, 112, 175–76

Seneca Falls, women's rights convention, 107, 108

sex, 21–27
   and advertising, 115, 173
   and birth control, 44, 67–69, 289
   and birthrate, 44–45, 68
   "crimes" related to, 35
   and dancing, 23
   and dating, 38
   double standard in, 46–47
   experimenting with, 8, 36, 46, 289
   free love, 106, 107

   liberating effect of, 64
   media stories about, 23, 61, 64, 115, 122
   "petting parties," 46
   premarital, 118
   in primitive societies, 158
   redefining, 45, 243, 289
   "sexual revolution," 289
   songs about, 23–24
   women's right to enjoyment of, 106–7

Shakespeare & Company, Paris, 96, 271

Shawn, Ted, 189, 248, 249

Shawn, William, 283

Sheik, The (film), 262, 276

Sherwood, Robert, 84, 252

Shirer, William, 271

Sims, J. Marion, 140

Smith, Ina, 32–33

Smith, Mary Rozet, 119

smoking:
   by film stars, 261
   and public relations, 172
   and women, 6, 106

social Darwinism, 73

social psychology, 197–99

sports, women in, *136,* 142–45

standardization, 168, 170, 171, 290–91

Stanton, Elizabeth Cady, 107, 108, 141

Stars and Stripes, 82

Steichen, Edward, 89

Stein, Gertrude, 270

Stewart, Donald Ogden, 97

stock market collapse (1929), 277, 279

Stubbs, Francis, 24

Sullivan, Mark, 77

Sun Also Rises, The (Hemingway), 272–73

Symes, Lillian, 105–6

Talmadge, Norma, 214
Tarkington, Booth, 84
taste:
    in fashion, *see* fashion
    national habits of, 9
    New Yorker as arbiter of, 82
technology, of nineteenth century, 33,
        162, 181–82, 223–24
Tender Is the Night (Fitzgerald), 287
Thalberg, Irving, 228
This Side of Paradise (Fitzgerald), 27,
        39, 41–43, 47, 51, 53, 61–62
Thomas, Olive, 232–33
Thompson, Denys, 179
Thurber, James, 116, 271
Toohey, John Peter, 84, 85
Toomer, Jean, 83
Tracy, Spencer, 281
"Transformation of a Rose, The"
        (Wellesley), 41
True, Ruth, 32
Tynan, Kenneth, 283

United Artists, 229, 257
urbanization, trend toward, 29–30,
        31, 81

Valentino, Rudolph, 259, 262, 276
Vanity Fair, 84, 85, 89, 185, 189, 190,
        248
Van Vechten, Carl, 268
Victorian era:
    chaperones in, 32
    courtship in, 32–33, 34, 35, 37
    domestic partnerships in, 119–20
    etiquette for ladies in, 21
    fashions in, 137–39, 150
    gender roles in, 108, 109, 110,
        118, 120
    makeup in, 205
    movie depiction of, 223, 226–29

    neurasthenia in, 139–40
    parents born in, 42
    romantic culture of, 33
    throwing off the shackles of, 65
    upholding propriety of, 74, 100,
        289
    values of, 65, 69, 223, 227
Vionnet, Madeleine, 159
Vogue, 89, 168, 183, 189, 205
Volstead Act, 102
voting rights, *104,* 105, 107, 109,
        110–11

Wanger, Walter, 254–55, 279
Ward, Artemas, 182
Warhol, Andy, 56
Warner Brothers, 254, 255, 279
Watson, John B., 200
wealth gap, 54, 55, 171, 290
Weidman, Charles, 248
West, Nathaniel, 257
Wharton, Edith, 270
What Ails Our Youth? (Coe), 44
White, Katharine, 101, 116
Whittemore, Mrs. E. M., 23
Wilder, Laura Ingalls, 181
Wilkin, Josephine, 144–45
Wilkinson, Charlotte, 192
Wilson, Edmund, 53, 57, 84
Wilson, Harry Leon, 84
Wilson, William, 74
Wilson, Woodrow, 197
Windsor, Duke and Duchess of, 285
Wister, Owen, 143
Wolfe, Thomas, 83
women:
    and birth control, 44, 67–69, 289
    and birthrate, 44–45, 68
    choices available to, 68–70
    in cities, 29, 30, 31
    in college, 45–46, 143–44
    and consumerism, 183, 185, 290

women (*cont.*):
 and diets, 262–64
 double standard for, 36–37, 46–47
 equal rights for, 7–8, 69–70, *104,*
  105–13, 208
 and fashion, *see* fashion
 and gender differences, 110–12
 immigrants, 265
 independence of, 7, 8, 9, 30, 31,
  68, 79
 KKK threats to, 74
 and labor laws, 110–11
 makeup used by, 204–8
 marriage vs. career for, 119, 120,
  121
 and moral obligation, 70
 and motherhood, 65
 and movies, 260–63
 and other women, 118–23
 of poverty, 109
 roles of, 7–8, 64, 108–10
 and sex, 21–27, 35, 38, 243, 289
 smoking cigarettes, 32, 106, 172
 social activism of, *see* feminists
 social control of, 6, 8, 9, 37, 100,
  137–41, 264
 in sports, *136,* 142–45
 unmarried by choice, 119, 120

 wages of, 67, 92–93, 105, 109, 110
 working, 23, 29, 30, 31, 36–37,
  67, 92–93, 109–12, 142, 154,
  164, 170, 205
Wong, Anna May, *258,* 265
Woodbury cold cream, 206
Woodward, Charlotte, 108
Woodward, Helen, 178
Woollcott, Alexander, 84, 85
Woolley, Mary, 119
Woolworth's, 169
workplace safety, 105, 110
World War I, 5, 107, 167, 197, 199
Worth, Charles, 149
Worth, Gaston, 149–50
Worth, Jean, 149–50

Young Degenerates, 255
Youth and Sex (Bromley and Britten),
 35
youth culture, 44–46, 61

Ziegfeld, Florenz, 253
Ziegfeld Follies (revue), 246, 249, 252,
 253
Zukor, Adolph, 243

About the Author

JOSHUA ZEITZ has taught American history and politics at Cambridge University, Harvard University, and Princeton University. He is the author of *Lincoln's Boys: John Hay, John Nicolay, and the War for Lincoln's Image* and has written for the *New York Times, Washington Post, The New Republic, The Atlantic, Dissent,* and *American Heritage*. He lives with his wife and two daughters in Hoboken, New Jersey.

Printed in the United States
by Baker & Taylor Publisher Services